Change Lobsters—and Dance

Change Lobsters—and Dance

AN AUTOBIOGRAPHY

LILLI PALMER

❀

Macmillan Publishing Co., Inc.

NEW YORK

Macmillan Publishing Co., Inc.
866 Third Avenue, New York, N.Y. 10022
Collier Macmillan Canada, Ltd.

First published in 1974 by Droemer Knaur under the title *Dicke Lilli—gutes Kind.*
© Droemer Knaur Verlag
Schoeller & Co., Zurich, 1974

Library of Congress Cataloguing in Publication Data

Palmer, Lilli, 1914–
    Change lobsters—and dance.

    Translation of Dicke Lilli, gutes Kind.
    1.   Palmer, Lilli, 1914–   I.   Title.
PN2658.P3A3313 1975   791'.092'4 [B] 75–15924
ISBN 0–02–594610–2

FIRST AMERICAN EDITION 1975

Printed in the United States of America

FOR
Carlos

Contents

"Will you walk a little faster?" said a whiting to a snail,
"There's a porpoise close behind us, and he's treading on
    my tail.
See how eagerly the lobsters and the turtles all advance!
They are waiting on the shingle—will you come and
    join the dance?
    Will you, won't you, will you, won't you, will you
    join the dance?
    Will you, won't you, will you, won't you, won't you
    join the dance?"

LEWIS CARROLL,
                    Alice's Adventures in Wonderland,
                    "The Lobster Quadrille"

Change Lobsters—and Dance

1
Departure

THE BOAT TRAIN was to leave Victoria Station at twelve noon. Both contingents, the British and the Central European, had assembled to see us off.

Rex naturally chatted with his British relatives, his sister and her husband, while I clung to Central Europe in the shape of my mother and two sisters, who hung back a little—an old habit. Occasionally I darted from one group to the other as a sort of liaison, although there was no lack of friendly feeling between the two, just a difference.

Departures and arrivals tend to emphasize people's personalities. The British group stood relaxed and unperturbed. All three members of my family, on the other hand, seemed to bend forward a little in an attitude of nervous apprehension. No wonder. They had lost so much that even a temporary departure was a minor disaster.

The last minutes on the platform dragged on. Everything had been said and resaid. My mother fell silent and just looked at me. "I'll write a lot," I said once again, "maybe every second day—like in Paris, remember?" She nodded, close to tears.

Thank God for the train whistle. We hurried into our compartment, but by the time we realized that the windows were still fastened shut, as they had been during the war (only six months past), the train had begun to move. Good. I hated waving from open train windows. It never failed to bring back two occasions that didn't bear thinking about.

We were alone in our compartment. Was nobody else traveling to New York on the *Queen Elizabeth?* Yes indeed, as we were to find out a few hours later. Thousands, in fact, American troops returning home, but they didn't travel by boat train. The *Queens* were still troop carriers in November 1945, and hardly any civilians were allowed to sail on them. Our permits had been specially granted in a hurry, for Rex was to play the lead in a film called *Anna and the King of Siam,* his first American movie.

The offer had come out of the blue. Leland Hayward at Twentieth Century-Fox had had a brainstorm about casting the King of Siam (a historic figure, not a fictional character). A new face was needed, a new star personality, somebody who spoke English fluently yet didn't sound American. Rex fitted the bill.

Where was he? In England, of course.

What was he doing? Was he still in the RAF? No, he had been released and was living in a small house outside London making British movies.

Get him.

He has a wife. She's an actress.

Bring her over with him; perhaps we'll find something for her, too.

They have a baby.

The baby must stay behind.

Such were the orders that reached us one day in September 1945, as we stood in the garden of The Little House, Denham, Buckinghamshire, picking raspberries. We were stunned. We'd been living in the little house (our first) for only five months. We loved it, we had whitewashed it, I had sewn all the curtains (crooked), the baby was tottering across the lawn followed by William the Sealyham, last week we had gone to the opening of our first film together, *The Rake's Progress,* which had turned out to be a hit, we had lots of plans for the winter—what did we need Hollywood for? Nuts to Hollywood.

The agent called again. Twentieth was offering Rex four thousand dollars a week, plus options for seven years with salary increases to astronomical heights; and there was an offer from Warner Brothers for me, though for much less money. Could we possibly afford to pass up that sort of thing? What about our back taxes and the mortgage on the house?

We reconsidered, took back the nuts, and signed on the dotted line.

"Okay," said the agent, "let's get on with it, they're in a hurry over there. Put your affairs in order, sell the house and the car and the dog—" "And the baby," I said. "No, you can keep the baby," said the agent, "he'll join you later. Children are not allowed on troopships." Troopships? Yes, troopships. No other boats were crossing the Atlantic as yet. Minesweepers were still busy.

We did as we were told, sold the house, the car, the dog. (The baby would stay with my mother.) We traveled light, each with a single suitcase; all our other clothes were left with family and friends. There hadn't been that much, anyway. Wartime rationing coupons had cut everybody's wardrobe down to a minimum. Besides, we wouldn't need our old clothes. Hollywood, oodles of money, nylons, Kleenex, and new clothes were waiting for us.

Yet when the car that was to take us to Victoria Station drove through the gates of The Little House, I cried. Why, in God's name? To start afresh in a new country was old hat to me, surely. And this time I wasn't going, as I had twice before, penniless and on spec; this time I went with a contract in my pocket, sent off in style and eagerly awaited—and, above all, not alone! So why the tears? No particular reason. Just the old atavistic suspicion of "good news."

When the boat train got to Southampton, it rattled at a snail's pace through the streets leading to the harbor until it reached the dock where the *Queen Elizabeth* was berthed and crawled alongside. We were too close to see the shape of the ship. All that was visible through the train window were rows and rows of black portholes in the gray blue hull, still in its wartime camouflage.

We clambered down to the platform, watched with amiable curiosity by what looked like an entire battalion of soldiers sitting on the dock, their luggage around them, waiting. No ship's officer in sight.

We parked ourselves on top of our suitcases and tried to assume the same expression of cheerful boredom as that of the troops. Everybody still operated under the standard wartime procedure of patient waiting anywhere, anytime, as if you were under a gentle anesthetic. Eventually something was bound to happen.

Rex got out his script of *Anna and the King of Siam*, which was uppermost not only in his suitcase but in his mind, all day long. Ever since it had been delivered, it was never out of reach. He already knew most of the text.

Once again, sitting on the dock in the shadow of the huge gray whale of a ship, he handed me the script and I gave him the cues.

Finally somebody appeared from inside the ship's belly, and the soldiers lumbered to their feet and lined up at the various gangways. We got right in among them and were slowly pushed forward and finally upward. Surely, I thought, those boys must be keen as mustard to get back home, but there was nothing in their behavior to show that this wasn't just another assignment. Maybe they had been stationed long enough in England to be conditioned by the general atmosphere of understatement. Just like me.

The agent had done his homework. We were shown to a tiny single cabin for just the two of us. Two bunks and a basin and john, no furniture whatever, not even a table or a chair. No matter; it was only for five days.

Rex went out on reconnaissance and returned with the news: the ship was full to bursting, uniforms only, you had to fight your way through the passages. Meals would be in shifts, the food was British rations (oh God!)—but there was a bar, full of decent booze by the looks of it, so all was well, really. And since it was already past six o'clock, how about heading in that direction?

We pummelled our way through the soldiery, who with every mile away from the shores of England seemed to rediscover their boisterous spirits, punching and flailing about and shouting at the top of their lungs. Now that the ship was moving, it must have dawned on them at last that they were actually getting nearer home with every passing second. Home! For good! On this, their first night aboard, they got plastered *en masse,* and nobody tried to restrain them.

We made it to the bar reserved for officers, who were also feeling no pain by the time we arrived, and didn't give up until there wasn't a drop left in any of the bottles. The last shift for dinner was sparsely attended. The boys couldn't make the steps. They were lying about in happy piles, snoring or glassy-eyed; we stepped gingerly across hundreds of "casualties" on our way back to the cabin, fell onto the bunks, and passed out.

Next morning on deck, not a single deck chair to be seen. Few uniforms about. The gangways, too, were empty of bodies, as if some giant garbage-disposal squad had been at work during the night.

I sat on the bare, scrubbed planks, leaned against a funnel, and looked out on the ocean. "I'm traveling on the Atlantic Ocean," I said to my father, who had died eleven years before. He had never seen it. His holidays had been spent in Italy, the land of a German's dreams for a thousand years past. His mind had been German through and through, his upbringing classical, Latin and Greek; he didn't speak a word of French or English. What would he have said if I had told him why I was sitting aboard a British troopship sailing for America? "You see, Vati, Germany has lost the war . . ." That would have been quite enough for him. Lost the war. Again!

Of course, if he had lived through the last eleven years, he would have known that it was a simple question of survival versus extinction and that Germany's defeat meant that the world could breathe again. Yet I suddenly remembered an evening, way back in 1941, when Rex had looked at me in a very special way while we were listening to a news broadcast about the first wave of British bombers sent to destroy Hitler's war machine. It was Cologne that had received this particular load of bombs, and the description of the ensuing devastation was pretty graphic.

"What are you looking at me like that for?" I had asked.

"Well now," said Rex, pulling his nose, which meant he was stalling, "well now . . . doesn't it make you feel a bit . . . peculiar when you hear . . . I mean, didn't you tell me about that cathedral in Cologne which you used to go and see . . ."

"But don't you understand," I said, "that I want Cologne destroyed even more than you do?"

He stared at me. "No," he said finally, "I don't understand. You ought to feel something, some kind of regret . . ."

"My God!" I said, "you really don't understand! Now let me try to explain: suppose Oswald Mosley and his thugs took over in England, and suppose they murdered or imprisoned everybody who was . . . say Protestant, and you and your family had to flee and you suddenly found yourself in France . . ."

"Oh, I wouldn't have gone to France," said Rex, "I can't make with the lingo."

"Okay, suppose you had gone to America and America made war on England to get Mosley and his assassins out—"

"I see what you're getting at," said Rex. "Still, I assure you, I would have minded like hell if I'd heard that bombs had fallen on Piccadilly Circus!"

I suppose it was a poor comparison. There was no way to make him feel what I felt.

And my father, who had spent four years at Verdun helping defend every sacred inch of the fatherland he loved, would have had the same reaction as all the other refugees, namely, *down* with Cologne.

But how good that he was never put to the test.

2

A "Decent" Family

❊

AROUND SIX o'clock in the evening my father would say, "Come on, let's take a little walk." My mother would drop whatever she was doing and hook her arm into his like the little tail on a capital Q, and they would walk down the main road past the station towards the woods. Time: the mid-twenties. Place: Berlin.

After the First World War, Germany was slowly recovering from revolution, turmoil, inflation, and paralyzing poverty. Schoolchildren still received a glass of milk and a spoonful of cod-liver oil every morning at ten o'clock "with the compliments of the American Quaker Society." (I had a written paternal dispensation from the cod-liver oil, because it made me sick. Even so, I felt queasy from ten to a quarter past, for you could still smell it in class every time a child opened his mouth.)

We lived in an apartment in West Berlin, in one of the comfortable, old-fashioned houses built around the turn of the century. Rooms were numerous, large and high-ceilinged, walls thick, the parquet floors a status symbol of bourgeois society. Bathrooms: only one. And a separate john for "domestics." I can't remember any bathroom for them; maybe they never bathed. We children did, twice a week at nighttime. The "Fräulein" bathed us until we reached our tenth birthday. From then on we were allowed to have our baths alone, and behind locked doors, too.

Fräuleins were frequently changed. I don't remember a single face. They never seemed to measure up to my father's demands, and he probably ruined whatever initiative any of them had by summoning each one into his study on the day of her arrival. She was never to beat us or kiss us. And he made it clear that he would prefer a box on the ear to a kiss on the cheek.

He was much easier on our various cooks. The first one, when he was newly married, was called Frieda, and he addressed all succeeding ones by that name.

He believed in healthy living and always chose "the golden middle road," carefully avoiding any form of "extremes." Every day, on their evening walk, when they reached the pine woods on the outskirts of the city, he would remind my mother to breathe deeply and "clear her lungs." They usually chose the same path through the forest; it led to a wooden gate in a wire fence encircling a large compound. It was through that very gate that I rode my bicycle to school every day. They liked to stop there and peer through into the greenery. Pines, birches, beeches, and a few brightly painted pavilions, a soccer field, a kitchen garden, a pool where the boys and girls—segregated, of course—could swim in the summer. That was my school, the Open Air School in Grunewald, Berlin.

According to my mother, every time they stood at the gate, my father would say, "When I think back to my childhood! Those dismal classrooms in those musty old barracks! What a lucky child she is!"

Sometimes the timing was just right. The school bell would ring out 6:30, and "the lucky child" would come pedaling through the gateway, whooping and yelling among the other bicycle riders, waving to her parents as she went by. My father and mother would wave back and walk on into the woods.

I had chosen my parents with care. Totally different in character and mentality, they offered a wide choice of guidelines, and I helped myself. My father was serious, reserved, meticulous to a fault, sometimes explosive, always impatient. My mother was serene, forgetful, communicative, and tolerant. I took after my father, both outwardly and inwardly. Which is probably why I loved my mother at first sight. Just as he did.

She was born in the little fortress town of Ehrenbreitstein on an island in the Rhine. My grandfather, a wine merchant, a tiny, handsome, volatile man, had always passionately wanted a son. Every time my grandmother produced a girl, his lamentations grew louder, until the midwife refused to set foot in the house, because she didn't feel equal to the emotional strain. There were already four girls in the nursery, but grandfather wouldn't give up; he simply had to have a son. Grandmother Julie secretly jumped off the kitchen table, hoping for a miscarriage; she broke a leg but remained obstinately pregnant. When the hour of her delivery arrived, the entire adult population of Ehrenbreitstein sank to their knees in fervent prayer. It didn't help.

The midwife's voice was barely audible as she announced the arrival of the fifth girl. Grandmother turned her face to the wall. Grandfather's wailing could be heard all over Ehrenbreitstein. The child, tiny and discouraged by the lack of a warm welcome, didn't make a sound, not even the traditional entrance cry. It grimaced as if it were trying to laugh. That was the first appearance of my mother, Rose Lissmann.

Grandfather was not a good businessman, and five children cost money. He had to give up his wine business and Ehrenbreitstein along with it and move to Dresden, Saxony, to try his hand at making and selling straw hats. His five daughters were sent to public school. They learned penmanship—my mother's handwriting was "like copperplate"—reading, counting, and the simple multiplication tables. In geography, all my mother knew about the world was the boundaries, cities, and rivers of Saxony. In history she learned only things that concerned that tiny kingdom. Even in her old age she could recite the names and dates of the kings of Saxony forwards and backwards.

Meals were of Spartan simplicity: dry bread and cocoa in the afternoon; dessert only on Sundays. No toys except one doll, which lacked both hair and arms by the time my mother inherited it. No vacation trips. Just daily walks in the public park. Yet for the sisters, those childhood days were pure gold. "We were so healthy, you know, and there was so much to laugh about . . ."

Of the five girls who romped about the Dresden public gardens every Sunday at the turn of the century, Hannah was the eldest and my mother Rose the youngest. In between, at regular yearly intervals, came Cilly, Ella, and Marta. Right from the start, Cilly, the second sister, mothered them all.

Even as a young girl, Cilly had a quiet authority, an outward serenity that made her look after, protect, and promote any person who came her way. The husband her father had picked out for her seemed at first quite a pleasant fellow. But when he started to go deaf at an early age, he made up for his growing isolation by keeping company with his shopgirls, getting them pregnant in the process. Aunt Cilly had to pay frequent calls on the authorities of the small Bavarian town of Landshut, where they lived, to keep him out of prison. Those interviews weren't much fun for her, though the townspeople acted as if they knew nothing. They loved her.

The bond among the five sisters was so strong that, long after they were all married, they would not entirely let go of each other. So they invented the "sisters' vacation." Every year in springtime, all five of them would spend two weeks at some small resort, usually in the Bavarian Alps. Husbands and children were excluded, makeup taboo. They wanted to be just the way they used to be on their daily walks in Dresden, and they would roam the countryside in sensible shoes, arm in arm, all looking somewhat alike, stopping from time to time in passionate argument or laughing uproariously, oblivious of onlookers.

Only once did the "sisters' vacation" come to a premature end: when Grandmother Julie died. The five daughters grieved, had her cremated, and Hannah, the eldest, took charge of the urn. All five of them got onto the train that was to take them from Frankfurt, where the funeral had taken place, to Landshut, near Munich, where they were all going to recuperate at Aunt Cilly's house. With a sigh of relief, they settled themselves in their compartment, took off their black-veiled hats, and blew their noses for the last time. As the train picked up speed, cigarettes were lighted and spirits revived. Soon they were as deeply and noisily involved with one another as ever.

When the train stopped in Munich, they collected their belongings and changed trains for Landshut, where they arrived an hour later. On the distant platform they could see two husbands waiting. At that moment, Aunt Cilly, thunderstruck, turned to her eldest sister. "Where's Mama?" Aunt Hannah jumped. "Don't ask me, I haven't got her." The sisters looked at one another aghast. "Who's got Mama?" shouted Aunt Cilly, usually so calm and soft-spoken.

The train stopped with a jolt. The little Landshut station was only a three-minute stop, but that was time enough for them to make sure that Mama really was missing. They clambered down from their compartment in a daze. The locomotive whistled, the train pulled out. On the platform stood two sons-in-law, hats in hand, condolence on their faces. But instead of a family scene of quiet handshakes and wordless embraces, five agitated ladies in black were shouting, "We've lost Mama!"

Then and there, on the platform, they retraced their steps and worked it out that Mama had last been seen on the luggage rack on the Frankfurt Munich train. They dried their tears, took the next train back to Munich, consulted the stationmaster, and finally caught up with Mama in the luggage rack of their first compartment, which had been shunted to a far corner of the vast Munich railroad yard. In the middle of the night, minus hats and veils, the sisters went stumbling across the perilous maze of tracks, convulsed with shameless laughter, dodging approaching trains by the skin of their teeth, until they finally made their way back to the main terminal. Tucked safely under Cilly's arm was Mama.

Shortly before the outbreak of war, Aunt Cilly visited us in London. It was not a happy reunion. During the few days she spent with us, my mother did her best to convince her that she must on no account go back. She had some money in Switzerland, a dangerous thing now that Hitler had ordered all foreign investments to be returned to Germany. It would have been quite feasible to get her deaf husband to Switzerland for the time being.

"No," said Aunt Cilly. She had taken it upon herself to pack a hundred food packages a week and mail them to relatives, friends, acquaintances, and strangers in concentration camps. She could still do that, but only from inside Germany.

In the taxi on the way to the station, we still kept trying to change her mind. We pointed through the window at people in the street. They were free; we were free. This was her last chance! My mother put her arm around her neck. "Cillychen, I beseech you, stay!" But she just shook her head, her cheeks flushed. "I must send my packages."

Soon after her return, three men from the Gestapo appeared at Aunt Cilly's house and told her to come along. She asked if she might fetch her coat from upstairs, while her deaf husband, who had no idea who the visitors were, sat in his rocking chair smiling at them.

She jumped from her bedroom balcony. The Gestapo men hurriedly made off, and Aunt Cilly died in the hospital the following day.

At the turn of the century people used to go regularly to the photographer. I still have a whole stack of photographs mounted on thick cardboard with an elaborate label on the back saying "Court Photographer, Dresden. Awards and honorable mentions from Princes and Ruling Sovereigns." My mother's little face looks at me, first with a short haircut like a boy's, later with long loose hair, always with the same expression of suppressed giggles. But her laughing eyes concealed a strong will, tenacity, and independence. As the youngest, she must have been my grandmother's favorite, for she managed to turn that conventional old lady into her co-conspirator. The plot was kept a deep secret: Rose, my mother, wanted to be an actress.

All his life my grandfather had a secret passion for the theater. As a young man he had sold programs to pay for a seat in the gallery. Yet he was shocked to the depths of his soul when my mother confessed to him after a full year of secret lessons. He was convinced that becoming an actress was the first step on the road to prostitution, and he died without having seen her on the stage and before she could prove to him that, while prostitutes often have to be good actresses, good actresses don't have to be prostitutes. Grand-mother's secret savings paid for the teacher, a retired actor from the Dresden state theater who predicted a great future for his pupil. When she was able to tell her father that Aschaffenburg, a good, provincial repertory theater, had offered her a contract as an ingenue, he knew that he had lost, because she had just turned twenty-one.

Though she looked much younger. The first time she tried to go into a rehearsal by the stage door, the doorkeeper blocked her way. "No children allowed backstage." Her professional photographs show a small figure with curly hair, eyes that narrowed to a blue slit when she laughed, and small, regular features. That type of face was very popular at the turn of the century, and my mother clung to this early ideal of beauty long after it had gone out of fashion. "The nose must be narrow," she used to say, "and the mouth small, as if you were saying 'pooch.'" As a punishment for her obstinacy, she was forced to bring into the world three daughters with large, wide mouths, who in this respect resembled their father. I don't know what my mother did to us when we were small, or whether our noses were narrow enough to please her, but I often watched her bending over her grandchildren's cribs, trying to press the tiny nostrils closer together. "The nose is too broad," she would sigh, shaking her head as she walked away.

She made such a success of her first engagement in Aschaffenburg that she was offered a contract for the following season at the Municipal Theater in Breslau, a major step forward. That same year a young doctor from Posen in East Prussia accepted a position as first assistant to the head surgeon of Breslau's medical school. He was a lucky young man. His parents were well-to-do, and after getting his medical degree at Würzburg under Professor Röntgen, the discoverer of the X ray, he could afford to spend several years as an assistant to eminent surgeons before going into practice. When he was not on night duty, he went to the theater. The greatest of Germany's future actors, Joseph Kainz, was a member of the Breslau company, as was a new ingenue named Rose Lissmann. The problem was getting to know her. Flowers sent to her dressing room produced no reaction. At last the stage doorkeeper relented and divulged her ad-dress. New problem: the landlady. She opened the door and gave the young man a stern look. "The young lady does not receive gentlemen visitors." The door closed, and he was left standing outside, more determined than ever.

When he finally succeeded in meeting her (a friend of a friend knew one of her girl friends), the impact was explosive on both sides. "I must get this young man out of my head *at once,*" wrote my mother in her diary that evening, while the young doctor wandered alone through the dark streets and vowed to himself, "That one or no one." Provided, of course, that she came from a "respectable" family—and was a virgin. She qualified.

Their marriage lasted only twenty-five years, but each day counted double because of the intensity and completeness of their relationship. The fact that my mother was virtually uneducated (apart from her store of information about the Kingdom of Saxony) didn't bother my father. Besides, she began at once to educate herself so as not to embarrass him in front of his friends. One of my earliest memories is of her sitting at a table in front of a large globe, peering at it through thick glasses and imperiously, in her role of instructor, asking questions such as "How do you get from Berlin to Calcutta?" And then, in her role as pupil, trying her best to determine the route and to repeat the names of countries, rivers, and oceans to be crossed.

But right from the start, the road to Calcutta meant nothing in comparison to her eagerness to learn something of her husband's profession, so that he could come home and talk to her about his cases without her getting on his nerves with asinine questions. She began to study the rudiments of medicine and insisted on watching him operate, complete with sterilized mask and white smock. The first dozen times he stationed a nurse behind her to catch her when she fainted, but she gradually got used to the smell and the blood, and within a year the memory of her life in the theater had been obliterated by the drama she could witness daily on the operating table.

We owed our happy childhood to the fact that my parents made no secret of loving each other more than they loved us. They were devoted to us, worried over us, were sometimes proud of us, but on the whole they were interested in each other first and us second. As a result there was a relaxed, balanced climate of independence, where nobody felt "loved" obsessively or possessively. Children—normal, healthy children—demand and receive their quota of love as a matter of course. Let them wangle an extra share out of their parents, rather than saturate them with it as though it were a birthright. Children of all ages should woo their parents; both parties thrive on it.

We certainly thrived. My two sisters and I had a happy, noisy, affectionate childhood, though we didn't know at the time how exceptional this was. We took it for granted that we would never hear our parents speak a single angry word to each other. There were no grievances, no "moods," never even a hint of "Well, dear, you know how your father is. . . ."

When he came home late for lunch from the hospital and we had already started on the soup, my mother would have one ear out for the front door. "Here he is," she would suddenly exclaim above our chatter, and putting down her spoon, she would sit quite still, as if she didn't want to be distracted from the profound, ever-new satisfaction his arrival brought her.

Of course it hadn't always been like that. Long after my father's death, my mother told me, hesitantly at first, then, when I didn't seem at all shocked, more confidently, that once he had actually been unfaithful to her. With one of his nurses. She told me how she had found out, how unhappy he had been, and how she had forgiven him on the spot. "When something like that happens," she said, "it's important to forgive absolutely and for all time. Never bring it up again later on, no matter how nicely it might suit your purpose."

She tried to keep her shape and stay slim—a losing battle—because my father detested fat people. He would visualize them strapped down on his operating table, and himself struggling to cut through thick layers of fat. Inwardly, she regarded the passing of time as a gain, not a loss, rejoiced over every year that had "gone well" and only demanded that it be lived through "with awareness." "The worst thing of all," she said, "would have been to be happy without realizing it."

For this reason I was very "aware" of her presence, particularly after she turned seventy. I tried to imagine the time when she wouldn't be there any more, hoping to get used to the idea. It didn't help when the time came. But at least I was able to keep a promise.

"Who'll tell me the white lies when the time comes?" she had asked once or twice. "Who'll pull the wool over my eyes?" She was convinced that she knew all the tricks and ruses that doctors and nurses use to deceive the terminally ill patient, and she swore that she herself would never be taken in, because she "knew all the symptoms." "I'll tell you the white lies," I promised her. "Maybe I'll manage to fool you. I'm an actress, remember?"

She was over seventy when she came to stay with me in Italy. The very day she arrived, she fixed her narrow, light blue eyes on mine and said, "Now tell me what you don't like about me."

No use answering that I liked everything about her.

"I'm serious. You've been gone three months. You can see me through new eyes. Maybe I've acquired some repulsive habit. Maybe I make noises when I eat or snort when I laugh. Old people sometimes do, you know. I wouldn't notice and nobody would tell me. That's why I'm asking you. You'll tell me."

I promised to watch her carefully.

A week later: "Well? Tell me without pussyfooting."

"Well, I've noticed that you make faces and giggly sounds when the maid serves you at table, as if you were apologizing for sitting there eating while she has to stand and hand you the dish."

"Right," she said. "That's exactly the way I feel. You see what happens when one lives alone and isn't used to being waited on. How right you are! I must watch that. What else?"

"Don't try to jump out of the car whenever I stop. You'll only ruin the door handle by pulling at it so frantically. You must get used to being an old lady and being treated like one. Stay in your seat, calm and dignified, and wait for me to open your door and help you out."

"*Ach,*" she sighed. "That's the hardest thing of all. But you're right. I've got to learn. It's high time."

She never did learn. There wasn't much time left. Shortly afterwards she said, "I'm really quite ready to go. I'm failing, you know."

That same year she developed cancer of the liver. "Has the bell rung?" she asked, when she had to take to her bed. I laughed gaily and pointed out all the symptoms of "acute hepatitis."

The doctor wanted to put her in the hospital. My sisters and I refused, because she would immediately have known what that meant. Should we get a nurse who could give her the necessary injections? Even that would have looked suspicious. We argued and fretted, invented and rejected all kinds of plans and subterfuges, didn't find a solution, kept up a facade of unperturbed cheerfulness, avoided any sign of anxiety, and deliberately neglected her a little. In the evenings we sat together, at our wits' end.

Then a miracle happened. The doorbell rang. A stranger in nurse's uniform smiled uncertainly at us. For a moment we didn't recognize her. Then we fell on her neck and cried. Sister Rosa, father's operating-room nurse! No one had heard from her for twenty-five years. She had emigrated to South Africa, where she had spent the war. This was her first vacation back in Europe. She had seen my films in Johannesburg and had come to London especially to visit us. It had taken her weeks to find our address. Would she stay with us? Of course she would.

She immediately took over the nursing, since she "happened" to be our houseguest. My mother was as happily surprised as we had been, asked few questions, smiled, and let her do whatever was necessary. The "bell" had obviously not yet "rung," since she didn't have to go to the hospital.

Carlos, my husband, whom she had loved from the start, was working in a Hamburg film studio at the time. One evening he suddenly felt that he had to see her at all costs. He jumped into his car and drove full speed all night long to Calais, where he managed to bribe his way aboard a departing ferry. From Dover he drove straight to London.

He arrived in the nick of time, although my mother was already unconscious. She died in his arms.

As we were walking home from the cemetery, I said, "Now I shall never hear her call me 'my Lilliche' again."

"Yes, you will," said Carlos. "As soon as we get home, if you're up to it."

I made him tell me at once, although he had intended to keep it for later, when I would be calmer. Months earlier, when my mother's illness had first been diagnosed, he had sat himself as often as possible on her bed with his left arm under the pillow and around her shoulder. Then he would ask her all kinds of questions: "How did you come to go on the stage? Tell me about it." Or "Now I'd like to hear how you got to know your husband." And my mother would tell him, breaking off from time to time to speak to Sister Rosa, and to me, too. On his left wrist Carlos wore a big watch with a microphone concealed in it. "So when we get home you can listen to her saying 'my Lilliche' again, if you feel up to it."

My father, on the other hand, died before I could make friends with him.

I was the second of his three daughters, and I knew him the least well. During the first years of my life he was away at war, and when he finally returned home, I insisted on calling him "Uncle." We had missed the early years of intimacy, and we were never able to make up for them.

I took it for granted that my mother loved him and that our large circle of relatives and friends regarded him as the final authority on all questions. And it didn't surprise me at all that on occasion he would give even grown-up members of this circle "a piece of his mind" without arousing any protest on their part.

My mother alone enjoyed a privileged position. Never did he raise his voice to her, and his impatience was always curbed where she was concerned. She was clumsy with her hands, something that drove him mad in other people. During an abdominal operation, a nurse once handed him the wrong clamps. He gave her a murderous look over his mask and hurled them through the window. (Fortunately the operating table was beyond the range of the shattering glass.) My mother, however, could spill the coffee in his saucer and provoke no more than an amused smile.

His patients, who were only briefly exposed to his skill and wisdom, were often reluctant to break away and would have liked to stay in touch with him for life. Some of them would jog his memory at least once a year by sending him presents on the anniversary of their operation. Several times a month packages used to arrive at our apartment, and we children would cluster around like dogs at a feeding bowl while they were unpacked. Perhaps there would emerge from the shredded paper a box of chocolates, which was traditionally our share of the loot. The accompanying letters spoke of "eternal gratitude," which we took as much for granted as the glowing, often tearful speeches occasionally made to him in our presence. There was never a moment in which he might have asked himself, "What is the purpose of my life?" It was spelled out to him every day. The epitaph on his gravestone says, "He was blessed."

But to me he was "Vati," and that meant unchallengeable authority and large, serious, sometimes threatening eyes. He always had a cheerful smile for us at mealtime, wanted to know what had happened in school, and was interested, friendly, and approachable, though he lacked the serenity that radiated from my mother. Now and then we would hear his impatient footsteps in the hall because the noise from our nursery had penetrated into his library. Then our door would open and you could have heard a pin drop, for my father's voice would be alarming and his large eyes full of indignation. These explosions were always brief, and the door would quickly close behind him again. We would crouch together on the floor, trying to pass it off with a giggle, mimicking his rolling eyes—but we didn't speak above a whisper. At least for the rest of the afternoon.

My mother scolded us much more often and sometimes quite angrily, but we accepted that as our daily bread and butter. She was so small and soft and round, so easy to hug, whereas my father was tall and hard to the touch when you put your arms around him to kiss him good night. Whenever one of us children rang the doorbell and the maid let us in, there was always the same hurried question: "Mutti in?" He could hear us from his study, and it hurt him, my mother told me later.

Two subjects were taboo in our lives—money and sex. Money had to be discussed now and again, though only reluctantly and briefly. We were what used to be called "well-off," though certainly not "affluent." In those days people had different ideas about what were "necessities" and what were "luxuries." My father was against luxuries. A cook, a Fräulein, and a housemaid were necessities; a car would have been a luxury. At dinner parties there were never fewer than five courses, but to eat in a restaurant was considered frivolous. When I left Berlin, after I graduated from high school, I had never set foot in one.

My allowance was seven marks fifty a week, which was tight after I turned sixteen and began to be invited out to an occasional movie by "boyfriends." This required special permission, which meant knocking discreetly at the library door and going in quietly, looking worried.

"Well, *mein Fräulein?*" The chair would be pushed back from the desk.

"May I go to the movies with Peter?"

"That will be one mark, right?"

"But Peter . . ."

" 'But Peter' nothing! Here's one mark and twenty pfenning for your subway there and back."

"But Peter won't let me . . ."

"You're not thinking of letting a young man pay for you!"

"But the subway . . ."

"You're to pay your own fare."

"Yes, Vati."

To my father, living beyond one's means was a crime, going into debt a mortal sin. Only once did I break the law. I had bought a hat for nine marks fifty and promised to pay for it the following Saturday (allowance day). I forgot. The bill was sent to our address. My father came into my room, holding the piece of paper in his fingertips as if it were a dead frog. A torrent of biblical rage broke over my head. His daughter was beyond doubt a juvenile delinquent, an adventuress, a fallen woman. Ever since then, any bill is a thorn in my flesh until it has been paid. Father is watching.

My mother wasn't quite so fussy about money, but her attitude toward sex in any form was the same as his: silence. While this was typical of the time—none of my girl friends was taken aside and told the facts of life—one might have expected a more clinically factual attitude in a doctor's household. But where his three daughters were concerned, my father was downright old-maidish, and my mother even went so far as to cram our developing bosoms into rigid brassieres that wrapped them up squarely like a parcel in order to disguise any hint of "shape." I even had to wear mine under my bathing suit. "It looks so conspicuous if you don't," she said.

My parents probably assumed that one day we'd find out something from somebody and draw conclusions. And that's exactly what happened. I discovered a few odd bits and drew absolutely wild conclusions. My friend Vera, two years older than I, said that her mother had told her that "what happened between man and wife" was the most beautiful thing in the world. Very reassuring, but what was it, please? Vera had no more to contribute. Sometimes I worried that I might be run over by a truck before I could find out.

Girl friends with brothers were ahead of me in anatomical knowledge. I, on the other hand, had never so much as seen my father in his dressing gown. Even on Sundays, when he normally didn't operate, he appeared at breakfast completely and impeccably dressed. In the end I became so self-conscious that when I looked at Greek statues, I stared them exclusively in the face.

Many years after my father's death, my mother, whose attitude had changed radically in the Anglo-Saxon environment, told me that her favorite sister, Cilly, had once said to him, "Fred, I'd like to ask you a question that no one in Landshut can answer. But I think you as a doctor will know and be able to explain it to me."

My father, always ready to instruct the medically ignorant, said: "I'll be glad to."

Aunt Cilly plunged in. "What do homosexuals actually do?"

My father got up and left the room. Aunt Cilly never found out.

3

One of the Lucky Girls

❀

I FELL IN LOVE for the first time when I was eight. The object of my affection was my German history teacher.

Our school was an unusual one for its time—a kind of boarding school, except that we didn't sleep there but went home at six in the evening. There were about three hundred pupils, mostly boys. I was one of the lucky girls.

Every morning the children formed a long line, four abreast, at the local station and marched one kilometer through pine woods to the school's main entrance. Those who lived in the neighborhood, like me, came on bicycles. I either rode close behind the platoon or threaded my way through it, creating havoc in the ranks, in order to stick as close as possible to the object of my affection, thereby getting on her nerves first thing in the morning.

She was a tall, thin woman from an aristocratic Prussian family, impoverished during the inflation after the First World War. She was not at all pretty, with an oval face and straight hair pulled back into a bun, leaving one soft wave just above her temples, her only compromise with fashion. When I saw her again after the war, twenty-five years later, she still wore her hair the same way, including the wave, though instead of brown, it was now gray. Her name was Elisabeth von Prusinowski, but we called her Prusi (Proosee).

When I fell in love with her, she was already quite old, at least twenty-eight.

We had another teacher, Fräulein Kaufmann, who was prettier and younger and funnier, but I loved Prusi, her quiet, reserved ways, her soft voice and her rare smile. Some of the other girls loved her too, but I don't think any of them suffered the way I did. Before I was ten, I had already undergone all the tortures of the unhappy lover. I remember staring with helpless yearning after the streetcar that was carrying her away from me and praying to God to keep that streetcar afloat, in case He was planning another flood.

It was my sole ambition to be head of the class—at least in Prusi's subjects, German and history. Sometimes I managed it, though never in other subjects, because there was a girl called Renate who could beat me in everything except drawing. She was tall and had two impeccable pigtails, a turned-up nose, and cool, critical eyes. She was the best at sports, too. She could jump higher and farther than I could and run and swim faster. When the report cards were handed out, she was invariably first in the class and I was invariably second. (Except for one unforgettable occasion when her bicycle fell on her head—bicycles used to be suspended from the ceiling during the winter—and she was out of the running for the term with a concussion.)

When I returned to Germany in 1954 to make my first German film and the first accounts of my life appeared in the press, I received letters from many of my old classmates, including one from Renate. I recognized her handwriting at once. It conjured up the countless times a teacher had entered our classroom carrying a stack of homework and my eagle eye would immediately detect Renate's on top, as usual.

I opened up her letter first. How had our Renate, our all-around top girl, made out? Her letter was brief, though loaded with drama. She had been married twice and had lost both husbands, one in the war, the other of war wounds not long afterwards. Her second husband had been a relative of one of the members of the twentieth of July conspiracy against Hitler. She bore his name, Baroness von Trott zu Soltz, one of the oldest names in Germany, and was trying her best to bring up her three children. She has since become, to nobody's surprise, a renowned official of the German government.

One morning I was bicycling to school as usual, with Renate next to me. Our conversation was to have extraordinarily interesting consequences: my "enlightenment." (At the age of twelve.) Prusi had asked me to prepare a talk on Frederick the Great, and I had explored my father's library. There were plenty of fat books about Frederick, and one which leaped to my eye because it had a picture of a dog on the jacket: *Days of the King*, by Bruno Frank. It dealt not only with the King's well-known love of dogs but also with his homosexuality.

It was a short book. I skimmed through it quickly and liked it, especially the passages about the greyhounds. But there was one chapter, apparently an important one, which I couldn't make head or tail of. I read it through once, twice, but it still didn't make sense to me. I took the book to school with me the next day, and when I met Renate, I told her about Frederick the Great's love problems. For my difficulties came from a chapter entitled "The Scar," in which the aged Frederick confesses to his friend Marshal Keith that in his youth he "had had an excessive love of women." The result, "of course" (why "of course"?), was that he fell ill and had to have an operation.

"Now, what I want to know is this," I shouted to Renate through the pines. "What did they operate on? His heart?"

Renate was concentrating on keeping her bicycle clear of the thick old pine roots that lay next to the path. "Why don't you learn the damn thing by heart?" she shouted. "Then you can't go wrong."

Now that made sense. I used the short recess before the history lesson to commit the questionable passage to memory, and thus was able to watch Prusi enter the classroom in my usual state of ecstasy.

"Well, Lilli," she said, "you were going to tell us something about Frederick the Great." She beckoned me to take her place on the platform while she herself sat down at my desk, as she liked to do on occasions like this. I climbed up, sat behind teacher's desk, surveyed the yawning class, and let fly at Frederick. When I got to the critical passage, I bravely recited: "As a young man, Frederick the Great had an obsessive love of women. Whenever he came too close to their skin or the fragrance of their hair, he was completely carried away . . ." At this point I realized that the drowsy class was suddenly wide awake and that Prusi was rummaging under my desk, looking for any notes I might have left there.

She found the book. I watched her leaf through it but couldn't see her face, because she kept it carefully hidden behind the covers. Never mind; I knew I was on the right track, so I kept going. About Frederick having the operation. I finished with a splendid climax of my own: "And that made him what he was."

The class stared at me with eager attention. Some of the boys snickered. I looked uncertainly at Renate, who nodded encouragement. Dramatically, and with a generous closing gesture, I repeated, "And that made him what he was," and climbed down from the platform.

Halfway back to my seat I met Prusi, who was holding my book in her hand. Her normally pale face was pink. "Thank you, Lilli," she said. "That was . . . er . . . a very interesting talk. But won't you tell us what Frederick actually was after the operation?"

Ay, there was the rub.

"He was a . . . a great king," I stammered. The class snickered again, and I was allowed to sit down. No further questions about surgery. But during recess Prusi told me to ask my mother to come and talk to her at the next parent-teacher meeting.

I worried about that meeting. Usually I was eager for my mother to make one of her rare appearances there, because I was proud of her and liked to show her off. This time I hid behind a tree, my heart pounding, as close as I dared get to the two of them. Prusi was talking and my mother was listening, openmouthed. Then they both burst out laughing, catching hold of one another to keep from falling off the bench; and the outcome of that afternoon was that Prusi was elected to acquaint me with the facts of life: only the elementary ones, of course; no details.

Many years later, at a Hollywood dinner party, I was seated next to a handsome, bald old gentleman. "Mr. Bruno Frank," read the place card beside his napkin. He looked at me in amazement when I opened the conversation by remarking that he was directly responsible for my being acquainted with the facts of life at the age of twelve. To prove it, I was still able to quote his own text to him, starting with "As a young man Frederick the Great had an obsessive love of women. . . ."

I had worked out my own intelligence system to keep me informed as to where Prusi might be located at any time of the day. The school grounds were extensive, but I always knew whether she was in the teachers' room or still at lunch, making the rounds of the pavilions or on duty at the swimming pool. She generally wore a lime green cardigan. That green beacon in the distance was the pole of my compass, and I worked out my bearings with the vigilance and cunning of Sherlock Holmes. During my afternoon activities, usually some sports contest, I never for a minute lost track of that green piece of wool, because there was always a chance that it might suddenly appear in time to witness my occasional triumphs over all the other girls (and boys). I was insanely ambitious and dreamed of Walter Mitty deeds of glory for Prusi's sake alone. Jealousy gnawed at my vitals like poison, and when I saw her pat another girl's head I would feel physically sick with rage. I think she must have known about the torture my passion caused me, because she bore with me quite patiently. Her gestures of affection were rare and deliberate. But if she happened to put her arm around my shoulders on the way to the lunchroom, my day was made.

Only once, when I was eleven years old, did she lose her temper with me. The class had been told that we were all going to the theater to see Kleist's "Käthchen von Heilbronn," with Reinhardt's young actress Tony van Eyck, who had only just turned eighteen. For me the most exciting part of the news was that Prusi would be in charge. And to crown it all my friend Kate and I were chosen to present a bouquet to Fräulein van Eyck after the performance, on stage, before the whole audience, which on this occasion would consist entirely of schoolchildren. In my closet was a new "best" dress, brown velvet with a pink silk collar, and Prusi would see me in it! On stage! Bearing flowers! I was having sleepless nights.

The great day dawned. Me in my brown velvet. Prusi not in her lime green cardigan but in black sealskin. I was quite overwhelmed at the sight, although she seemed a bit embarrassed as she rounded up her flock, all self-conscious and completely unrecognizable in their Sunday best. The foyer was full of children and teachers trying to find their seats. We had tickets for a box right next to the stage. At the end of the performance the stage manager would come and fetch Kate and me and take us backstage. First we were supposed to curtsey to Fräulein van Eyck and then, "in a loud, clear voice," I was to say, "With best wishes from the Berlin Youth Council."

My previous visits to the theater had been confined to Christmas pantomimes, and of course I had never been backstage. It was all like a dream. I followed Prusi into the box in a state of trance.

There my ecstasy was considerably dampened by the fact that there was room for one more child, and Prusi had chosen Inge, a tiny, very pretty classmate of mine and a dangerous rival. I managed to manipulate her into the back row, although she complained, quite rightly, that she couldn't see because she was so little.

The curtain went up. Golden-haired Fräulein van Eyck seemed to me a veritable goddess of beauty. I didn't hear a word she was saying, because I was wondering more and more anxiously how I would ever dare approach her and hand over the huge bouquet with its flowing ribbons. The intermissions were devoted to rehearsing "With best wishes from the Berlin Youth Council" and to holding Inge at bay. Then came the last act, curtain, applause—and the stage manager.

Paralyzed with fright, I held on to the bouquet and followed him. And before I could say "Please don't!" we were pushed mercilessly into the void—and a deathly silence fell. So, this was the stage! This stretch of glaring, empty hayloft. And was that small person over there the goddess Fräulein van Eyck? It was. She beckoned, and we advanced hesitantly towards her. She looked quite different, really rather peculiar, and I was wondering why she had painted a red dot on either side of her nose. No time to speculate; here was my great moment. I made my curtsey. Kate made hers. I wondered how I looked in my brown velvet, turned around to glance back at the box, and began, "With best wishes from the Berlin You—"

That was as far as I got. I stood transfixed, staring. There, in the box I had just left, sat Prusi, and on her lap—my knees were shaking—on her lap, bold as brass and grinning from ear to ear, sat Inge, with Prusi's arm around her! No one, no one in the world, had ever sat on Prusi's lap before, so help me God!

To this day I don't know exactly what happened. I still can't believe that I didn't finish my speech. But that's what they all told me, especially Kate. It could be that I dropped the flowers, because I don't remember handing them to Fräulein van Eyck. Kate picked them up, she said, dusted off the bow, and presented them. It is also possible that I rushed offstage amid uproarious laughter and applause (according to Kate). Otherwise, how could I have made my way back to the box so fast and launched into a hysterical tirade against Inge!

There, in full view of the audience, and very audibly too, Prusi lost patience with me, and when my brown velvet finally got back home, it was all wrinkled from my tears.

Prusi's reign lasted until I was thirteen. And then, one cold and foggy winter morning, the roll was being called, as usual, right after prayers. The first name echoed through the room: "Adam, Hans." Instead of the usual "Present," there was no response. Once again: "Adam, Hans?" No reply. "Absent," said the teacher and made a note. Somebody piped up, "He had a sore throat yesterday." The teacher nodded and went on with the roll call.

I sat there, miserable. And at the same time surprised. Surprised that I was miserable. What was Adam to me? Hans Adam, a big, fair-haired boy with pimples, who had never addressed a word to me apart from the usual daily incivilities.

All right, so Adam was absent because of a sore throat, and the only thing we could do about it was to go on with our geography lesson without him. After all, I'd lived through innumerable geography lessons in his presence without particularly appreciating it.

Next morning, before I even got off my bicycle, I was looking for the long blue woolen scarf by which you could recognize Adam a mile off. No scarf to be seen. I began to feel like an orphan again, and the worst of it was that not even the sight of Prusi's green cardigan could cheer me up. Maybe I was coming down with a sore throat, too.

Next day Adam showed up, the woolen scarf wound twice around his neck, his nose red, more repulsive than ever. When I saw him, my heart began to pound madly—and then calmed down. He was really too unattractive. Why ever should I have cared whether he was present or not?

I didn't know. But I knew for sure that I didn't care.

A week later I fell in love with a boy named Anselm. It lasted three months. We held hands and exchanged letters.

Prusi's reign was over.

* * *

Only once a year was I reminded that I was Jewish, at Christmastime.

The rest of the year I was a bouncing German child, true to the spirit of my father, one of many thousands of German Jews who loved their fatherland above all else. The dates on his ancestors' gravestones went back to the eighteenth century. His grandfather had watched Napoleon ride into Berlin. His father's unforgettably happy memories of the Franco-Prussian War made up for his own unforgettably terrible ones of World War I. When he returned to his clinic in Posen, he found the town annexed by Poland, in accordance with the Versailles treaty. The Poles were eager to have professional men stay on in their positions and offered my father considerable advantages if he would stay and become a Polish citizen. Unthinkable. He left at once for Berlin and found a good position as chief of surgery at a major hospital; my mother started to pack and we left Posen forever.

His heritage was no less German than anyone else's; he unquestionably "belonged," and he was convinced that worldwide assimilation was the only solution for all Jews. He was a surgeon and an agnostic, and neither religion nor dogma had any place in our family life. Twice a year he made concessions and took us to dinner at his parents' house to celebrate the two chief Jewish holy days, for these things were important to his father. I hated those gatherings. I had to sit still for hours on end, listening to my grandfather chanting Hebrew, of which I understood neither words nor meaning.

A child can't absorb its heritage by occasional teaspoonfuls. I held fast to being German and sang "Deutschland über Alles" just as fervently as the other children. Until three weeks before Christmas.

Right in the middle of our lesson there would be a knock on the door. A teacher (always the same one) would get up on the platform and read out a list of names in the tense silence of the classroom. The chosen children were to act in the Christmas play and thus were excused from all homework and other chores. Not to mention the fun they had during rehearsals.

I, the second-best student in the class, never heard my name called. On all other occasions they relied on me, whether it was to recite a poem, greet an important visitor with a speech, or play the lead at our annual theatrical performance. But when that man appeared early in December with his crumpled piece of paper, it was as if I didn't exist. Every time he left, I sat there shattered. The worst blow was always the casting of the Virgin Mary, the role I longed for with all my heart. Year after year it went to the same moon-faced girl with blond pigtails, called Ilse, who didn't have an ounce of talent as far as I could see. Condemned to sit in the back of the auditorium among the other children, I boiled with indignation at the constipated bleating with which this Virgin Mary replied to the Archangel Gabriel. The Annunciation might just as well have been a ticket for parking her bicycle in the wrong place.

One memorable December morning, however, the teacher with the notebook did in fact read out my name, even if it was last on the list. I was to play one of the angels.

Two ladders were mounted on the rehearsal stage, meeting at a sharp angle above the nativity stable. On every rung stood an angel. I was on a low rung—two angels below me, multitudes above. We were all dressed in nightgowns and had cardboard stars attached to our heads with yellow ribbons. But the really sensational feature was a tiny electric bulb in front of each star, connected by a wire running down the nightgown sleeve to a battery held in our devoutly folded hands. At the crucial moment, modest spotlights illuminated the stage, the choir praised the Lord, the angels flipped their battery buttons, and the golden stars formed a halo of soft light above the stable—our director's favorite stage effect.

I hated my nightgown and my tiny star. The size of the stars decreased with every rung of the ladder. The top one was large and brilliant; the bottom ones twinkled miserably. At least I should have been on top with the big star! I balanced, fuming, on my third rung from the bottom.

I had, of course, asked Prusi why I couldn't play the Virgin Mary. She hesitated for a moment. "Well, dear," she said finally, "we think the Virgin Mary ought not to be played by a Jewish girl."

"Why not?" I demanded. "Mary was Jewish, wasn't she?"

"Yes, she was," Prusi replied. "She certainly was." She looked at me unhappily.

"Well, then! Please, Prusi. Please."

But she shook her head and said, sadly but firmly, "Christmas has become a Christian festival, you know, and the Virgin Mary is a Christian symbol now. You understand?"

I didn't. What was a symbol? "But Ilse can't act for little toffee apples!" I burst out. Whereupon Prusi put her arm around me, which at any other time would have been a great consolation.

I had even gone to see my father about it. This took courage, because you didn't disturb my father in his study unless you'd fallen off your bicycle and cut your knee. This time, however, I felt I had every right to interrupt him in his medical studies.

"Well, *mein Fräulein?*" he said, visibly surprised when I suddenly burst in.

"Vati," I said, "I must talk to you about a matter of the utmost importance."

He looked at me seriously with his large gray eyes. "I'm all ears, *mein Fräulein*," he said.

"Vati, I want to become a Christian. At once. Before Christmas, please."

"That urgent?" he said. "Why?"

"Because I want to play the Virgin Mary in our nativity play. I'd be so good in it! And they won't let me. Only if I'm Christian. Can I be baptized somewhere, quickly?"

He drew me toward him and lifted me onto his knee. "I'm

afraid not, *mein Fräulein*," he said. "Time's too short. You can't change your religion like your gym tunic. And that's just as well, for you might have second thoughts—"

"No, I won't, Vati, my mind's made up."

"Well, I'll make you a proposition. If you still feel the same way on your twenty-first birthday, I won't stand in your way. But we'll have to wait until then."

"Ten years!" I wailed and burst into tears on his lapels, which always smelled faintly of ether. There was nothing left but to put on my nightgown, climb up on my rung, and wait for the big night.

There were no lessons that morning. Everybody was busy trimming the three big Christmas trees and setting up chairs and coatracks in the lunchroom, which served as our theater. Scenery was hammered into position on the stage, right through the choir's final rehearsal. We angels had been running around in our costumes all morning, powdered and rouged, getting in everybody's way and growing dirtier by the hour. At noon there was a final run-through, which went off without a hitch. I awaited zero hour in a state of deep melancholy, unrelieved by our Christmas ration of gingerbread with chocolate icing.

As darkness fell, parents, friends, and nonparticipating children took their seats in the auditorium, and we angels finally climbed onto our ladders. During the first half of the play we were hidden behind a screen. Later, when the manger came into view, a spotlight suddenly illuminated us, revealing to the audience twenty-one green nightgowns forming a triangle above the stable roof. Not until the end, when the three wise men and the shepherds knelt in adoration, were our thumbs to go into action on the batteries, producing a spectacular final climax during the three verses of "Silent Night."

Everything went smoothly. Even Ilse's Virgin Mary got applause after the Annunciation scene, which made me even more desperate as I balanced, dim green, on my rung. The gingerbread rumbled around in my stomach while I jubilated and hosanna'd away. And then at last came the cue to flick the battery button upwards. We did it in perfect unison, and an "Ah" came from the audience.

To this day I don't know what made me suddenly push my button downwards again just as my lips were breaking into a rapturous "Silent Night." I knew, of course, that all eyes would now be focused on the one gap in the chain of lights above the nightgowns. I quickly switched on again—and off once more. On, off, on, off, right through the sacred hymn. The audience could only watch me, spellbound, while the children giggled.

My fellow angels, of course, had no idea of what was going on. And I, on the other hand, didn't know that my battery had given up the ghost during the second verse and that I was switching on and off for nothing. All during the third verse I was still frantically keeping it up, but I remained dark green.

The tactful little battery came to my rescue a few minutes later, when the curtain had fallen and the director, followed by a bunch of angry teachers and gleeful children, came storming on stage. No amount of innocent eye-batting would have saved me if my claim— "But I didn't do anything! The battery must be defective!"—hadn't proved true. When they tested it then and there, they couldn't get a glimmer out of it. So instead of punishing me, they patted me on the head and gave me some more gingerbread.

Only Prusi gave me a long searching look, but I calmly returned it, for there was no doubt in my mind: the Lord was clearly on the side of His chosen people.

There was never any doubt in my mind that I would become an actress. My first performances took place under the pine trees at the Open Air School when I was ten. We were half a dozen tragediennes—boys would never have joined in anything so soppy —and we used to rush directly from the lunchroom to "our" place in the farthest corner of the school grounds, where, hidden under a cluster of trees, we would act out our version of "The Nibelungs," based on Fritz Lang's silent film, which every one of us had seen. Not so much *seen* as lapped up. We were absolutely crazy about that movie—the story, the actors, the music—and if the others were enthusiastic, I was possessed. I was the instigator and organizer of the performances we put on every day for many months. As a reward, I was the only one allowed to play two parts—Siegfried (of course) *and* the dragon. The scene where Siegfried fights his duel with the dragon required hectic efforts on my part. As Siegfried I would leap madly about, clutching a pine branch in lieu of Notung, the magical sword, and a few seconds later I would be crawling on all fours as the dragon, snarling and belching fire in all directions. Kate, the prettiest of us, as Kriemhild, wore a wreath of green leaves and moved sedately, eyes modestly down. Renate, the sports ace, was Brunhilde, because she could jump farther than anyone else. The casting of the role of one-eyed Hagen was an everlasting bone of contention, because no one enjoyed having her eye plastered over with green moss and spit.

But it was not only during the afternoon recreation periods that I distinguished myself. In the morning, in class, it was taken for granted that I would learn by heart not just the assigned verses of a poem we were reading but the whole thing. It took no effort on my part, because I had a good memory. The class took a dim view of my diligence. "Jesus, do you have to yap on like that?" they'd say in desperation. I had to. To stand up front, face the class, and declaim was my passion, and I could never get enough of it. Other children would slink to the platform, red-faced with embarrassment, and stammer out the lines as badly as possible, deliberately adopting a monotonous, droning voice, because it was considered corny to recite poetry with the proper intonation.

All that had nothing to do with me. I felt I was above the law, and I was so unashamed and brazen about it that the class gave up on me in despair. Thus I slipped into the vacant role of the school's entertainer, and when I bicycled home at night, I took my histrionic talent with me and tried it out on my mother whenever I got a chance. She smilingly put up with me, occasionally correcting my terrible intonation, whereas my father refused to listen or take me seriously. Until I cornered him one day. Like most girls, I wanted to leave school at sixteen and go to drama school for two years. "Out of the question," said my father. "You'll graduate from high school and then we'll see."

His dearest wish was for me to study medicine, and he tried to steer me in that direction right from the start. I was barely five when he would take me to the hospital with him and sit me at the bedside of his newly-operated patients. He hoped to kill two birds with one stone: I was to amuse his patients—this was before the days of radio or television—and at the same time get used to the hospital atmosphere. I did what I was told and played guessing games with the quiet, yellow-faced patients—"I spy with my little eye something beginning with . . ."—but all the time I was counting the minutes until the door would open and my father would appear, surrounded by assistants and nurses (never mind if they did smell revoltingly of ether), and take me away again. When he swept into the room with his beaming, extra-optimistic smile and the sick people beamed weakly back, I was finally liberated and allowed to ride away, perched on his shoulders.

One day I was sitting in the waiting room. I sat perfectly still, not daring to move. The only other person in the room was a big man who sat in the corner, sobbing into his huge handkerchief. I had never seen a grown-up cry before. I wanted to cry too, but I didn't dare. At last the door opened and Sister Elisabeth, the operating-room nurse, came in. Without paying any attention to me, she quickly walked up to the man and put her arm around his heaving shoulders.

"Remember," she said quietly, "the doctor told you right from the start that there was no hope."

It was a little while before he could answer. "But one always thinks . . . the doctor might be wrong."

I was seven at the time. From then on I refused to set foot in the hospital, and my father, deeply disappointed, shook his head. Perhaps I would change my mind later. Never! I couldn't imagine spending my life among people I was supposed to save. What if I couldn't? To hear every day, "Doctor, my wife . . ." or "Doctor, for God's sake, my only child . . ."

A doctor has to fight hard over the years to acquire a mental balance about the terminally ill. Only when a patient had died unexpectedly would my father go straight to his study when he came home, and my mother would immediately follow him. He wouldn't want anything to eat, and we children would know why. It happened very rarely and always disturbed me deeply. In my mind's eye, I always saw that man crying into his handkerchief.

I just didn't have what my father called "the vocation." He had it, together with the necessary thirst for knowledge. Even as a little boy he upset his sisters by cutting open their dolls' stomachs to see what was inside. It was obvious that I lacked his zeal for scientific research. Nonetheless he insisted that I get my high school diploma, in case I should see the light later on.

"But Vati," I said in despair, "I can't wait to study acting until I finish high school. I'll be much too old!"

He thought for a moment, looked at me appraisingly, and said, "You can do both. You can go to high school in the morning and drama school in the afternoon. How you manage it is your own business."

School lessons were over at one o'clock, but we were given a lot of homework. I simply had to get it done at the acting school or in the evening. The result was that between my sixteenth and my eighteenth years I lived an exciting double life. In the morning I kept Shaw's *Saint Joan* hidden in my logarithm tables, and in the afternoon I spent my breaks at drama school brooding about the negative trade balance of the Balkan states. Nobody showed me any sympathy. I had got what I asked for. After a while I became accustomed to it. The rushing back and forth was fun; so was the constant risk of being caught.

The drama school consisted of two teachers and twenty-four students. The teachers, Lucie Höflich and Ilka Grüning, both in their fifties, were among the best actresses in the German theater of the time. Every year they selected from a long list of candidates twelve girls and twelve boys between the ages of fifteen and twenty to receive two years of training, first in speech and voice production, then in the study of roles.

I appeared at the first session, outwardly blasé but inwardly vigilant lest any one of the twelve girls could hold a candle to me as far as talent was concerned. One of them could. Not only could she hold a candle to me, she snuffed me out completely. Her name was Juanita, Juanita Sujo, born in Argentina of Russian descent. She hardly needed training. At the most a little supervision. She was very popular, even with the girls. We forgave her her talent because she wasn't pretty and we all were, God be thanked. She had short black hair, small, deep-set eyes in a round, coarse Russian face, and a large, generous, loosely defined mouth. Her most beautiful feature was her feet, tiny and delicately shaped, and although she was as poor as a church mouse—her tuition was free, of course—she somehow managed to wear decent shoes. Occasionally Frau Grüning would interrupt the class to ask with a smile, "Juanita, what size shoes do you wear?"

"Three," came the proud reply.

It was a turning point in my life when we became friends. I only had girl friends from my own background—average middle-class families. Juanita's brother and sister were musicians; they studied violin and piano in Berlin with Szigeti and Schnabel. Juanita's Russian mother cooked and cleaned for the family.

The first time I went to see Juanita, I couldn't even find the place. Finally, in a rear building at the back of a courtyard, I noticed a door opening into a kitchen. At the stove stood a fat, Slavic-looking woman who grinned at me and kept on stirring. The mother. She was canning green tomatoes. Neither my mother nor my friend's mothers had ever canned green tomatoes with sloppy old house slippers on their feet.

Juanita and I talked in sign language, because in the next room somebody was playing the piano at ear-splitting volume. Juanita's sister, Anita, was practicing. Without looking up, engrossed and unapproachable, she nodded to me as we entered. This tiny room was the living room, but only the big piano lived there, though there was space for a few music stands. Piano and violin scores were piled up all over the floor—Beethoven, Mozart, Bach, and Brahms.

"Where do you eat?" I whispered.

Juanita shrugged. "On the piano—when we have company."

Anita was hacking away at two bars, always the same two. I had never heard anyone practice the piano like that. For eleven years I had had a piano lesson every Wednesday; I had to practice half an hour every day, and I hated every minute of it. Anita began to take the two bars apart, talking to herself in the process. "Oh yes, yes," she cooed, "that's it!" Then she suddenly frowned and murmured, "No, no. Never!"

I looked at Juanita. "There are always questions and answers in music," she whispered. "Anita is talking to Beethoven."

Questions and answers in music? When I practiced at home, I sat all alone on the piano stool, whether I was doing finger exercises or murdering a sonata. Neither Beethoven nor Mozart had ever addressed a word to me.

During my two years at acting school, I hung onto Juanita, watching her effortless, free-and-easy way of life with fascination. She often came to our apartment, and when she sat down at the piano, although she couldn't compete with her sister, even my father would emerge from his study, though he never failed to express his disapproval of the cigarette that hung from a corner of her mouth during her "questions and answers."

Listening to Juanita one evening, he suddenly decided to stop my expensive piano lessons. He played the cello himself and loved his chamber-music evenings, when members of the doctors' orchestra would meet at our house. He had hoped that some day his daughters would accompany him. My sister Irene did quite well, but the stern glances from behind the belly of the cello always made me strike so many false notes that he would end by laying down his bow. Nevertheless it was a hard decision for him, because music was his religion. Every Sunday morning he took us to the eleven o'clock concert of the Berlin Philharmonic, the way other people go to church.

He looked at me for a long time as I jumped for joy at being liberated from the boring old piano for good. Perhaps he knew that the day would come—thirty years later—when I would buy myself a piano, watch full of excitement as it was carried into the living room, and modestly and laboriously make a fresh start with finger exercises and scales and spend hour after hour tinkering away at a little Mozart sonata, cursing the lazy, dumb bonehead I had been when I had made my father cancel my lessons.

In the second half of my eighteenth year, things got a bit hectic. I couldn't get spherical trigonometry through my head and sat up half the night cramming, because I was having trouble with physics and chemistry too. I dozed at school, swallowed my lunch, and rushed to catch the bus to drama school. My father occasionally gave me a searching look. "Well, *mein Fräulein,* how's it going? Wouldn't you rather postpone your final exam at the drama school until next year?"

"But Vati, why?" I exclaimed indignantly. "Everything's fine."

In April things came to a head. My high school final examinations were scheduled for the first week, followed at the end of the month by the public performance that would conclude my two-year course at the drama school. On April 5, 1932, we assembled in our high school classroom, bleary-eyed and washed-out, and were told that we had all passed the written examination. A great Indian yell, unworthy of dignified seniors, rent the air, and our old professor smiled. The oral exam was child's play. Two days later I leaped about our apartment shouting "Hurrah," pushed my schoolbooks, one by one, into the tiled stove in our living room, and collected fifty marks from my father. I thought I could see a sad smile in his large gray eyes. "Just wait, Vati," I said. "You'll see. You'll see!"

And he saw, together with my mother and the proud parents of the other twenty-three boys and girls. The more important sector of the audience was made up of the directors of Germany's repertory theaters, who had come to Berlin especially for the occasion. Each one of us appeared in two different roles, to show our versatility. I did the bells monologue from *Saint Joan* and a comic scene from Sardou's *Cyprienne.* Juantia did Aase's death scene from *Peer Gynt* and a Josephine Baker role from a popular farce. Even before the final curtain fell, every one of the two dozen budding stars had a contract, the usual result of this school's public performances. We scattered in all directions, Juanita to the Munich Kammerspiele and I to the Darmstadt State Theater.

4

The Iron Cross

❀

EVEN BEFORE I presented myself, radiant and excited, at the office of the State Theater of Darmstadt (one of the best repertory companies in Germany) on August 1, 1932, things had begun to simmer and bubble in the political life of the nation. Suddenly people were actually reading those ridiculous newspapers published by the Nazi party, instead of just making fun of them. My father, with his love of Germany, refused to believe that his country would ever allow itself to be represented by "that kind of man." And when he was finally forced to recognize that Germany would indeed allow it, he sought refuge in the hope that, once in the saddle, "that man" would drop his mad ideas and "behave decently," as befitted the leader of a civilized country. It never occurred to my father to emigrate. As chief of surgery at Berlin's biggest Jewish hospital, he was irreplaceable anyway.

In those early days only a few farsighted people thought of moving to another country. Those few closed their bank accounts, packed their belongings, and left Germany as if an alarm bell had sounded. The majority stayed where they were and waited.

My salary was tiny, a hundred and twenty-five marks a month. After all, I was a beginner, just turned eighteen. My father added another hundred so that I could live, though only just. "I don't want to stand in your way," he had said when I triumphantly showed him my Darmstadt contract, "but I still don't think you'll last long on the stage."

"Oh, yes, I will, Vati," I exclaimed. "All of my life!"

I was immediately put to work in all kinds of productions. Unfortunately I could dance and sing a little, and that was my undoing. I was cast in musical comedies, although neither my dancing nor my singing was even halfway adequate. *White Horse Inn,* for instance, was going into its third season in the repertory of every German theater, and twice a week I "sang" in that. Since my numbers placed me opposite the tenor who sang Tristan on other nights, nobody was surprised that my voice never quite came across.

I also appeared as Stasi in Kalman's *Gypsy Princess,* a role that includes several world-famous songs. I managed to scrape through because the conductor was used to my "voice" and held the orchestra down to a mere whisper whenever I opened my mouth. Suddenly an SOS came from nearby Frankfurt. They, too, were doing *The Gypsy Princess* at their opera house, and their Stasi was ill. Could I replace her? Of course I could! (Twenty-five marks extra per performance.)

On the early morning train to Frankfurt, I tried to cheer myself up. Caruso had sung in *Aida* at this very same Frankfurt Opera, as a helpful colleague had reminded me just before I left. So what?

From the station I headed straight for the opera house for a quick run-through, stepped from the wings onto the stage, and looked at the huge, empty auditorium. I suddenly felt very cold. Even the orchestra pit, where eighty instruments would be accompanying me, looked like a great, black, unbridgeable abyss. Would I be able to see the conductor clearly enough to follow his baton? My new colleagues reassured me. The conductor, they said, was a good man who could enhance anybody's voice by the uncanny sensitivity of his accompaniments.

Nobody seemed worried about me as we ran through our numbers at the piano. They probably thought I was holding back to save my voice for the evening. Little did they know that I was giving my all! I spent the rest of the day gargling and doing breathing exercises, and then went to the theater early and put on my costume, which was prettier than the one in Darmstadt. That pepped me up a bit, and when I heard my cue, I strode out to the footlights convinced that a miracle would happen and a brilliant voice would issue from my mouth, as long as I opened it wide enough and breathed deeply.

The friendly audience greeted my entrance with applause for the guest performer. Courage! A short exchange of dialogue, and then my leading man and I sat down side by side in a hammock for the duet "Let's Do as the Swallows Do," rocking gently back and forth and keeping an eye on the conductor. That good man, who had never laid eyes on me before, led his orchestra through the opening bars of the famous tune and threw me an encouraging smile. But the awe-inspiring sound of those opening measures had already scared me to death, used as I was to the muted orchestral murmur of our Darmstadt conductor. No time to protest, explain, or beseech—go! I opened my mouth and sang, "I'm waiting for the happy wonder, tralala—"

The conductor stopped conducting. He leaned forward as far as he could and cupped his hand behind his ear in order to hear better. Had I started on cue or not? He thought I'd just moved my lips, because, as he told me later, not a single note had reached him.

After a few ragged chords, the orchestra gave up. In the deathly silence, a faint cheeping became audible: ". . . tralala, I've heard so much about . . ." The conductor looked at me desperately, his hand still behind his ear. I stared back just as desperately and struggled on, unaccompanied but undeterred, since no one had told me to stop.

In the meantime the audience had caught on. There was some whispering and a few guffaws. Someone in the gallery shouted, "Hey, Miss, have another go!"

On stage all was quiet, because my part in the duet was finished. Now it was my colleague's turn. But the poor man, who all this time had been holding my hand (soaking wet), according to the stage directions, didn't want to follow my example and sing without the orchestra. Silence. Gaping, black, deathly silence. Endless. A sort of rigor mortis gripped me. I could only stare at the conductor the way a rabbit stares at a cobra.

Suddenly the cobra moved, raised his baton, forced a smile to his colorless lips, and uttered the magic phrase, *"Da capo."* Once again the orchestra plunged into the introduction, this time held firmly in check by the left hand of the wiser and sadder conductor. It is therefore possible that a few of my notes did actually reach the audience, because there was some spontaneous applause when we finished the duet. My colleague had to lift me out of the hammock so that I could take a bow. I curtseyed blindly in all directions and made my exit as fast as I could, to more applause and laughter.

Six months of my contract had elapsed, and I hadn't exactly set the town on fire with my talent. Then out of the blue came my big chance. I was offered a part in another operetta, Kunnecke's *Happy Journey*. No classic, thank God. They could overlook my singing, because the role was primarily an acting one. *Happy Journey* was a hit and earned me the first reviews I could send home.

It opened early in 1933, soon after Hitler came to power. Until then there had been only vague rumblings and rumors. In our immediate neighborhood, no dramatic incident had occurred. Everyone went about his work and hoped for the best. My contract had another six months to run, and the managing director had already mentioned a possible renewal. But after the premiere of *Happy Journey,* the Frankfurt Playhouse offered me a two-year contract at double the salary, not as a junior member of the company but as juvenile lead. I overflowed with excitement, in spite of the hitherto unknown and quite frightening daily spectacle of Brownshirts parading with their swastika flags. Now that Hitler was actually in power, he would surely realize how complicated everything was and stop screaming. Of course he would; everybody said so. The terrible things he'd said in *Mein Kampf* were only party propaganda; everybody said so. No responsible politician would ever dream of turning thousands of good German citizens against him just because they happened to be Jews—people like Einstein and Max Reinhardt and Elisabeth Bergner. Germany surely wasn't going to try to get along without *them?*

Admittedly the new Nuremberg "racial laws" made ugly reading: everybody was required to produce his four grandparents' baptismal certificates. If you couldn't, you were declared "non-Aryan" and were eliminated from all areas of public life and held unfit to own any business, public or private. Did they really *mean* that? Of course not. It was inconceivable that any of these new "measures" would be put into effect. That was all just party politics. Propaganda. Nothing to worry about.

The following week, however, my Frankfurt contract was cancelled in a letter stating that, owing to the anticipated "reorganization," which would involve changes in the repertory and the company, the management regretted, but . . .

So it was true after all. I read the letter sitting on the sofa in my digs. I loved my digs. Two tiny furnished rooms on the edge of town and a nice old landlady who was accustomed to theater tadpoles like me and knew how to keep up their morale before first nights by shouting kind if confused encouragement from her kitchen. "You'll do all right, my girl, I know you will—oh Lord, my cauliflower's burning—happy landings!" I knew she'd been subscribing to the *Volkische Beobachter,* the official Nazi newspaper, for the last two months, but she took to emptying her mailbox very early in the morning so I wouldn't see it. Her affection for me remained unchanged, although she knew that I didn't measure up to Goebbels's Aryan standards.

What now? No more chance for a career in Germany. Hard to swallow, because my stupid, stubborn optimism wouldn't accept it. What if the Frankfurt theater was being honest with me after all? What if it were true that they hadn't decided on next year's repertory? Nonsense. They needed a juvenile lead; the general manager had told me so himself. I might as well get used to the idea: *they didn't want me.* Was there really nothing one could do except leave the country?

My landlady stuck her unhappy face around the door to offer me a cup of coffee. She had shared my jubilations over the Frankfurt contract and she'd seen the envelope and my face that morning. Perhaps she had known what to expect. "It's really a shame," she ventured cautiously from behind her steaming coffee cup, "because you can't deny that Hitler is a good man. You bet your life he'll make Germany great again. Too bad he has this—this thing about the Jews . . ."

That night I decided that it really was too bad. I'd better get it over with: give up the apartment, leave Darmstadt, leave Germany, go to England and make a new start in English. Luckily my father had sent me to England every year during the long summer vacation until I spoke the language fluently.

I put on my good blue dress and instead of going to morning rehearsal I went straight to the general manager's office, although I knew that Gustav Hartung, the man who had hired me, whose avant-garde productions were admired throughout Germany, was away. As I waited outside, it occurred to me that he'd been "away" for quite a few weeks—most unusual for a man so dedicated to his theater. (He never returned. He was one of the few who "knew.")

His deputy, a kindly man, received me with friendly courtesy. I told him briefly about the letter from Frankfurt, and he stared out the window for a while before turning to me with a sigh.

"Yes," he said.

I waited, but he didn't go on. Whereupon I said I was sure that under the circumstances Darmstadt would also prefer to dispense with my services. Could I consider my contract terminated as of now? To my surprise he shook his head and replied that he had no authority to let me go. After all, I was appearing in at least four current productions, one of which, *Happy Journey*, was the theater's current hit, and he must therefore refuse my suggestion. My contract had another four months to run, and as far as he was concerned, I would be obliged to spend them in Darmstadt, working.

My second attempt to get in line with the new Germany was nipped in the bud just as fast. When I tried to replace my landlady with one who didn't subscribe to the *Volkische Beobachter,* my old one was so upset that I had to unpack again.

The following weeks went by as usual, at least outwardly: rehearsals during the day, performance at night. But I had a feeling that a certain change had taken place in the behavior of my colleagues towards me. Most of them were making a point of being extra friendly, and this made me nervous. Before, they had ignored me in the friendly fashion in which junior members of a company are meant to be ignored. Now I fancied that they spoke more loudly to me than to other people, as if they wanted to make sure it didn't go unnoticed. They never missed an opportunity to say hello and ask me how I was. A very few avoided me.

Hitler had been chancellor for only three months, but the drastic change, the radical revolution, the upheaval, that was to affect every single German—man, woman, and child—was already making itself felt. Looking back, one assumes that all Germans must have recognized from the outset what Hitler and National Socialism meant. But at the time most people—unless they were already Nazi party members, and there were only about ten thousand of those—held aloof, were undecided, looked cautiously into the future, hastily made sure that their grandparents' baptismal certificates were to hand (all four of them), heaved a sigh of relief if they were, waited, read the papers, and listened to rumors.

Of course there were a few who wouldn't fall into line without protesting, or at least speaking their mind. At the Darmstadt theater they were represented, loud and clear, by a few intrepid young directors and stage designers who expressed their contempt and their derision. One of them in particular, Arthur Maria Rabenalt, the young director of *Happy Journey,* loved to make fun of "dedicated" and newly surfacing party members in the company and didn't care who heard him.

The most amazing element was the appearance of those "new men." Where did they all come from? Brand-new, completely unfamiliar faces—unless you happened to remember seeing the new "Herr Direktor" delivering groceries a week or two ago or recognized the new "Herr Conductor" as a former singing teacher at the local high school. Now conductor and director sported the brown SA uniform with the red and white swastika armband, their heavy black leather boots tramping loudly and insolently up and down the halls of hallowed institutions. Their orders from behind their splendid desks were easily understood by one and all: they didn't care what their underlings did as long as it was "different" from what had gone on before and, of course, as long as no non-Aryan persons were involved.

Non-Aryan. That definition became an overnight status symbol and was liberally used, though not universally understood. My mother, for instance, who had to engage a new cook at that time, told the honest Bavarian peasant woman at the end of the interview, "I must, however, draw your attention to the fact that this is a non-Aryan household." To which the good woman replied with a broad and friendly smile, "Oh, madam, it's all the same to me, Aryan or non-Aryan! The main thing is, no Jews!"

The replacement of people in leading positions began with those at the top in important political, commercial, and cultural functions and worked gradually downwards. But it was thorough. It left no business or establishment, however insignificant, untouched, and it became uglier as it went down the scale. The people who "took over" from the rightful owners were no longer those one had known locally in menial jobs, but seemed to have crawled out from underneath a stone. They all had low party registration numbers and were now being "rewarded."

The next piece we were rehearsing was called *When the Young Wine Blossoms,* a semiclassic from the middle of the last century. Director: A. M. Rabenalt. I played a young girl who makes her first entrance right at the opening of the play. This scene was staged as a kind of folk dance. The whole cast was divided into two equal groups, each of which started from one side of the stage, the actors holding hands and dancing towards the center of the footlights. The groups passed each other and danced off at the opposite exits. All this by way of "introduction to the audience."

Rehearsals had gone well, and the dress rehearsal was at last announced on the blackboard by the stage exit. This was good news to me. We were in mid-April. Ten more weeks till July 1 and the end of my contract.

The dress rehearsal went off satisfactorily. The play's mild, nineteenth-century humor and quaint sentimentality were vintage German and could not possibly offend anybody, even in these touchy times. The nervous man who was deputy general manager—no big noise had as yet officially replaced our absent former boss—watched from the stalls, very pleased, and made a little speech at the end, expressing the hope that our "heartwarming, carefree gaiety" would not be lost in tomorrow's first-night nerves.

I took off my white muslin crinoline, caught the last streetcar home, and prayed that this might be my last opening night at that theater. It wasn't likely that they would cast me in any new productions. I would appear twice a week, once in my good old hit *Happy Journey* and once in this new play, and that would be it until I could pack my suitcase for good.

There was the usual run-through in the morning. On the day of a premiere, the actors would assemble in the foyer of the theater to go through their lines while finishing touches were added to the set and the lighting. The moment I entered the foyer, I knew something had happened and that it was something to do with me. Everybody was standing around in groups, talking, but when I came in, they suddenly stopped abruptly. No one said good morning. Rabenalt was nowhere to be seen.

I hung up my coat, sat down, and pretended to be busy with my script. There was a menacing, totally inexplicable, endless silence. I read one page of my script over and over again so as not to make a noise by turning the page.

At last the door opened and Rabenalt appeared. In the deathly hush, he asked me as casually as possible to follow him. I picked up my coat, feeling everybody's eyes on my every movement. He walked very fast to the general manager's office and entered without knocking. "Here she is," he said, "she's all yours!" And made for the door. But the man behind our former boss's desk sat with his head in his hands and called after him, "Don't go, for goodness' sake! I need you! We've got to work something out!"

"Well, hurry up then," said Rabenalt, and fell heavily into an armchair. "Make it short. I have an opening night tonight, and now this goddam business!"

I was bidden to sit down and the unhappy deputy allowed himself a short pause before he finally addressed himself to me.

"Was your father in the last war?"

"Yes," I said, mystified.

"Thank God!" he exclaimed and sat up a bit. "Do you happen to know if he received a decoration?"

"Yes," I said. "The Iron Cross."

"What for? Do you know?"

"Because he ran a field hospital at Verdun for four years."

"Did you hear that?" said the deputy, filled with sudden enthusiasm, to Rabenalt. "That might make a difference, don't you think?"

"It might," said Rabenalt, and they both looked at me as if I were the one who had run the Verdun field hospital.

"Would you mind telling me . . ." I began.

They told me. That morning they had received a memo from the commander of the local Storm Troops saying he had just been informed that a new play was to open that night at the State Theater in which an actress of non-Aryan extraction would appear. This was a contravention of the order that such persons were permitted to appear only in old productions in which they could not be replaced by Aryan performers. A platoon of twenty-five Storm Troopers would therefore occupy the front row of the stalls that evening. At my entrance they would demonstrate "in an appropriate manner" and reserve the right to take "further measures."

For the last three months such "spontaneous" demonstrations had been nothing new in the German theater. We had heard of several similar outbursts of patriotic indignation throughout Germany, though so far nothing of the sort had happened at Darmstadt. If a local Storm Troop commander or his group leader didn't like a play or its author, or if actors were suspected of "cultural Bolshevism" or had been members of the Communist party or even friends of members (although until three months ago the Communist party had been a perfectly legal organization), the commander would send a detachment of Brownshirts to demonstrate. This could mean a variety of things: they might throw rotten eggs, or interrupt the performance, or jump onto the stage, beat up the actors and haul the particular target of the evening off into "protective custody." "Protective custody" was the euphemistic name for that new institution—new to Germany, at least—the concentration camp. There,

according to the newspapers, "unreliable" people would be "protected" from the legitimate wrath of their fellow citizens.

Even in its mildest form, such an evening at the theater was
pretty frightening for the audience, not to mention the actors. Now
I understood my reception in the foyer. They all knew.

The deputy manager sprang to life and issued orders into the
telephone. He demanded to speak immediately to the chief of the
local Storm Troopers, as he had vital information concerning tonight's demonstration at the theater. The Nazi boss, however, was
nowhere to be found. Word was left for him at his office, at his
home, all over town, to please contact the theater immediately.

Seconds later the telephone did indeed ring and the manager
jumped, but it was only the box-office lady reporting that twenty-
five seats in the front row had been requisitioned by the Storm
Troopers, which meant reseating twenty-five ordinary ticketholders.
Should she? Yes, she should. There was nothing else to be done
for the moment. I was sent to my dressing room, where I was to
wait.

The simplest course would have been to replace me, but I had no
understudy and Rabenalt resolutely refused to start rehearsing
somebody else. The question was, were the actors willing to go
through with the opening under these conditions or would they
refuse and demand that the premiere be postponed until a replacement could be found? Insults, rotten eggs, a possible beating up, on
top of the usual first-night jitters—wasn't it too much to ask?

I sat in my silent dressing room and tried to keep calm. The fact
that within a few hours I might be taken off into "protective
custody" did not enter my mind. Things like that just didn't happen
to me!

My father's decoration. I remembered having read somewhere
that non-Aryans who had served at the front in World War I could
claim "special privileges." I also remembered dimly having once
seen the box containing the cross and its ribbon. Only once. He
never wore it. No one wore medals in the Weimar Republic. My
father rarely spoke about his war experiences, but I knew that they
had been as harrowing as those of millions of others. All the

same, he had come back. Throughout my school days, the "free tuition inspector" used to show up in our classroom every few months. At the command "All war orphans please stand up," seven out of twenty children would rise to their feet, self-conscious and resentful, all of them shabbily dressed and peaked. Seven out of twenty . . .

Hours went by, and I was still sitting in my dressing room. My dresser came in, bringing sandwiches and coffee. No, she hadn't heard anything new. Yes, they'd had the run-through with the prompter reading my part. I was to stay here until further notice. Did I want anything? I wanted a whole lot of things, but nothing that friendly old soul could provide. I pushed a couple of chairs together, lay down, and fell asleep.

Toward evening the silent theater started to wake up. I heard footsteps and colleagues' voices in the halls. At last my door opened and Rabenalt came in. He looked exhausted. "Well," he said, "there's nothing else to do but go through with it. The others are willing to take the risk. What about you?"

I nodded.

"Good. We haven't been able to reach the Storm Troops' commander, but we're still trying. There's still plenty of time before the curtain goes up. So get ready—and good luck!"

He left. I began to lay out my makeup in my corner of the room. Two other actresses, playing minor roles, appeared and nodded to me. There was none of the hectic chatter of an opening night. Both of them remained grimly silent.

As I began to put on my makeup, I suddenly lost my nerve. From one minute to the next. I stared into the mirror, scared and furious with myself for having said yes so thoughtlessly. Why, in God's name? And for whom? I shot dirty looks at the other two, as if it had been their fault. If only somebody would come and tell us something!

Nobody came. Only the call boy, making his rounds, calling the hour until curtain time, then the half hour, and finally fifteen minutes. There wasn't a sound to be heard on our floor.

We had finished our makeup, and the old dresser came to help us into our crinolines. "No news," she snapped as she came in, cutting off any further conversation.

"Five minutes!" shouted the call boy outside the door, and we trooped downstairs.

On stage they were all crowding around Rabenalt, who was giving them a last-minute pep talk. He looked up when he saw me, tried to smile, and continued, "As I was saying, it's a good thing you all make your entrance together holding hands. I don't think anything will happen as long as Frau Menz is on stage." (Menz was our leading lady.) "Everybody loves her. Honestly, I don't think there'll be any violence. Be prepared for catcalls and whistling and that sort of thing and try to carry on as if nothing had happened. And . . . er . . . if they throw things, try to ignore it and keep going. Only if they actually jump on stage—then I think it would be better if you'd all stop. I've given instructions for the fire curtain to be rung down immediately."

The leading man interrupted. "Are you sure they're actually in the house?"

Rabenalt nodded. "They got here fifteen minutes ago. Lined up outside and filed in in double ranks. Take a look! You can't miss them. Front row center."

The actor went and looked through the peephole into the house. He came back without a word.

At that moment, the houselights dimmed and the call boy shouted, "Places, please." No more time for anybody to question or argue. We took our places in the wings on either side of the stage, hand in hand, ready to make our entrance, while the orchestra struck up a short introduction.

And then it happened. The actress whose right hand I was to hold, a woman in her late twenties who played one of the leads, pulled her hand free and faced me, her eyes desperate. "You don't really count," she said as loud as she dared, "you're only a child, but as far as most of the Jews I've met in my life are concerned, all I can say is—" and she spat with great precision on the floor between us.

"For God's sake, Dorothea!" hissed the actor next to her, aghast.

But she turned once more to me. "Enough's enough," she said, trembling. "I just want to make it quite clear where I stand."

The orchestra stopped, and a loud rushing noise told us that the curtain was going up. In a flash the stage was bathed in brilliant sunshine, and the first daisy chain of actors, Frau Menz in the middle, danced toward us, laughing gaily. Dorothea grabbed my hand—she grabbed my hand!—and we too, with joyous guffaws, began to skip in the direction of the footlights. As I was propelled speedily forward, my heart was pounding like a kettledrum. Any minute now . . . would they? . . . would they? . . . now! Here was the crucial moment: the footlights! Now? Onwards, halfway across —I almost flew . . . ten more steps and I would be able to disappear into the wings on the other side . . . still nothing . . . three more steps . . . made it! There was our goal, our deliverance, our haven: the stage manager's little stool! (With the poor man standing next to it, his prompt script, his glasses, and both hands convulsively clutched to his stomach.)

Breathless and sweating we collected ourselves in the darkness of the wings while the action continued onstage between blessed Frau Menz and a couple of minor actors. In their excitement nobody noticed that I was right among them, one of them, so to speak. Why had nothing happened? Was our entrance too fast or were there too many people onstage at the same time? Was it all over or was it still to come?

At that moment Rabenalt joined us. He had been sitting in the stage box physically sick with anxiety, so he said, and had rushed backstage through the secret connecting door. He could hardly speak, as he was holding up his hands in biblical gesture of rejoicing. "They're gone!" he whispered hoarsely. "They all got up during the overture and left! I saw somebody in uniform arrive and hand a message to the one nearest the exit. After that, they just got up and filed out. In formation! Didn't you know?"

No. No one had known. Everyone had aged a few years in the course of that short dance across the stage. Our "heartwarming, carefree gaiety" was gone. We drooped.

The evening dragged to its close. The audience was obviously disturbed, too. What was the meaning of the conspicuous exit of all those uniforms in the front row? Leaden silence hung over the performance. When the curtain fell, there was barely polite applause, followed by a rush towards the exit.

Next morning, I received a letter from the deputy manager: my father's Iron Cross had done it. The Storm Troops' commander had received the message in the nick of time. He, too, had spent several unforgettable years in the trenches at Verdun.

But the writing on the wall stood out in capital letters as far as I was concerned. Get out, it said. Get out of Darmstadt. Get out of Germany. At once! The only question was where to go.

The day I returned to Berlin, my father and mother and I sat up late into the night, arguing. Paris was their choice, because my sister Irene had been there for a month already, trying to get a foothold somehow. London was mine. But not my father's. "You're going to join Irene in Paris," he said. "You're still a child; you're too young to live alone in a foreign country. There's no more to be said."

At that point the "child" was just going through the ups and downs of her first love affair: Rolf Gérard, painter and medical student. "Aryan." Our love affair was already one year old. I had met him in a café on the Kurfürstendamm in Berlin shortly before my high school finals. I was sitting alone at a table looking at my wristwatch, waiting for a girl friend. So was he. We had both been stood up and started ogling each other instead. He joined me forthwith at my table, we drank a coffee together, went for a long, long walk, and fell passionately in love. I was seventeen, he was twenty-three. When I left for Darmstadt a few months later, he contrived to inscribe himself at the University of Heidelberg, an hour's train journey away. We visited each other as often as we could afford it, wrote hundreds of letters, and talked on the telephone. When I broke it to him that I was going to emigrate to Paris, he said, after a moment of contemplation, that strangely enough he had planned to go there too, to continue his studies at the Sorbonne. At Heidelberg University, he had been forced to attend a certain number of lectures on Nazi ideology every week, without which he wouldn't have been eligible to take his exams. ID cards were stamped at the entrance to the building, to prevent cheating.

Rolf had shown up at the first session as required, but from then on, as soon as he had had his card stamped, he jumped out of a window to avoid sitting through the lecture. The third time he sprained his ankle.

That did it. There was only one solution for both of us: Paris.

5

The Steel Corset: Paris

❈

M Y FATHER saw me off. He never doubted that I'd make it, somewhere, somehow. At least that's what he said there on the drafty station platform, looking up at me as I stood at the window of my compartment. Every month he would send two hundred marks to us in Paris, the maximum one could send abroad from Nazi Germany at that time. Enough for the rent and one hot meal a day. Everything else would be up to us.

"You'll need a steel corset, *mein Fräulein*," he said, fixing me with his large, gray, hooded eyes as the train started to move out of the station. He held up his hand without waving, and grew smaller and smaller as we picked up speed, until the train rounded a bend and I saw him no more.

All I saw before me, as I closed the window and sat down, was Paris. Paris, waiting for me as I'd seen it in René Clair movies, radiant and beckoning. No matter if you had lots of money or none at all. The Champs-Elysées, the Bois de Boulogne, lovers walking along the Seine—how could life be anything but wonderful? In Paris you had to be young. Young and—bulletproof. That's how I felt—bulletproof. I took out my sandwiches. Much too soon. I'd just gotten on the train, but for me a package of sandwiches always meant one thing: unpack and eat at once.

Contemplating my prospects at leisure, I could see only one

56

obstacle in the way of a meteoric rise to fame—the language. That would have to be tackled and mastered without delay. And then Paris would be conquered. On the spot. Darmstadt? A thousand miles away. Who knows, maybe it was really a stroke of luck that they'd kicked me out.

The main reason for my cloudless state of mind was Rolf. Within a few weeks he would be in Paris to register at the Sorbonne. In the meantime, I'd find a job, if necessary as a movie extra. We'd be together. What was there to worry about?

Early in the morning the train pulled into Paris. I climbed down onto the platform and looked around. Good God, what a place! The earsplitting din of trains, hundreds and hundreds of people swarming, shoving, shouting in a foreign language—and at last, thank God, my sister Irene. "Everything's quite different here," she said. "But you'll get used to it."

Our headquarters was a small hotel right next to the Bois de Boulogne, the Hôtel de la Muette. We had a tiny bedroom under the roof, cramped but cosy. I opened the window and looked out over the iron railing of the narrow balcony onto treetops. Delightful.

I was hungry. It had been a long journey, with endless customs and hotel formalities, and my stomach demanded its favorite meal. Even in Darmstadt, under the constant pressure of rehearsals, breakfast had always been my mainstay. It had to be plentiful and varied, and my Nazi landlady had always brought it to my room herself on a huge tray, thus setting me up for the rest of the day both physically and mentally.

"Can we order breakfast?" I asked.

My sister looked at me.

"All right," I said. "Where shall we go?"

We went down in the tiny, rickety, open elevator. "Where's the restaurant?" I asked.

"There's no restaurant."

"Well, where are we going to have breakfast?"

"Next door, at the bar."

"At a bar? Breakfast at a bar?"

A couple of barstools were empty, and we pushed our way in among taxi drivers and workmen. When the harassed barman finally got around to me, I was ready with my order in my best high school French: "Hot coffee with hot milk, two soft-boiled eggs, three and a half minutes, orange juice, freshly squeezed, please, toast and marmalade."

The barman, speechless, looked first at me, then at my sister.

"*Café crème et croissants,*" she said calmly, and he poured a grayish mixture of coffee and watery milk into thick white cups and shoved a basket of croissants toward us.

"You can butter yours if you like," said Irene, "but nobody here eats butter."

I stared at her.

"Most people here don't eat any breakfast. They just grab a cup of coffee somewhere. Lunch is the first meal of the day. Try a croissant. They're rather nice, and better without butter."

Worse things have happened to me in my life, but rarely has anything knocked the stuffing out of me as completely as that first French breakfast. I cried openly into the awful coffee, in which I dunked the unspeakable croissants. My steel corset had temporarily buckled.

In view of this inglorious beginning, my sister hesitated to tell me about the truly serious problem that confronted us. But by the evening of my first day in Paris, I knew the worst. "The trouble is," said Irene, "you need a work permit for everything, and you can't get one unless a French employer makes a special application for you and declares that you can't be replaced by a French girl. You can't even work as a dishwasher. We'll be lucky to get you a residence permit."

So instead of going to see the Arc de Triomphe and admiring the view, we took the bus to the Cité and the Alien Registration Office at police headquarters. First, however, we had to make a purchase: a little bottle of perfume for Mademoiselle the registrar. It had to be small enough to hide in your palm as you handed her your passport. Everybody knew, of course; still, you couldn't do it too openly. We also took along sandwiches; Irene was a seasoned refugee, hardened after two months of battle with the authorities.

That was the first of many days I was to spend standing in endless lines at police stations, waiting for registration or for a work permit.

Deprived of my main prop, a decent breakfast, I felt my steel corset buckle again as I looked at the masses of people lined up in the vast room or sitting along the walls. No one seemed to move a step forward.

"Come on," said my sister. "Let's get in that line. I know the Mademoiselle at the window. Watch how the others do it."

We got in line and I watched as we inched forward. The lines in front of the many windows were all made up of refugees of some sort. A number of them—the better-dressed ones—obviously came from Germany; others, often clutching small children, were from the Balkan countries. Almost every case became a drama when it reached the window. Passionate pleading, first in broken French, later on in wild accents of the mother tongue. I kept my eye on the little presents. Irene had been turned away several times before she caught on. Sure enough, bearers of little gifts passed the window relatively fast, without much talk. But there were only a few of them.

We took turns standing in line and sitting down. There was plenty of time to eat our lunch, because "our" window went to lunch and there was no sense changing Mademoiselles in midstream. Other people, too, ate their lunch on the benches, or even on the dirty floor. Several children looked enviously at our sandwiches.

My turn came at long last. "Our" Mademoiselle could have been anywhere from twenty-five to fifty-five. Everything about her was thin—face, hair, eyes, nose. She had no mouth at all. She eyed me coldly, frowned when I handed her my passport and tiny package, made some unpleasant French noises, opened a drawer under the counter, and added my package to several similar ones. Still muttering ominously, she grabbed a series of rubber stamps and banged them viciously on an empty page in my passport, thereby giving me the kiss of life. Now I could walk about the streets like other people, and take a bus or sit in the park without even glancing up if a policeman passed.

I was allowed to live. But not to work. That was quite another, and a far more difficult, hurdle. No use going to the Ministry of Labor, said Irene, with packages large or small. Without a contract with a French firm in your hand, you couldn't even get through the front door. Still, for the time being, we had my father's two hundred marks a month from Berlin to keep the worst wolf from our door.

And then Rolf arrived, as he had promised. Early one morning I hugged him ecstatically at the Gare du Nord, and right there on the platform we discussed the most important question: Where was he going to live? Somewhere near us, I suggested. Rolf had a better idea; he and I would take a little apartment, just for the two of us. After all, he was getting a weekly allowance from his mother for his tuition at the Sorbonne. Not much, but two could live as cheaply as one, couldn't they? I stood there, jostled by shoving, yelling travellers. A little apartment—with Rolf—alone—was I ready for that sort of thing? Yes, said Rolf emphatically, picking up his suitcase and pushing his way through the crowd.

We found exactly what we were looking for. It wasn't hard in those days. In the rue Greuze, near the Bois, five minutes from my sister's. One room, a midget's kitchen, a midget's bathroom with an ancient tin tub. Princely. A hot meal a day in one of the innumerable good, cheap little restaurants patronized chiefly by taxi drivers—French taxi drivers know about good food—served on a paper tablecloth, without napkins. Sandwiches for supper.

We had few friends. Most of the people we knew were acquaintances, German refugees, of course. We had no contact whatever with French people, nor did the other refugees. Real Parisians lived in a fortress, and we were outside, beyond the moat. Naturally, we always spoke German together. I soon realized that we'd have to cut down on our contacts with refugees, no matter how comforting it was to huddle together like chickens under the barn door, sheltering from the storm.

I was blind to the beauty of the city. I looked at the Place de la Concorde, illuminated on Saturday nights by hundreds of street lamps, with indifference, even hostility. Paris was beautiful all right, but I wasn't a tourist. I didn't have a return ticket to take me back home. I had come to work.

I started at once to make the rounds of the theatrical agents, sitting day after day in anterooms among French actors, waiting and listening until someone sent me away. That's how I learned the language. My high school French, with its terrible accent and mingy vocabulary, was as good as a sick headache. What if I knew that Louis XIV had outlived all his children and grandchildren, when I wanted to find out if some director might be looking for an actress with a foreign accent?

At first I tried the direct approach: "I'm a young German actress, with plenty of experience. I've played leading roles. Here are my reviews." (Painstakingly translated into French.) "Have you any work for me?" Or the sly one: "I happened to be in the neighborhood, so I dropped in on my way to such and such a studio, where they've got a part for me. Would you be interested in representing me—if by chance it doesn't work out?" Their first question was always, "Are you married to a French citizen? No? What about your work permit?"

Of course I always had my answer ready: "Just get me an introduction to the producer. I'll audition for him—and he'll take care of the work permit, you'll see!" This admirable self-confidence didn't fool the hard-boiled agents. They would give me a long, searching stare, under which I tried to look irresistibly beautiful. Then they'd tell me to drop by again next week.

When I look at my photos from this period, I understand their lack of enthusiasm. Some women are at their best in their teens, the famous youthful bloom bursting from every pore. I was a fat and friendly Girl Scout, with a moon face, an enormous mop of frizzy hair I was very proud of (natural curls!), and a double chin. During my teens, I starved my way from one reducing diet to the next. Long before mealtime, I was usually to be found at the as yet unset table, hands folded, stomach fiercely growling, eyes on the kitchen door, drooling in advance like a dog. Every time I managed to lose five pounds, I gained them back within a week, mostly in an orgy of milk chocolate with nuts. To atone for these transgressions, I would swallow a double dose of laxative with the last mouthful of chocolate—and spend the night on the toilet, wrapped in a blanket to protect me from the cold outside and the cramps within.

Not until much later, when my first love affair took its inevitable downhill turn, did the stubborn fat gradually dissolve and bone begin miraculously to emerge in my face. But in the days when I was making the rounds of the Paris theatrical agencies, there was no hint of future promise. All that could charitably be said about me was that I was cheerfully persistent, breathtakingly cocky, and very oddly attired, mostly in bobby socks and colorful blouses and skirts. And yet, thinking back, I remember clearly that I always had an unshakable conviction—factual evidence, such as photographs or my mirror, to the contrary—that I was very, very pretty.

And then, of course, it happened, as it was bound to by the law of averages. One dull morning at some dull agent's, I had not even finished asking the routine question, "Is there anything, perhaps?" when I was told, yes, as a matter of fact, there was. A French theatrical producer had bought the rights to a famous German operetta, Paul Abraham's *Victoria and Her Hussar,* and was planning to present it at the Moulin Rouge Theater. Did I know the piece? Of course I did! Did I remember the role of the Japanese princess? Did I remember! Well, then, would I get myself to the Moulin Rouge tomorrow morning to audition for the part.

In my excitement I forgot to ask where to get the music, and rushed home. The truth was that I had never seen the operetta, but we had had the records at home, and I knew them by heart. I spent the afternoon with a pianist friend, memorizing the music as best I could.

Promptly at ten I went through the hallowed stage door of Toulouse-Lautrec's Moulin Rouge with my pianist in tow. We hardly had to wait. *"Mademoiselle Palmer et son pianiste"* were loudly proclaimed, and I propelled myself onto the enormous music hall stage while my accompanist made for the piano in the corner. I advanced to the footlights and peered at some gentlemen sitting together in the vast, empty auditorium. *"Allez-y, mademoiselle!"* I was told, and I went into my version of the first song.

Maybe it was the German text that fooled them, or maybe the Moulin Rouge acoustics were as miraculous as those at Epidaurus, where to this day tourists can hear the sound of a coin dropped on the stage echoing up to the topmost row of the amphitheater—the fact remains that the gentlemen out front actually heard me sing and unanimously declared that I was simply splendid. They consulted excitedly in voluble French while I reclined against the piano, trying to strike an attitude midway between modesty and nonchalance. Finally, a call came from the seats. "Mademoiselle, would you show us a dance?"

A dance! That was the last thing I wanted to show them. If my singing was no great shakes, my dancing was nonexistent. Once more I advanced boldly to the footlights and declared that unfortunately, owing to the short notice, there had been no time to prepare a dance routine with my pianist, but that I was willing to show them some acrobatics, if they didn't mind seeing my knickers. Delighted laughter from below. "*Allez-y, mademoiselle!*"

Ever since my early coeducational schooldays, I could turn cartwheels, stand on my head, and perform some minor acrobatic exercises. I therefore threw myself with desperate abandon across the filthy stage of the Moulin Rouge, cartwheeling from one end to the other and landing in a spectacular split at the feet of my speechless pianist. "*Assez, assez, mademoiselle!*" came a chorus of agonized voices from the stalls. "*C'est merveilleux!*" They probably had caught the wild look in my eye as I went flailing past, and feared for their stage equipment.

Then and there, I was told that I was engaged. They were bamboozled into thinking that I must be a good dancer by the sheer mad energy of my cartwheels. I drifted out the stage door in a haze of glorious dreams, reading and rereading the piece of paper someone had hastily scribbled in lieu of the forthcoming contract. Oodles of money, or so it seeemed to me, star billing, etc., etc.—I nearly missed my metro stop and arrived home in a state bordering on delirium.

All our problems had been solved in the couple of hours since I had left for the audition that morning. Work permit? No difficulty at all, they had said. They would get it for me within forty-eight hours. In my mind's eye I could already see huge posters advertising *Victoria and Her Hussar* and its new star, Lilli Palmer. Paris had been conquered; *veni, vidi, vici;* Paris was the world's greatest city, incomparably intelligent, appreciative—I ran out of adjectives and demanded to know how much it would cost to buy a little car.

I had to be hit over the head and reminded that I couldn't drive anyway and told to wait, for goodness' sake, until the play had proved to be a success. But even in my hysterical condition I realized that it was imperative from now on to spend every free minute at one of the dancing schools (open at night, too) that turned out by the hundreds chorus girls with a proper knowledge of tap-dancing routines. Of these I had only the haziest notion, but they were indispensable in the musical comedy of that time.

Rehearsals began almost at once. Luckily, we started with the dialogue scenes, which were comparatively easy for me. I was reminded to speak up—the Moulin Rouge is a vast barn of a place —but otherwise they seemed to be pleased with me, accent and all. Every night I went straight from rehearsal to dancing class, and to the tune of "I'm Gonna Sit Right Down and Write Myself a Letter," I tapped along in a row of would-be chorus girls in front of giant mirrors that showed only too clearly that I was not exactly God's gift to the class. While most of the girls easily passed on to the second and third routines, I still wrestled mightily with the first, hopping on the wrong foot on the wrong beat time and again. "Don't worry, *chérie*, you'll get the hang of it soon enough!" said the others. But I never did. I watched them in growing despair, because I wasn't just going to dance in the chorus line, as they would, but in front of it, as a soloist, and there I was, floundering around, incapable of going through the simplest routine without tripping over my own feet.

The harder I tried, the worse I got. Dance rehearsals at the Moulin Rouge were officially scheduled to begin the next week, and the Italian choreographer had already asked me where I had danced before and what my specialties were. Our interview had been so unsatisfactory that I had left him full of dark forebodings.

When the day of reckoning came and I showed up at the Moulin Rouge dance studio along with the specially hired troupe of thirty fantastically trained chorus girls, mostly American, his worst fears were justified within the first five minutes. He asked me to execute a step that he casually demonstrated once. (Once!) It was obvious that I hadn't a clue, while the two gorgeous, long-legged dancers on either side of me acquitted themselves with the greatest of gum-chewing ease. The others stood around in small groups, pretending not to be interested, while the Italian and I had a little heart-to-heart talk. Actually, there was little talk but plenty of heart.

"I can do some acrobatics," I said, crestfallen.

"I know," he replied, "but this isn't a circus."

I had no comeback to that one, and just stared at him dumbly. He stared silently back. I put a lot of things into my stare, finishing up with WORK PERMIT in large telepathic letters. He was an Italian. Maybe he too had once stood in line at the Cité with a little gift in his hand. He must have gotten the message, for he let me stay, an unwise decision which caused him no end of trouble from then on.

I was given a few infantile steps, kindergarten-style, while the two splendid girls on either side of me diverted the audience's attention with some extra-special routines. And of course the entire troupe was clicking and tapping away behind us, easy, smiling—I couldn't get over it.

There was a noticeable cooling off in the general attitude toward me. The dance instructor must have said something less than enthusiastic about me to the powers in control. Desperately, I rehearsed my silly little dance steps in remote corners, even during lunch hour—and that was my undoing, for I clearly overdid it and tired my untrained muscles beyond endurance.

The day finally came when the little notice I had been dreading appeared on the board. "Costume rehearsal Thursday," it said. As such, this was nothing to be alarmed about—on the contrary, I was excited about my beautiful Japanese outfit but after the costume rehearsal would come the final dress rehearsal and then, next day, inevitably, opening night. God help me.

Thursday came, and my dresser wrapped me into my Japanese costume—slit up the side for dancing—and put on my black wig. My round eyes, anything but Japanese and rounder than ever from stage fright, stared into the makeup mirror. God help me.

The struggle was quickly over. My feet, accustomed to old sneakers during rehearsals, had been crammed into new silver slippers with heels, and during the very first number my swollen ankles gave up the ghost. I just keeled over and fell between my two gorgeous American satellites, who never missed a beat but tapped daintily all around me and over me, and since I couldn't manage to get my left foot out from under my right one, I lay where I had fallen, a limp Japanese bundle, till the end of the number, when the curtain came down.

Even then I couldn't move, because my left ankle turned out to be broken. As I was carried into my dressing room, I was suddenly flooded by a feeling of enormous relief. Lying on my sofa with my leg bandaged, I could hear the orchestra far, far away. I stretched luxuriously, secure in the knowledge that no one could possibly come in and tell me to get ready for my next number. Somebody from the chorus had taken over my routine, a girl called Gladys. Good girl, Gladys, I thought drowsily (they'd given me something for the pain)—she can't act her way out of a paper bag, but she can dance.

The next day dawned rather gray for me, with one leg in a cast and what was left of my four weeks' rehearsal pay. But I still had my work permit, good for the run of the show. Surely they wouldn't cancel it? Surely they wouldn't remember that?

They remembered. Forthwith. A policeman appeared and asked for the slip of paper. He looked at my face, then at my cast, and decided to stay for a cup of coffee. Which turned out to be important for the future. From then on he got into the habit of dropping in around the first of the month, accepting with dignity a *café crème* and a hundred francs, and leaving again with a "*Merçi, mademoiselle.*" He wasn't the only policeman dropping in for coffee with refugees in those days.

A month later my sister and I did indeed start working. Hitler had just issued a new order that not a penny was to be sent abroad, thus abruptly cutting off my father's lifeline to us. There wasn't even time to lament; the rent was due. Was there really no way to get around the work permit?

There was. We found out that the only places the police never checked were nightclubs, which employed mostly foreigners for short engagements, too short to interest the authorities. So while my ankle was healing, we began to work out a "sister act" in five languages. Irene, with her pretty voice, carried the tune, and I sang the harmony. (Less conspicuous.)

Our program was anything but ambitious. We diligently rehearsed a dozen songs, half of them Viennese waltzes, because we planned to bill ourselves as "Les Sœurs Viennoises." ("Les Sœurs Allemandes" would have been unpopular at the time. "Austrian" softened the blow.) So we sang "Wien, Wien nur du allein" and similar Viennese schmalz. For Americans and Englishmen we had a sure hit. I sang "Did you ever see a dream walking?" to which my sister answered "No," and I sang brightly, "Well, I did!" etc., etc. Then there were one or two Spanish and Italian songs and a few French ones, including a translation of Disney's "Who's Afraid of the Big Bad Wolf?" (*Qui craint le grand méchant loup?*)—worth mentioning because it proved later to be a turning point in my life. In Russian we sang the inevitable "Ochi chornye," coached by a Russian, a refugee of an earlier vintage.

But what were we to wear? We needed two identical costumes— evening dresses, something theatrical, something Viennese, above all something that cost nothing, because we hadn't a penny to spare. At a haberdashery at the foot of Montmartre we found the solution—a few yards of light green taffeta, probably curtain material, at a bargain price. A friendly neighborhood sewing machine made it up into dresses with puff sleeves and frills all over the place. We looked like two large, lime-flavored lollipops.

The first nightclub we hoped to conquer was called the Monte Cristo. We had read about it in the paper. It was a new *boîte,* recently opened, and a Monsieur Max promised all tourists a warm welcome, dimly-lit tables, and a discreet orchestra. We put on our "good" coats and squeezed into a bus going to Montmartre. We got out at the Place Pigalle and easily found the place, on the rue Pigalle, small but splendidly illuminated, guarded by an enormous Russian doorkeeper. It was eleven o'clock at night, too early for customers, but the right time to approach the management, we had been advised. Monsieur Max, a Greek gentleman of shiny black appearance in immaculate evening attire, was informed of the presence of "Les Sœurs Viennoises" and threw an unappreciative look at our "good" coats. He listened patiently to our eager self-advertisement and agreed a bit doubtfully to our coming back next day at three o'clock in the afternoon to audition.

We left his office jubilant, lingering for a moment in the entrance since the "discreet orchestra" had just started its first number. What a marvelous place this was! I had never seen anything so seductive and cosy in my life. A small room, no more than twenty tables, all lit from beneath, dark red silk walls, candles everywhere, soft music—so this was a nightclub! I could hardly tear myself away.

At three o'clock sharp the next day, "Les Sœurs Viennoises" were back at the Monte Cristo. I hated to admit it, but in the daytime the *boîte* was a letdown. Light filtered through small slits in the ceiling, the silk hangings looked dowdy, and a charwoman was vacuuming between the tables. We draped ourselves around the piano until Monsieur Max finally showed up and ousted the charwoman. He, too, should have been on view in artificial light only. He slumped heavily into an armchair and wearily waved his hand toward us both in greeting and as a signal to begin, for God's sake, and get it over with.

We plunged brightly into our repertoire, starting with a Viennese waltz. His eyes stared glassily at us from over his heavy six o'clock shadow with a mixture of incredulity and unconcealed horror. In his hung-over state, our waltzes-in-harmony must have just about done him in.

Yet, as he later explained, the thought struck him as he looked at us that we were obviously sisters—a brilliant observation, as there is a strong family resemblance among all of us. Also, he felt, we looked "different" from the usual nightclub act, and there he was most certainly right. There must have been some sunny, hillbilly quality about us which he probably mistook for "Viennese"; anyway, after our last lingering chord and pearly smile, he roused himself to a sitting position and waved us to his side.

Ten minutes later we left, hugging each other for joy. We were engaged as of the next day for two weeks, with options for further extension "if the customers took to us," at a salary of one hundred francs (about ten dollars) per evening. A fortune.

Rolf was less happy about my new line of work, but he had no alternative to offer. His schedule was already established. Every morning he went to the Sorbonne for the courses needed to finish his medical degree, and also some that weren't needed, such as physics with Marie Curie, then in her last year of teaching. She was a poor teacher, he said. The students always greeted her appearance on the platform with an ovation of foot-stamping that lasted several minutes, but her shyness would never let her acknowledge it. Eyes riveted on the floor, she would make at once for the blackboard, rapidly filling it with her physicist's hieroglyphics, making no attempt to explain what they meant. When she did occasionally turn to say something, it was inaudible. Nonetheless her lectures were crammed to capacity, for the tiny figure on the rostrum was already legendary.

Monsieur Max had not asked about our work permit. He had also not asked about our costumes, and that proved a mistake. For when we turned up the next evening in our green taffetas, he did a double take. But it was too late to send us away and get somebody else, so he gritted his teeth and had us announced: *"Mesdames, Messieurs, maintenant nous allons avoir le plaisir d'entendre Les Sœurs Viennoises,"* and we wafted into the bright spotlight to the enthusiastic applause of the headwaiter. The couples at the twenty tables looked up, probably felt a bit sick at the sight of so much light green, and went on with their conversation. This was disconcerting and had to be digested; customers' bad manners must be ignored with a dazzling smile. We dived headlong into our schmalziest waltz, and a couple of tables actually stopped talking. Emboldened, we graduated to our English and French numbers, which were tolerated, and when we arrived at the eternal Russian "Ochi chornye," quite a few tables were actually singing with us, which did not exactly enhance the musical quality of our number. Never mind, the customers had "taken to us," no doubt about it. Even the green taffetas were allowed to stay. Maybe they, too, were "Viennese" and *gemütlich*. Monsieur Max had no intention of questioning his customers' tastes; he was amazed, that's all. But he let us stay and paid us our hundred francs every night.

Every morning, that is, for we had to stay from 11:00 P.M. until

5 A.M. For the first week I found that timetable simply marvelous. Never having stayed up past midnight, except on New Year's Eve, I was thrilled to find myself listening to soft music at four in the morning in a nightclub. But by the time the second week started, my enthusiasm had begun to wilt a little. We found it difficult to get enough sleep during the day. The noise from the street or the telephone woke us up, and we were bleary-eyed and tired when we set out for work at 10:30 at night.

A small corner table was reserved for us, with an unopened bottle of champagne in a cooler and four glasses—in case. In case a customer might want to sit down with us. Only then would the champagne be opened. The first time this happened and some friendly chap from Iowa joined us at the table, the hovering head-waiter swooped. But when the American asked us what we would like to drink, we didn't know the routine, and Irene answered, "Nothing, thank you," and I said, "A glass of milk, please!" where-upon the headwaiter was overcome by a coughing fit. Afterwards, we were called into Monsieur Max's office and told a few facts of life. We were always and automatically to ask for champagne.

"But I can't drink champagne," I said. "It doesn't agree with me. And it makes me sleepy."

Monsieur Max glared at me. "Pour it on the floor while your sister is dancing with the gentleman. Pour hers, too—and his. Then fill all the glasses again."

"I can't do that!" I cried indignantly. "That's . . . that's . . ."

"That's a nightclub rule," said Monsieur Max firmly. "What do you think the thick carpets under the tables are for?"

Fortunately, unaccompanied gentlemen rarely paid any attention to us. They usually concentrated on the ladies sitting at the bar alone, the *entraîneuses* hired by Monsieur Max for this purpose.

At 5:00 A.M. we could finally take a taxi home. At that hour no other transportation was available. Wan and bleary-eyed, we would sit side by side and avoid looking at each other. Apart from the bellowing of an occasional drunk, there was only the rattle of the milk carts clattering slowly through the streets in the early morning light. Irene got out first. We waved shakily to one another, and then I drove on to our apartment around the corner. On my pillow

I usually found Rolf's contribution to my night's work in the form
of a drawing graphically and lovingly depicting the day's events.
I was represented as a flounder wearing a beret, while Rolf saw himself as a frog with glasses, carrying a briefcase under his arm. The
drawings showed Flounder and Frog coping with their daily problems: Frog flunking his exam, Flounder being harassed by rich,
passionate nightclub habitués. I would pick up the day's drawing
and admire it in the bathroom by the gray morning light. After
which I went to bed, tired and content. Nothing could happen to
me. Bulletproof.

The two weeks at the Monte Cristo went by like lightning. What
next? Were they satisfied with us? Did the patrons like us well
enough? We didn't know and were scared. The headwaiter read it
in our faces and casually told us not to worry. "*Ça va aller.*" And
sure enough, on the very last day, when we were beginning to
shake in our shoes, Monsieur Max condescended to tell us that our
contract would be extended. For how long? His answer was non-
committal: a week, two weeks, maybe longer. It would depend
entirely on the reaction of the clientele, on whether they still liked
the act or were getting tired of it. By the way, could we change
our program? But of course! And those . . . costumes? Unfortunately
not.

By the third week, our lack of sleep was beginning to tell on us.
I knew every tune the orchestra played, backwards; the atmosphere
of the *boîte,* once so mysterious and seductive, was by now stale;
I began to look at my watch every half hour. Still, we were making
a living.

But what were we to tell them at home? Our parents kept asking
questions, waiting to hear all about everything, but they got only
vague answers. Neither my father nor my mother had ever set foot
in a nightclub, so what was the use of upsetting them? We wrote
that we were appearing in a "cabaret," and they were surprised and
thankful that we were managing to live at all. They worried about
us, and we worried about them. We read French newspapers, so we
knew better than they did what was going on in Germany, and
above all what was in the making.

At night at the Monte Cristo there were of course the usual problems, as well as the unusual ones. From the first we had no trouble dealing with the usual ones. After all, there were two of us, which meant that we had "rearguard cover" even when the guest who sat down at our table took us for *entraîneuses.* They never stayed long. Nightclub patrons, most of them tourists, didn't waste their time on two frosty Girl Scouts when there was livelier company to be had at the bar. The unusual problem came to me in the form of an order from Monsieur Max to see him in his office, alone, please. Without any preliminaries, he tried to push me backwards onto his black leather sofa, while I resisted vociferously. "*Au secours!* Help, help!" I screamed at the top of my voice, and a few moments later there was a pounding from the outside on the black leather door, and the headwaiter called nervously that mademoiselle's voice was audible above the orchestra. Whereupon Monsieur Max released me abruptly and announced, "*Je n'insiste plus.*" I was allowed to leave the office without further ado, green taffeta slightly crushed but head high and full of dignity.

Monsieur Max never referred to the incident with so much as a look. We stayed at the Monte Cristo about five weeks, saved a little money, and even more important, established new contacts. It made all the difference to be able to drop into another nightclub just before opening time and say casually, "We're appearing at the Monte Cristo. Why don't you stop by and take a look at our act?" But before we could move on to another *boîte,* fate had something in store for us, so devastating that all our plans for the future came to a standstill.

One afternoon as I was carrying a shopping bag to Irene's flat, the concierge, instead of hiding behind her small window as usual, fluttered out to greet me, wringing her hands. "News from Germany," she called. "Bad news."

The trip up to the fifth floor in the rickety elevator was endless, and there on the landing stood Irene. "I thought you'd never come," she said, crying. "It's Vati. He's . . . ill."

I stopped, frozen.

"He's dead," she said, and ran into her room.

A few hours later we were on the train to Berlin. My father had died the night before, suddenly, within a few minutes after his first heart attack. All I could think of was my mother.

She greeted us at the door, all in black, as I'd never seen her, her face unrecognizable. "My only one is gone and he is not coming back," she said.

There were many hundreds of people at the funeral, so many friends, so many patients. I remember a few with canes, or helped by nurses—people on whom he had recently operated. Someone performed a cello solo of his favorite piece, Schumann's "Träumerei," and I remembered his playing it and my accompanying him on the piano. It was almost too hard to bear, and I forced myself to conjure up his gray eyes and the tone of his voice when he said, "You'll need a steel corset, *mein Fräulein!*"

Later we kept up a front in the big apartment, which had lost its soul and its sense. On my father's desk lay a volume of Schiller's poetry. The morning after his death, my mother, still stunned and barely able to walk a few steps, had been looking for his keys and had found the book, the page opened at his favorite poem, "Die Ideale." He had often quoted it. She fetched her glasses and read the passage he had underlined:

> Extinguished are the clear bright suns
> That lit my youthful path.
> Vanished are all the high ideals
> That filled my loving heart . . . .

The "clear bright suns" had certainly been extinguished. He died on January 31, 1934, exactly a year after Hitler had come to power. In the face of the devastating evidence all around him, he had been forced to give up his last vestige of hope about "the man." His personal tragedy was to stay at his post in the country that he had loved so passionately and where he had in the end been an outcast. My mother told me that once, not long before his death, he had come home very late, refused all food, and gone straight to his study. She had followed him and sat down on the sofa, where he was stretched out. His eyes were closed, and he looked gray and utterly exhausted. That morning, several young men had been brought to his hospital, which happened to be the nearest—all of them young

Communists who had been beaten up by gangs of Nazis. "I went through four years of war," he said, "and I've seen people torn apart by bombs and machine guns, but I never thought the day would come when I would have to try to sew up bodies torn apart by human hands—in peacetime."

We didn't realize it at the time, but fate did him a good turn by letting him die. He wouldn't have made a good refugee. He was too old to learn a foreign language in order to take medical examinations and begin all over again. Later, in London, I met refugee doctors and scientists of his generation whose wives ran boarding-houses for other refugees. The husbands answered the doorbell, said "Hope you'll like your lunch" to the paying guests, and helped with the washing up.

Outwardly, life would continue as before. My father had plenty of life insurance, enough for my mother and my youngest sister, Hilde, to live on. We wanted to stay on with them, at least for a time, and make sure my mother ate something, try to talk to her about Vati or, if she couldn't do that, simply sit with her and take turns sleeping next to her in Vati's bed.

Then for the first time she awoke from her apathy. We must return to Paris immediately, she said; every day in Hitler's Germany was a loss for young people with their lives before them. Impossible, we said. She couldn't remain alone with little Hilde, aged thirteen, who sat frightened and apprehensive in the nursery, dressed in black for the first time in her life. A few weeks before my father's death, my mother had been asked to come to the Open Air School. The principal, Wilhelm Krause, had known my parents for years. First Irene, then I, and now Hilde had all bicycled happily through that wooden gate. Herr Krause stood staring out the window when my mother entered. After a long silence he said that he was obliged to ask her—or rather to tell her—though very regretfully, to take Hilde out of school. The new regulations—he really didn't know himself what to make of them—she must realize how difficult . . . So for the last few weeks Hilde had been attending a "private school," one of many children in the same position, all dejected and hushed, because they didn't understand what it was all about. And now Vati was gone, too; the anchor one had always been able to cling to had vanished.

After the funeral Irene and I sat up with my mother until late at night, repeating over and over, "We can't leave you alone *now*."

"Yes, you can," she answered stubbornly. "Yes, you can. First thing tomorrow. No one can help me now. And it would make everything much worse if I knew you were risking your entire existence just to stay with me. What do you want to do all day long? There isn't anything left to do."

She was right, and we knew it. Our foothold in Paris was precious and still very shaky, and we must on no account lose it if we wanted to survive.

The last time I had gone out of our front door carrying my suitcase, my father had been with me. Only four months ago. Was it possible? Only four months? This time my mother went with us to the station and waited on the platform, a little black figure waving until the train rounded the bend.

We closed the window, sat down, and made a vow. From now on we would take turns writing home every day, every single day, good long letters, telling her all about everything. Then she would always find something in the mailbox when she got up at dawn, for of course she couldn't sleep. In this way she would share our lives, our hopes and disappointments, just as if we were coming home at night to report. Every Friday we'd send her a special-delivery letter, so that she'd get something on Sundays too. For two years and three months we kept our vow.

Back in Paris, we took off our black clothes and plunged into the fray again. Another nightclub had to be conquered, because our days at the Monte Cristo were numbered.

We would have been fired there long before if it hadn't been for an eccentric young Frenchman with a passion for Viennese waltzes who dropped in nearly every night to hear "Wien, Wien, nur du allein." Baron Nicky de Ginzbourg and his girl friend Denise Bourdet, wife of Edouard Bourdet, the famous playwright, had taken a fancy to us, probably because we so obviously didn't belong. While Nicky and Denise were still checking their coats, the orchestra would strike up the first waltz and we would have to start warbling. Afterwards we were allowed to join them at their table, and Nicky would always order something special for us to eat. But when he left Paris on a holiday, Monsieur Max took advantage of his absence to get rid of his two green canaries.

No choice but to look elsewhere. We had a picture of our "act," showing us back to back in green taffeta, and with this photograph, of which we were very proud, we went in search of a new job. This time we aimed higher. The "Casanova" was the most famous and the most expensive nightclub in town. It wasn't far from our home base, the Monte Cristo—most nightclubs were within walking distance of the Place Pigalle—but the Casanova was different in style. Very discreet on the outside, hardly any lights showing except the famous name in a soft red glow. At the door, of course, the giant shape of the Russian doorkeeper. We were shown into the office. No shiny black leather here; old ikons and costly tapestries on the panelled walls. The manager, Monsieur Nicolas, a dapper, well-dressed little man with a Russian accent, could just as well have been an English bank manager. He listened to us politely and said that he was always on the lookout for new talent and that we could have a two-week tryout at a hundred and twenty-five francs a night.

Easy as pie. Would you believe it? If only we had other costumes! We racked our brains and came up with a solution: a refugee friend in the wholesale raincoat business offered us two specimens, rather pretty ones, white with velvet collars. The contrast would be sensational—green taffeta for our first appearance, raincoats for the second.

Monsieur Casanova, as we called him, wasn't too keen about either of them. But he didn't say anything, only winced a bit when he first heard our version of "Ochi chornye." The clientele was even more exclusive than at the Monte Cristo, more international and more blasé. Especially during our act. They talked loudly right through, nobody deigned to sing along with us, and there was only scanty applause. We were followed by the famous Hildegarde, an excellent singer who accompanied herself on the piano. Nobody talked during her number, except for a few drunks.

They put up with us for ten days. Then we were summoned to

Monsieur Casanova's office. He made it short: we didn't fit into the atmosphere of his club. He paid for two full weeks.

We simply didn't have time to mope. The very next day we presented ourselves at another Russian nightclub, the Schcherazade. There must have been an acute shortage of nightclub acts in Paris at that time, for once again we were hired on the spot—"it so happens that we've just finished our engagement at the Casanova"— by the owner, an enormous Russian with red scars across his face. This time we lasted only five days, our shortest engagement. We accepted our dismissal with composure. They didn't like us? Okay, we'll go somewhere else.

"Somewhere else" included several nightclubs, the names and shapes of which escape me, until we landed in one which, for several reasons, did impress itself on my memory. We had tried all the more elegant places, where they didn't want us anyway, and were now concentrating on the more "popular" kind, with lower price of admission, clientele to match, and of course matching lower salaries for us. In these places we always stayed for the full length of our contract and sometimes longer. Our program had varied, but the green taffeta and the raincoats had not.

We had already been appearing for a month in this particular *boîte* and were glad of it, for we couldn't afford to be out of work for more than two weeks at most, in spite of the most rigorous economy. One night I had a stomachache and asked a girl behind the bar if there was anywhere I could lie down for a moment. Maybe a sofa in the manager's office? No, there was none. But she pointed vaguely to a staircase at the back, which I had never noticed before, and mumbled that I would find a place to lie down "up there." I climbed the stairs and was surprised to find myself on a long narrow landing with half a dozen doors leading from it. I tried the first door, but it was locked. So were the second and the third. The fourth, however, opened—and there was a sofa, all right, and a bed, too. But it was very much occupied by two people who stared at me the same way I stared at them. At last one of the two, the gentleman, spoke up and said, *"Eh bien, Mademoiselle,* want to join us?"

I scurried downstairs and back to our table. "Do you know what's going on upstairs?" I asked Irene, when I caught my breath. From that moment on we took a great interest in what went on around us, and before the evening was out we knew that downstairs the place was a respectable nightclub and upstairs a respectable brothel, and that our *entraîneuses* marched up and down the back staircase with different clients twice every hour, on the average. Downstairs, though, none of the ordinary patrons, the married couples or groups of tourists for whom we sang our Viennese waltzes, suspected anything. We decided that we wouldn't suspect anything downstairs either, as long as no one asked us to participate upstairs. No need to worry about that. The owner, whose wife kept the cash register, treated us with professional indifference, and the *entraîneuses* with icy disdain.

But at that very nightclub it happened. Every night, as I was putting on my green taffeta, I said to myself, today's the day! Tonight Sam Goldwyn is going to be there with a whole crowd of people. He'll take one look, point to me, and say, "That one over there!" But when it actually happened, I didn't recognize it, because it wasn't Sam Goldwyn.

We had just finished the French version of "Who's Afraid of the Big Bad Wolf?" and were sitting at our table back in the corner when a small, fat man came up and introduced himself. He was Walt Disney's French representative, he said. Would we like to sing that song in honor of another Disney executive, who would be arriving the next day from Hollywood? A free dinner? Of course we would.

And a splendid four-course dinner it was, for a whole lot of people, most of them Americans, who had something to do with Disney. Without their wives. Which was probably why I was seated next to the guest of honor. Before dinner he had listened to our version of the Disney song with great pleasure, most likely because he didn't understand a word of French; now, after some lengthy tribute to Disney achievements—three cheers for Walt Disney—he revived himself with the excellent wine and turned to me. I had been busy all through with second helpings of every course.

"Well, young lady," he said by way of an opening ploy, "and what is your goal in life, if I may ask?"

I stopped chewing long enough to inform him that it was my intention to become, before long, one of the world's greatest actresses.

He roared with laughter, in which I didn't join. "In that case, young lady," he said when he had recovered, "let me help you take your first step up the ladder of fame."

My fork stopped halfway between my plate and my mouth. "How?" I asked, suspicious.

"Well, now," he said, "why don't you drop by the United Artists office tomorrow and meet the head of the casting bureau?"

"What's his name?" I asked, still unconvinced.

"Curtis Mellnitz," said my neighbor. That was all. I waited, but he did *not* ask me to join him for a drink later on. I forgave him his laughter.

"What time shall I be there?"

"Eleven o'clock. And bring a few photos if you have any."

The next day was sunny and cloudless, although I had prayed for rain so that I could wear my raincoat, by far the prettiest outfit I possessed. Photos? Yes, I had a few, dating back to my Darmstadt days, only a year ago. An eternity.

Promptly at eleven I entered the United Artists office on the Place Vendôme. Thick carpets, huge potted plants, many doors. "Mr. Curtis Mellnitz, please." Third door on the right—was that what the girl at the reception desk had said? In my excitement I wasn't sure, but I didn't dare to ask again. I ventured a tiny knock.

"Come in," croaked a hoarse voice. Behind a desk sat a man of about sixty with a large mane of white hair, looking at me suspiciously through owllike glasses.

"What do you want?" he growled, like a dog getting ready to pounce. I retreated toward the door.

"I've come to see Mr. Mellnitz—I have a recommendation—excuse me, please, I've got the wrong room."

"You've got the right room," he said. "I'm Mellnitz. Sit down. What do you want?"

When I looked more closely, the eyes behind the glasses were kind and the growling turned out to be something wrong with his vocal cords. As briefly as possible I told him what I wanted. He didn't laugh or make any comment, just looked at me without a word. Then he asked a few questions, where I lived and where I worked. I showed him my photos. He shook his head and handed them back to me. "They're bad," he said. "Don't show them." A long pause.

"You know," he said finally, "this is a most extraordinary thing—the way you came in here and the way the sun hit you as you were standing there at the door. It's happened to me once before, in Berlin, a few years ago. We were looking for the right girl to play Katya in *The Brothers Karamazov,* but we couldn't find anyone. One morning there was a knock at my door and a girl came in. Anna Sten, Russian. I knew she was our Katya as soon as I saw her standing there blinking in the sun, the way you did just now—why are you wearing a raincoat?"

I explained.

"I see," he said gravely. "Now look, United Artists don't make movies any more. They just distribute them. Otherwise I'd easily find something for you. Still, I know a lot of people in the industry. I'll see what I can do."

I stammered a few words of thanks.

"We must try to get you to London. You'll never get anywhere in Paris. London's the place for you. Where's your mother?"

I told him.

"Could she come here and talk to me? Give me your telephone number. You'll hear from me. Write to your mother. Good-bye."

Outside on the Place Vendôme I took off my raincoat and walked in the hot sunshine the short distance to the Tuileries. I sat on a bench and looked across the formal gardens of the Louvre toward the Arc de Triomphe. But I didn't see it. Instead, I saw my future quite clearly, for the first time. I didn't doubt for a moment that the old gentleman would keep his word. Somehow I'd manage to go to London and start there all over again. No more nightclubs, no singing or dancing, no more faking something I couldn't really do. I'd be an actress again. And when I had signed my first contract,

I'd bring over my mother and sisters, Rolf would follow, and I'd buy a black car and a black dog.

Before the week was out, I heard from Mr. Mellnitz. "Miss Palmer?" bellowed the receiver. "My old friend Douglas Fairbanks is here. I'd like to introduce you to him and see what he thinks of you. One o'clock tomorrow at the Ritz."

Douglas Fairbanks! The very first picture I ever saw in my life had been *The Thief of Bagdad*. I had sat enthralled and so completely transported that I had eaten off the entire right thumb of my woolen mittens, for which I caught it later from our Fräulein.

And now the same old problem: what was I to wear to lunch at the Ritz? I'd simply have to keep my raincoat on. Anyway, by now I regarded it as my lucky coat. At the Ritz, however, it failed me.

Douglas Fairbanks was shorter than I expected, with dark skin and startlingly white teeth. He didn't take any notice of me, just smiled once vaguely in my direction when I was presented. Instead, he concentrated on his food. It tasted gorgeous to me, but he didn't like any of it and sent it back several times, keeping the waiters on the double. He seemed thoroughly miserable, and nothing his beautiful wife or Mr. Mellnitz said could cheer him up. A few months later he was dead.

I prayed that Mr. Mellnitz wouldn't be put off by Douglas Fairbanks's lack of interest. He wasn't, for a few days later my telephone rang again. "A good friend of mine is passing through Paris," he croaked cheerfully. "His name is Alexander Korda. Drop by my office tomorrow."

Alexander Korda, Hungarian, one of the founding fathers of the British movie industry, a tall man with a mane of gray hair and eyes full of secret irony, looked me up and down and smiled.

"How old are you?"

"Nineteen."

"You've still got puppy fat all over," he said. "Do you know what I think? You'll look a lot better in ten years' time. Now don't look so unhappy! It's something to look forward to, no?" I didn't think so. In ten years I'd be old, done for, finished! "But I promise I'll give you a screen test if you come to London. We're actually on the lookout for a young girl for a certain part. Here's my card."

That card became my most sacred possession, the open sesame to my future. Alexander Korda, 36 Davis Street, London W. 1., would be my only toehold, the one person in the whole of England I could call up with the words "Hello. This is Lilli Palmer. Here I am."

But how to get there?

My mother came. Hidden in her suitcase were two valuable little paintings, a Corot and a Daubigny, which she wanted to sell so she could send me to London. There was nothing for it but to confess how and where we were earning our living (our brothel had just extended our contract), and she sat there looking very white.

The two paintings were quickly—and badly—sold, and the money divided between Irene and me. It was only about a thousand francs; the pre-Impressionists didn't fetch high prices in those days. My mother left again as soon as she'd seen Mr. Mellnitz. She didn't want to stay on and involve us in extra expense, because every franc counted.

We saw her to the train. "Take English lessons," I begged her. "You'll see! We'll all be together soon in England, and you'll make a new home for us in London. You'll see!"

She was still in black and still couldn't smile, but she nodded from the train window, and we could see that she liked the idea.

We didn't need to break up our sister act; it collapsed gently all by itself. There were no nightclubs left to conquer. Either we'd already appeared there or they had turned us down. When our brothel finally got tired of us, we had reached rock bottom.

The year in Paris, full of disasters, had been of great importance to me. I had come to know myself a little better and knew by now when I could rely on myself and when I would let myself down. Surprises either way were always possible, but I resolved as of now to take myself severely in hand. I would be more critical, both of myself and of other girls, less untidy, less sloppy—and above all *thinner*.

Out of the five hundred francs that were my share of the proceeds, I bought my ticket and put aside thirty-four pounds as a nest egg for conquering London. Fifty francs were spent on new photographs, which left a hundred and fifty francs for two new dresses, one for every day and one for "best." I was going to have them made, and I sought the advice of the best-dressed woman we knew, Babs Siodmak, wife of Robert Siodmak, the German film director, who was making movies in Paris.

"Black," she said, when I asked her what color my everyday dress should be. "A black and white tweed suit."

"And the good one?"

"Black," she said sternly. "All black. What else?"

Crestfallen but obedient, I gave up for good my enthusiasm for "cheerful" colors and let her do the choosing and supervise the fittings. When I finally stood in front of the mirror, the result was startling. There wasn't much left of the fat Girl Scout. I looked older, paler, and less moon-faced.

The day before I left, I dressed up in my new finery and went for a long last walk in the Bois with Rolf. Flounder and Frog, hand in hand, through the snowy woods. It was his last day in Paris too. He had registered at the University of Basel, in Switzerland, where he was going to take his medical degree. Everything suddenly looked different now that we were about to leave, more beautiful, more seductive, and more foreign—although the city had remained foreign enough to us in the fifteen months we had lived there. Not once had we set foot in a French apartment. Not once had a Frenchman invited us to his home. One took foreigners into a restaurant, never into one's home. I had come to Paris a complete stranger and I was leaving a complete stranger. Better that way. Less of a wrench.

But parting from Rolf weighed on me like lead. We stood by the frozen lake and promised to write every day. He would come to London as soon as his finals were over. But it would be a year from now, at the very least . . .

I crossed the Channel from Calais to Dover on one of those days when English papers used to carry the headline: "The Continent Is Isolated." For hours we were tossed about by waves as high as a house, while I lay prostrate in a deck chair, unable to move and violently seasick. Even the immigration officer at Dover realized that I was in no condition to answer questions, so he simply stamped a visitor's visa in my passport—though not a work permit, of course.

Green around the gills and feeling faint, I collapsed into the London train, revived a bit with my first cup of English tea, and collected my wits. I had a residence permit, thirty-four pounds, and a card saying Alexander Korda, 36 Davis Street, London W.1.

6

The Steel Corset: London

❀

T HE TRAIN STOPPED at Victoria Station with such a jolt that I
threw up once again. After a decent interval I walked out of
the station and looked around. It was undoubtedly the vilest night of
the year; the storm was still raging and rain was lashing the pave-
ment. No point in trying to economize, I'd have to take a taxi. I was
heading for a boardinghouse in Paddington, one of the less elegant
parts of London. The place, run by Lo Hardy, a German movie star
from the silent days, was a haven for refugees who were not exactly
opulent.

The taxi slithered through the storm from one traffic light to the
next while I tried to make out something, anything, through the
window. The city seemed endless, jet black, hostile. At long last we
stopped in front of an ugly old house, one in a long row of similar
houses. I lugged my suitcase out of the taxi, looked for the doorbell,
and got soaked from head to toe. Suddenly the door opened. I saw
a light and a tiny woman with platinum blond hair, and a voice
said in German, "For goodness' sake, you poor child! We'd almost
given you up." Lo Hardy.

She stretched out both arms to welcome me, thereby buckling up
my steel corset, which had come dangerously undone during the
day. After a hot bath and a good long night's sleep, I woke up in
a warm room, thirty shillings a week, including breakfast.

Fortified by my favorite meal, I boldly approached the telephone, crossed my fingers, and dialed the number on Korda's card. A secretary answered. I said my piece, spelled my name, and was asked to hold on. I held on. I held on for a long time, and began to sweat. I thought of last night's black taxi ride through hostile London. Suppose he wasn't there? Suppose he'd already found someone for the part? Suppose he'd completely forgotten me? I began to shake all over and was looking around for a chair when the secretary returned and spoke the blessed words: "Yes, Miss Palmer, Mr. Korda says welcome to London. He will be testing next week. The studio will send a car. I'll be in touch with you."

I sank, sobbing, onto my bed. London wasn't hostile, London was warm and friendly. London would be conquered forthwith.

The following week, bursting with self-confidence thanks to my black and white Paris outfit, I was taken in a big car to my first movie studio. I was made up and taken into a huge, dark hangar, the set, I was told. Another girl was being tested, and I watched intently. She looked like a magnolia blossom, with an extra-long neck, dark hair, and light green eyes. I managed to read the name on the clapperboard the boy was holding in front of the camera: Vivien Leigh. She only turned her head from one side to the other, but that alone was worth watching. Then she nodded daintily in all directions and disappeared.

My turn. A little man with a pointed nose and raisin eyes, walking with a cane, limped over to me and said, "I suppose you know what this is all about."

"No," I said, "this is the first time I've ever been in a film studio."

"Is that so?" He looked at me a little closer. "Well, what would you like to do? Do you just want to stand there and turn your head from side to side or do you want to recite a poem or—"

"I'll do the bell monologue from *Saint Joan,*" I announced firmly.

"Okay," said the little man and set about lighting me, for he turned out to be the cameraman. A famous American cameraman, Hal Rosson. After a while he said, "Let's go!" And I went into Joan's great monologue, one of my favorite pieces dating back to my days at Frau Grüning's school of acting. The little man sat under the camera, watching me intently with his black raisin eyes.

When I finished, he didn't move. I asked him if I should repeat it. "No," he said, "that was good enough for me."

My return trip in the glamorous car was one long dream of future screen triumphs about to fall into my lap.

Lo Hardy's paying guests assembled every night for a hot meal. Five shillings extra. Every room was inhabited by a German refugee, so we always spoke German. This didn't bother me, because my English was still fluent. Everybody's troubles were aired, everybody's hopes explored. Refugee life in London was tough, news from Germany terrible, money short, work permits—labour permits, as they were called in London—the common problem. Of course they all knew about my screen test, and I had to give a full account that evening. Lo Hardy in particular, reliving former glories, wanted to know all the details.

Suddenly the telephone rang. A call for Miss Palmer. Everybody looked at me while I sat mystified. I didn't know a soul in the whole city; who could be wanting to speak to me?

"This is Hal Rosson," said the voice. "I'm the cameraman who photographed you this morning. I had a lot of trouble getting your telephone number."

"Oh?"

"I just wanted to tell you what I said to Korda this evening. 'There's one girl,' I said, 'who did a scene from *Saint Joan*. I've had plenty of actresses in front of my camera with greater ability, but none with greater promise.' I thought you might like to hear that before you go to bed. Good-bye."

It wasn't easy to get through the next two days, until Korda had seen all the tests. But at last the telephone rang and the boss himself spoke to me. "I like your acting all right," he said, "but I don't like the way you were lit. Rosson agrees. He thinks he can do better. We'll make another test of you tomorrow."

Once again the big car came for me and I rode in luxury to the studio. This time a specal makeup expert worked on my face for a long while, adding all kinds of shadows and sticking on long eyelashes, and then a woman did incredible things to my hair, until I was completely unrecognizable. Maybe that was just as well.

Hal Rosson, waiting on the set, limped over to greet me like an old friend and set up his lights. They had told me his story in the makeup room. For years he had been unhappily in love with Jean Harlow, whose special cameraman he was at Metro-Goldwyn-Mayer. There came a time, however, when Miss Harlow went too far in her "unconventional" life-style, and she was bidden by the studio to get married at once in order to put a stop to the scandals. Hal Rosson was available. She left him after a few months, and he came down with a severe case of polio. Now, a year later, trying to escape from his Hollywood memories, he had signed a contract with Korda in London.

He looked at me long and searchingly. "Which is your good side?"

"Good side?" I asked in surprise.

"Yes. Everybody has two different profiles, and one is better than the other. Don't you know—I mean, as a girl, as a woman—don't you know how or when you look your best?"

I stared at him in bewilderment. I had no idea there were such things as good and bad profiles and that "as a woman" I was supposed to know which was which. Not getting any help from me, Rosson told me to turn my head from side to side and fussed for hours with his lights.

Finally he asked me to sit down beside him. "I don't know whether this'll come out any better," he said, "but I've done the best I can. You're still very young and you've got a long way to go. Two things will help you. First, a good agent—and I'm going to recommend one. The other you'll have to do for yourself. You must lose ten pounds. Then you'll be much easier to photograph."

I sat with a stone in my stomach while he scribbled a name on a piece of paper: Harry Ham, Myron Selznick Agency. "The best agent in town," said Rosson, "and a good friend of mine. I play golf with him on Sundays. I'll talk to him about you. Good-bye and good luck."

I didn't eat any dinner that night. If I had to lose ten pounds, I might as well begin right away. Next day I climbed expectantly onto Lo Hardy's scales; they didn't show the slightest change. Never mind, they soon would. While I waited for Korda's call, I combined artistic demands with necessary economy and ate practically nothing for five long days. Even so, the scales recorded a loss of only half a pound. The fat that had clung to me all my life refused to budge.

Five miserable days. I didn't even dare go for a walk for fear of missing *the call*. Hunger gnawed at my vitals, goulash with fried potatoes danced before my eyes—but I drank black coffee and ate only a slice of lean meat and a Kleenex-thin piece of cucumber. Most of my time was spent in front of the mirror, looking for my "good side" or trying to hypnotize the telephone into ringing.

At last! The secretary. Mr. Korda had seen the test and liked it. He was prepared to offer me a contract at a starting salary of seven pounds a week and to apply to the Home Office for a labour permit right away. I'd hear from him as soon as they had news. Good-bye, Miss Palmer.

Seven pounds a week! For a movie contract it wasn't much, but for me, living on four pounds a week, it was a fortune. In any case it would mean one year of complete security, and in the meantime I'd starve myself into the most beautiful wreck in London. I dashed off an ecstatic letter, special delivery, to my mother and rushed downstairs to tell Lo Hardy and the others.

Had I been less excited, I would have noticed that Lo didn't quite share my enthusiasm. She had lived in England for years and knew that the Home Office would never grant me a labour permit at that salary. In England, too, a foreigner was allowed to work only if no eligible British citizen was available. She had realized at once that Korda was letting me down gently but firmly, but decided to let me go on dreaming as long as I was still on my strict diet. At long last, after ten days of starvation, the fat actually began to melt away, and my morning trip to Lo's scales was accompanied by loud yells of triumph. I had lost five pounds and already looked a bit better.

The bad news came by mail, a small buff-colored envelope stamped OHMS: On His Majesty's Service. Inside, a piece of paper informing me that Mr. Korda's application for a labour permit had been refused.

Three precious weeks had gone by. I had about twenty pounds left. Something had to be done at once. I opened my suitcase and took out the letters of recommendation, about a dozen of them, neatly bundled, biding their time. Well-meaning people in Paris had pressed them into my hand before I left. "You're going to London? I know someone who's a big noise with So and So Films . . ." The someone was, of course, a German refugee who had made it as director or producer or writer. A very few had made it even as actors—but only those who were already famous in Germany. The letters all said one thing: Dear Mr. So and So, The bearer of this letter is a gifted young actress. Could you perhaps . . .

Not a chance. No refugee who had made it "could perhaps," even with the best will in the world. He had to stick strictly to English talent or he'd be accused of nepotism. Clear as daylight. I put the letters back in the suitcase and fished out Hal Rosson's note: Harry Ham, Myron Selznick Agency.

Several secretaries tried to get rid of me, but finally the name Hal Rosson lifted the right receiver. "Mr. Ham? Perhaps Mr. Rosson has mentioned my name to you . . ." He had. I got an appointment the very next morning.

Harry Ham, an American with blue eyes, tiny, chiseled features, and a bald head, received me preoccupied and in a hurry. He probably had more important clients. "Yes, yes. Rosson told me about you. Wait a minute—I have an idea. Are you a quick study?"

"Yes," I said eagerly.

He picked up the telephone. "Get me Warner Brothers, Teddington Studios. Ask for Mr. Irving Asher . . . Irving? About that part in *Crime Unlimited*—I think I've got the right girl here in my office. Yes! She can make a screen test this afternoon if you'll give her the script as soon as she gets there. Okay. I'll send her over."

He put down the telephone and turned to me. "This is only a class B movie, you understand. Nothing special. A run-of-the-mill gangster story. But it's the leading part, and it would be a good opportunity for you to learn the ropes. They'd already hired a girl, but she's ill and now they're in a fix. My car will pick you up after lunch."

Somehow I found my way to the door, but he called me back. "Do you need money?"

"No, thank you. Not yet."

"Fine. Good-bye. Take care of yourself."

That did it. He shouldn't have said that. I just managed to get out of his office before bursting into tears on the staircase outside. "Take care of yourself." What a beautiful thing to say! How thoughtful and kind! All right, from now on I was going to take great care of myself, starting this afternoon.

Harry Ham's expensive American car took me to Teddington Studios, where Warner Brothers shot their British movies. I was hurriedly made up and saw at once what losing all that weight had done for my face. This time no one suggested painting dark brown stripes sideways along my cheeks. They handed me the script to memorize, and in half an hour I was ready. I would have been ready before if it hadn't been for my opening line, a tongue-twister, to be shouted at great speed. I still know it by heart: "Tell Scotland Yard that Pete Borden is at The Withies, a country house near Owsley, Sussex!" That one took me twenty minutes. The rest of the dialogue, three pages, only needed reading through twice.

On the set a young actor was waiting for me in a chair marked "Esmond Knight." He had shiny blue eyes, which I was to remember all too well later, during the war, when I read in the paper that actor Esmond Knight had been blinded during the naval battle between the *Bismarck* and the *Hood*.

He stood up and smiled at me, so I decided to trust him. "I'd better tell you the truth, Mr. Knight," I whispered while they were setting up the lights. "I think Harry Ham, my agent, has said that I have made some films in France. That's not true. I've never made a film in my life."

"So what?" he whispered back. "Don't worry. There's nothing to it. Just relax and don't look into the camera." And with that we began our test scene, which gave me no trouble once that opening gambit was out of my mouth.

This time I didn't have to stay home waiting for the call. I barely had time to lose another pound before Harry Ham called to say that the test was a success and I could have the part at a salary of a hundred and twenty pounds.

"And the labour permit?" I gasped.

"No problem. They're in a fix. They *want* you. Get it?"

At Lo Hardy's dinner table, bets were laid on whether the Home Office would relent or not. Some pessimists thought it would not only refuse, for the salary was still low for a leading part, but would even deport me for "having violated the rules granted upon entry" stamped in my passport when I arrived, namely, not to seek employment. Lo, however, was optimistic, and she was right. His Majesty's Post Office brought the glad tidings in a buff envelope: permission granted to appear in the film and to be paid a hundred and twenty pounds for it. All of a sudden I was rich, secure for at least the next eight months. I hugged everyone within reach and called up my mother in Berlin and Rolf in Basel to celebrate. I was on the way! I was on the way!

Shooting began immediately and left me no time to marvel, for in those days one worked at least ten hours a day, especially if it was a low-budget movie. I enjoyed every minute of it and never missed the day's rushes, drooling with pleasure at the sight of myself, now at last minus the ten pounds that Rosson had demanded.

My part gave me no headaches. I was playing a girl working as an *entraîneuse* in a nightclub—echoes of a recently familiar milieu —who was a good girl, really, falling into the hero's arms in the end. Warner Brothers were obviously pleased with me, and toward the end of the shooting Harry Ham sent for me. They were offering me a three-year contract at a starting salary of twenty-five pounds a week, to be raised to seventy-five in the third year.

I left his office, sat down on the top stair again, and for a long time stared out at Old Bond Street in the pouring rain. All along, hand in hand with my cocky hopes and dreams, there had always run the great doubt: would it come true? Really and truly? It had. London was conquered. Career. Security. My mother would be able to come over right away, and my sisters too. Car! Dog! Within a year I'd be a great star, the most glamorous bag of bones in London. The ride home in the bus was one long, happy haze, and that night Lo Hardy opened a bottle of wine to celebrate the unforgettable day.

I didn't give my old enemy, the labour permit, a thought. They wanted me. The salary was good. Well, then! For once I didn't worry. His Majesty's Service arrived posthaste. Not only was Warner Brothers' application rejected, but I was invited to leave the country forthwith, i.e., within forty-eight hours.

Most of Lo's boarders had materialized out of nowhere when I fished the letter out of the mailbox. They stood silently around me as I read it and followed me upstairs to help me pack. Lo herself brought me my suitcase and saw to my ticket. "I'll be back," I said. "You'll see." They all nodded. (But when I did come back, the boardinghouse was closed. Lo had killed herself with an overdose of sleeping pills. No one ever knew why.)

Still, I had actually made a film. And I had more than a hundred pounds; no need to despair. I boarded the Channel steamer—the sea was calm and blue—and then the train for Basel. To Rolf.

In Switzerland spring had just broken out. We wandered through the woods full of early green, trying to sort out the future. Where to go? Try France again? Out of the question. America? The fare alone would cost more money than I had. Austria? The *Anschluss* was just a matter of time. Holland? No chance of a career in Dutch. Stay in Switzerland? No movie industry, and the theaters overflowing with German refugees. There was nothing for it: back to England.

Four weeks later I was sitting once more in the train. During the Channel crossing I braced myself for the impending battle with the immigration authorities, rehearsing various opening gambits and fitting answers to possible traps. I also vowed not to be hasty, as usual, but calm and observant, and to scan the officer's face carefully in order to guess my best mode of attack.

But when my turn came, I knew at once that I had no chance at all. This particular type of thin official face was impervious to overtures. Silence would be my best weapon. The man studied my gray alien's registration card, pored over the various entries, and saw fit to read them aloud: "Entered on a visitor's visa—applied for labour permit—permit refused. Second application granted . . ." He broke off and looked at me accusingly. I looked back without a word. Another officer joined him and together they peered at the offending document while the first man proceeded, raising his voice: "Applied again for labor permit—permit refused—alien requested to leave the U.K." They both looked up, satisfied.

"Could you possibly . . ." I began. "I would like a visa, please."

"No," they said firmly, handing back my passport and registration card. I refused to take them.

"Would you please tell me what I am to do?"

"Go back."

"Where to? Do you want me to swim around in the Channel?"

"Look here, miss," said the first one, "we're not here to solve your problems. We're here to see that aliens don't give any trouble."

"I'm not going to give any trouble. I've come over to see a film I made in your country. Is that against the law?"

Pause. That remark about swimming in the Channel had obviously worried them. They probably thought I was quite capable of jumping overboard. At last the second officer reached for my papers and said slowly, stressing every word, "We're going to let you have a visitor's visa for two weeks, nonextendable. And it's no good you asking for no labour permit. I'm warning you, Miss." With that he banged down the rubber stamp on my passport, making me a present of two weeks' life in England.

In those two weeks, something had to happen. And it did. Harry Ham hadn't been idle. Also, several people had seen the first cut of *Crime Unlimited,* and the "new girl" had come out well. There was always a demand for new faces, and Gaumont-British, a big English film company, had already shown interest. As soon as I arrived, they examined me under a magnifying glass and declared me worthy of a contract.

"But," I breathed, "I'm an alien! My labour permit—"

"Don't worry. We'll take care of that."

"Oh, no, you can't. You see, I'm not even allowed to apply."

They were amazed, puzzled, thought it over, and came up with a solution: I was sent out of the country at their expense while they applied for a proper permit to put me under contract, a seven-year-option contract renewable every year. In their letter to the Home Office, they stated that the alien Miss Lilli Palmer would unquestionably be "a valuable asset to the British film industry." Hallelujah!

What I didn't know was that Gaumont-British, cunning and cautious, applied for only three months' extension at a time. They told me that the Home Office would not grant a longer one, and I had to resign myself to shaking in my shoes every time the three months were up.

When I returned to England this time, I sailed through immigration with my head held high. I had a genuine labour permit stamped into my passport and big ideas in my head. The time had come to turn dreams into realities. My mother and Hilde were packing their suitcases in Berlin, Irene was buying her ticket for London—and I was taking driving lessons.

Irene arrived first from Paris, and together we pored over the classified advertisements looking for a suitable house. One gave Parsifal Road as the address, and being Wagner lovers, we tried that one first. We looked at dozens more, but in the end we came back to Parsifal. The rent was cheap, and it had plenty of bedrooms and a tiny back garden. From the start we referred to it as the second-ugliest house in London, allowing for the possibility that there might be an even uglier one.

Soon my mother and Hilde arrived from Berlin, having had to leave money and life insurance behind but having been allowed to bring some furniture, which turned Parsifal into a home for us all. Shortly after we moved in, my mother opened her bedroom window one morning and saw the three of us eating breakfast on the tiny lawn. "Good morning," she called happily. It was the first time we'd seen her smile since my father's death.

I bought my first black dog for cash and my first black car on installments, and proudly drove myself to the studio every morning. Gaumont-British put me in one movie after another, none of them memorable. Every three months, when my work permit had to be renewed, I would bite my fingernails with anxiety and wake up at night feeling sick with forboding until the little buff envelope with the extension arrived. Not until war broke out did England decide to change the status of refugees.

One morning as I was lying in the bathtub, my mother knocked at the door. A buff envelope had arrived. I sat up and called out, "Read it to me." She went to look for her glasses. I held my breath.

At last she came back and through the closed door she slowly and laboriously, in her thick accent, spelled out the announcement that the Home Office was herewith granting alien Miss Lilli Palmer a permanent labour permit in the United Kingdom.

I sank back into the hot water and floated, eyes closed, for a long, long time.

7

Elsa

❀

I'VE ALWAYS BEEN LUCKY. Whenever things have gotten tricky for
me, I've stumbled across people who knew better than I did.
Perhaps my most valuable possession is an antenna for instant recognition of such people, and my most useful quality is my willingness,
after token resistance, to surrender, submerge, *learn*—and emerge.

One morning I was walking down Old Bond Street with three
newspapers under my arm. It was a glorious morning, not just because the sun was shining but because I'd had a premiere the night
before, a Gaumont-British film in which I'd played my first lead, and
all three morning papers had praised me.

Around the corner came Beate Moissi, the daughter of Reinhardt's
great actor Alexander Moissi. I held the reviews under her nose, and
she read them without a word.

"Well? What do you say? Were you there last night?"

She nodded.

"Didn't you like it?"

She looked at me for a moment.

"The film is of no importance. But you're so bad that you even
look old, and that takes some doing when you're twenty."

I just stood there speechless.

"Listen," said Beate calmly. "I don't exactly enjoy saying this to you. But you asked me, didn't you? Also if you want me to—I'll tell you what I think you ought to do. Maybe you have talent, although just to be young is a kind of talent. But you have to *learn* too, and you don't know the first thing about that. You have no craft, no understanding, and no taste."

Fury restored my speech.

"And where does one buy a craft and understanding and taste?"

Beate got her little black book out of her handbag and turned the pages. "From Elsa Schreiber. She's in London. I'll give you her address. If you're lucky, she'll take you on."

I went home shattered. Beate Moissi knew what she was talking about. She was brought up in the theater—theater of the very best quality. If she said somebody stank, he stank. Yet after all, I had played leading roles in Darmstadt, I was a star (a small one) at Gaumont-British; what else did I have to learn?

Funny thing . . . just a few days earlier I'd been offered my first part in an English stage play. Perhaps it wouldn't do any harm to find out what Frau What's-Her-Name had to say. Gritting my teeth, I called Beate.

"Listen, Beate. That Frau . . . Frau Schreiber, would she help me with a stage part, too?"

"Of course."

"You see, I've been offered a great part in a marvelous play. It's called *The Road to Gandahar*. For instance, there's a scene where I go stark staring mad—you know, with a murderous look in my eyes . . ."

"Good God!" said Beate. "Send Elsa the script today so she can read it. And let me give you some advice: don't tell her anything. Let her do the talking."

Two days later I drove my little car across London, stood outside a door in a big apartment building, and rang the bell. I had made up my mind to be reserved and distant.

The door was opened by a small woman in her thirties. "Come in," she said briskly, and closed the door behind me.

"Well, now, Mrs. Schreiber—" I began nonchalantly, but she interrupted me at once.

"I know. Beate told me. Sit down. I read your play last night. It's awful. So is your part. Let's see what we can do about it."

My play awful? My part awful? The woman must be out of her mind. I looked at her more carefully. She was like a polished apple, round all over, aggressively healthy, as if she might burst out of her clothes any minute. Short black hair, a snubnosed face dominated by extraordinary eyes. And a voice! It flattened me right against the wall.

"Let's start," she said. "I haven't much time. And, to put you in the picture, I don't exactly enjoy teaching. I'm doing it because for the moment I have no choice. Here's your script. Let's begin with your first scene."

I rescued my last trappings of glamour and sailed to the door. "Well—this woman from the milliner's is at the door and I call out, 'Have you brought me some pretty hats, Mrs. Jones?'"

"That's right," said Elsa, adding pointedly, "and that's how I want you to say it."

I stopped dead in my tracks. "But I haven't acted it out yet!"

"That's just it," said Elsa, giving me a look. I became very familiar with that look over the years.

I rebelled. I had only just met her and I hadn't any idea what was in store for me.

"But she's glad she's getting some pretty hats. I mean, she can't just say it like nothing at all."

"Yes, she can," said Elsa, "unless you want to play her piss-elegant right from the start."

I suppressed an urgent desire to make for the door. Damn it, I was a promising young actress at twenty-five pounds a week from Gaumont-British! But that antenna was coming to life in the back of my head—so I turned around and started again. "Have you brought me some pretty hats, Mrs. Jones?"

"Better," said Elsa, "but still not good. Have the courage to say the line without showing me your talent."

That's how we began. It started out as a brawl and developed into a pitched battle, and when I think back I wonder how Elsa ever had the patience to cope with my ignorance and my pretensions.

"Don't show me your talent" became the leitmotif of my next two years. I loved showing my talent; I couldn't wait to demonstrate how clever I was, how well worth my salary. I had to learn that a good actor, like an iceberg, reveals only a small part of his ability on the surface. You suggest; you don't serve on a platter. You hold back. You don't expose it all to view. That's the way to put the audience's imagination to work.

Within a very short time, I had to admit that Beate had been right. "No craft. No understanding. No taste." Under protest, sometimes in tears, I had to accept it, losing every bit of my film star "poise" in the process. But Elsa taught in the only way you can teach anybody anything: by taking away but at the same time giving something in exchange. She never said "What on earth are you doing?" without immediately showing me how it ought to be done.

Up to then my acting rules had been simple. I was sincere. If it was a sad scene, I cried. (Easy.) If it was a gay one, I laughed. (Not so easy. Laughter on command is not easy.) It wasn't until I met Elsa that I learned to my amazement that a comic scene must be played dead seriously and that a smile on your face can make a sad scene even sadder.

It was a fight with no holds barred. After our long sessions, I would jump into my car and drive home exhausted and cursing loudly. I cursed Elsa and I cursed myself, in equal parts. But gradually, after several months of nightly drudgery—I couldn't start working with her until I'd finished at the studio—I felt I was beginning to understand what she was getting at.

In the meantime I'd grown accustomed to her devastating honesty and was soon forced to admit how right she had been about my play. The critics made mincemeat of it, but I was praised in superlatives never before used in connection with my name. This was nothing to be particularly proud of. Elsa could train complete duds in the same way, as one trains seals, so that they could make quite a good impression, at least for a short time.

There was, for instance, the case of a pretty model named Ilona, whose boy friend, a film producer, had persuaded Elsa to prepare her for a screen test. Elsa charged him double her usual rates, but even so she was often tempted to throw his money in his face and Ilona out the door. Sometimes, when I was waiting in the hall, I could hear Elsa exploding in stifled fury. Finally the door would fly open and the lovely creature, face flushed and hair disheveled, would shoot past me out the front door, while Elsa stood in the middle of the room beating her fists against her forehead. "I'm losing my talent! That moron makes me lose my talent!"

Came the day of the moron's screen test and Elsa's release. In the middle of my lesson, the telephone rang. "Hello . . . Oh, yes, Ilona. Well, how did it go? . . . You got the part? . . . They're delighted? . . . What's that? . . . What did they say? You're what . . . A great actress? . . . What do I say to that? I say, you can kiss my ass."

Her method was simple: she hadn't any. She hadn't even read Stanislavski's famous books on dramatic art. She had been an actress herself, but a bad one, she assured me. Hard to believe, because while teaching she could act superbly. But she insisted that as an actress she had had no staying power, just flashes of brilliant ideas. She was in effect a director, and these flashes could magically nail a scene, a line, sometimes only a single word, for the actor. But this was by no means all she did. She improved bad scripts by cutting or expanding and by making sense out of nonsense. "Don't be one of those actresses who complain all their life that they never get good parts. *Make* them good."

Above all, she taught me how to work on a role, how never to lose sight of the story line or my character. She showed me what to look for when I read a script, how to recognize and improve weak scenes ("The actor must help the author!"), how to turn deficiencies in the script into assets, and finally how to work on every single sentence, turning it inside out if necessary, always looking for the simple, and at the same time original, solution. Cute little tricks, funny giggles, special "breaking" of the voice—all personal mannerisms were taboo. What it all added up to, as I was to realize much later, was an actor's most precious possession: a technique and a taste of his own.

Naturally this often led me into bitter fights with directors who wanted clichés that Elsa would not tolerate. I fought as if I were being crucified and refused to budge, even over details, because at a decisive moment in my career Elsa had taken me apart, brainwashed me, and put me together again.

For instance, in any scene where you had to express fear, the director would inevitably demand that you breathe "heavily." Nothing could make me do this. Actors who breathed heavily were one of Elsa's pet aversions—unless, of course, they'd been running. "When you're really nervous or scared to death, exactly the opposite happens. You have *no* air in your lungs."

I breathed regularly and made myself unpopular, but when I complained to Elsa about my isolation, even among my fellow actors, she remained unmoved. "Don't compromise. Stick to the script and go your own way."

I "stuck," but it wasn't easy. The first two weeks of rehearsals would usually be hell, and I would continually be caught between the frying pan of the director's legitimate demands and the fire of Elsa's incomparably superior teachings. Sometimes I came close to being sacked because I stubbornly gave Elsa's reading and not the director's. I knew I had to endure his wrath until I could convince him—usually by the third week of rehearsals—that what I was doing was right.

Elsa for her part was a hard taskmaster, who demanded total subordination and unlimited capacity for hard work. I would rehearse onstage or on the set eight hours a day and then drive straight to her apartment, where she would have "something nourishing" waiting for me—usually a slice of meat with spinach. I had to eat enormous quantities of spinach, because it was "good for the nerves." Elsa was a health fetishist, and there was no arguing with her. While I chewed, she would read me difficult passages from the scenes we were going to work on, and then we would start battling until late at night. When I drooped, she would ask calmly, "Do you want to have a career—yes or no?"

Of course, she went way beyond our lessons. When the dreaded opening night drew near, Elsa came to the dress rehearsals in the guise of a "close relative," a role she hated. But she wanted to see for herself what was going on onstage, so she sat in an orchestra seat with a face of thunder. She didn't want to be spoken to, because she was making notes. Some of her reactions were quite arbitrary and got me into trouble. During one costume rehearsal, she decided that a certain white dress didn't suit me. At intermission she appeared in my dressing room and told me to spill ink on it. And I obeyed her, though with trembling hands, because I'd never in my life spilled ink on a beautiful white—

"Never mind, child. Just do it."

When I had to face the producer and pretend to be in despair about my "clumsiness," I hated Elsa. I even dared to protest, but she remained serene. "You'll love me tomorrow," she said calmly. And when I read the reviews in the morning papers, I did.

The lessons were expensive and far exceeded my budget. "I'm not a charitable institution," Elsa said. "I don't enjoy doing this anyhow. Besides, I'm baking you in a completely new mold, not only as an actress, but as a person!"

True. Occasionally she would put down the script, look at me seriously, and say, "Lilli, what I've just shown you represents the whole difference between dullness and charm. And I'm not just talking about this particular role. Remember: you *must* learn charm. Both on stage and in life."

Shortly before the war, she left England to work in Hollywood with her husband, the director George Shdanoff. (She still lives and works there for the benefit of a great many actors, even very famous ones, who all but owe her their careers, and their Oscars.) I took her to Victoria Station, feeling orphaned and lost. "It will be good for you to stand on your own feet now," she said. "You're ready for it. You know how to work on your roles. Don't worry if you don't get good directors. There are too few around. But listen even to the mediocre ones if they're still telling you that something isn't right when you're almost ready to open. A director is rarely so stupid as to criticize something that is obviously good. But, Lilli, never, do you hear, never listen to what they suggest you ought to be doing instead! That you will have to discover for yourself."

She hugged me and got aboard the train. The engine whistled, and the train pulled slowly out of the station.

I drove to the theater. How strange it would be not to have anyone to keep an eye on my performances. ("Never let me see you give a sloppy performance. Even if it's a hot day and a half-empty matinee. Make an extra effort for the few people who took the trouble to buy tickets.") How strange not to be able to run to the telephone and say, "Elsa, I've been offered a new script with a marvelous part. Can I come over right away?"

All that was left of her was a piece of paper she had pinned to my dressing table with a thumbtack on my first opening night. I was to read it through slowly every evening before the first scene. On it she had listed my ten principal shortcomings, all the things she wanted me to bear in mind and guard against:

1. Remember: you have no charm.
2. Don't *act* adjectives. No need to illustrate what you're saying.
3. Iron out those abrupt, hasty gestures.
4. Take your time. Then no one will be bored.
5. Don't mumble.
6. Listen to your fellow actors. That will make *you* interesting.
7. Stay dry. Sentimentality is Mortal Sin Number One.
8. Don't stand with your feet apart. Keep them together. You're not in the gym.
9. Stay vital. Monotony is Mortal Sin Number Two.
10. Courage—above all, courage!

I kept that sheet of paper for years. Long after I stopped working with Elsa, I still carried it around with me, pinning it up on every new dressing table until it was in shreds. In the end, all you could still make out was the beginning:

1. Remember: you have no charm.

8

War and Marriage

❀

ARLY on the morning of September 3, 1939, I drove to the studio as usual. But while I drove as usual, everything else was unusual. The streets were even emptier than they normally were at that time of day. I seemed to be the only person out and about. The guards at the studio entrance were nowhere to be seen, the corridors and sets were deserted. Yet the parking lot had been full of cars. Where was everybody? Not a soul in my dressing room. I finally ran some inmates to earth in the makeup room, all clustered in groups listening with feverish attention to someone "in the know." I joined them. Maybe somebody really did know something. At home nobody did; nor did friends or acquaintances or strangers in the bus, all of whom had for weeks been passionately debating one question: Would he or wouldn't he? "He" was Hitler. Was he bluffing again? Or did he mean it this time? All kinds of bizarre fantasies were put forward as gospel truth: Hitler was producing ten thousand airplanes a month; Hitler could never bomb London, because he was short of gasoline; Hitler had twice as many tanks as Britain and France together; Hitler would have a revolution on his hands if he declared war.

No one knew what was really going on. Every newspaper told a different story. What was one to wish for, peace at any price? Or war, to put an end once and for all to the intolerable tension of recent years? Most English people hoped, secretly, for peace at any price. Most refugees prayed, secretly, for war to destroy the monster for good.

Today at eleven o'clock we would all know which it was to be. At the last stroke from Big Ben, Chamberlain was to broadcast "an important announcement" to the nation. Four hours to go. We had no desire to work; we just felt like standing about like sheep, talking. An assistant director finally sent us packing, but he, too, first checked whether anyone had heard any news.

A couple of scenes were shot without anybody paying attention. Who cared about a silly script at this moment? The thing might never be finished, never be shown.

At 10:30 there was a tea break—a sacred ritual in the British working day. We sat down on a few square yards of artificial grass and drank our tea in silence. Now, as zero hour approached, no one had anything further to say. Maybe it was just one more false alarm, and the old chap with the umbrella would once again proclaim "peace in our time."

On the stroke of eleven, Mr. Chamberlain's familiar squeaky voice, trembling slightly with emotion, told us in a few arid words that the ultimatum had expired and that Britain, together with her ally France, was now at war: God save the King.

I had the feeling that my English colleagues removed themselves from me by a few inches of artificial grass. They also seemed to await some sort of "explanation" from me. All looked at me expectantly. After all, I was a German! No, my dear friends, I'm not a German. Would you like to see the letter I received several years ago from the German Embassy officially informing me of that fact? No one was interested in such a fine distinction. I understood German, didn't I? Well, then, would you please tell us what "that man" really wants. My explanations didn't satisfy them. They could read the same thing, much better, in the *Times* editorial columns every day. What they wanted to know were quite different things; for instance, did Hitler have an accent? At that time it was still of vital importance to speak the king's English, and they informed me that it was unthinkable for a chief of state to speak with a regional accent. Did Hitler, or did he not, have a vulgar accent? Not vulgar, I said, just Austrian.

Helping himself to another cup of tea, one actor said wistfully that he had his own theory about the man. He was sure Hitler's clothes didn't fit him properly; they probably "pulled" under the arm. And that for a chap who had to raise his arm all the time! Somebody ought to have sent over a decent English tailor long ago, and then the fellow wouldn't always be so bloody angry . . .

During the first weeks, nobody knew what to expect—whether one could calmly go about one's business in town or in the country, with nothing to worry about except rationing, the blackout, and having to carry gas masks everywhere, or whether the streets were going to be turned into rivers of blood because Hitler was planning a quick knockout by bombing us to smithereens. All the film studios were temporarily "resting." The London theaters closed, "just in case," and actors went on tour into the provinces. My contract with Gaumont-British was cancelled. War was a *force majeure*. Small personal catastrophe. I was lucky to find refuge in a new play that was also about to go on tour. Salaries were tiny, but enough to keep Parsifal Road going. In any case, my mother rented out two rooms to other refugees to help with the budget.

There was another reason why I was grateful for any job that would take me out of London. Rolf and I had broken up, and every square inch around Parsifal Road "reminded" me. We had been too young when we met. We couldn't last. Being refugees had bound us together for years, but once I was living at home again—at Parsifal —and lunch was served punctually at one o'clock every day, with meat, two vegetables, and dessert, Rolf began to yearn for the Bohemian life of a painter, and we grew apart.

I was sure it was the end of me. My mother thought differently. Though she never showed it, she had never believed that Rolf and I were made for each other. But when I told her, in floods of tears, that it was over, she was so happy that the next time she saw Rolf she proposed to his astonishment that from that time on they would address each other with the intimate *du*.

In the bleak weeks that followed, I tried to keep my head above water and not sink into black despair. Until then I had always torn throughout the day without looking right or left. I had never known the luxury of choice. My decisions had been dictated by urgent necessity, and I always felt as if I were walking along a precipice with my back to the rock. The rock had been Rolf. How was I to walk from now on?

The new play, a good part, rehearsals, the usual chaos, crises, and problems helped, and I gradually stopped crying. Dress rehearsal, general rehearsal, and a suitcase to be packed for Birmingham, where we were to open. It was now November, and though Hitler had devastated Poland, not a single bomb had fallen on England. Many English people were hoping for a separate peace. The refugees read the paper every morning in a state of deep depression, while their coffee got cold. Everything one did seemed pointless. All one could do was hold one's breath and win time, for the volcano might erupt any minute. Eventually you got used to even this state of limbo and carried on as though the daily routine had a meaning. I carefully avoided all discussion of the war with my colleagues. They were a bit self-conscious with me, because I couldn't be pigeonholed. A few understood my situation and in their tactful English way kept their mouths shut.

When we opened in Birmingham, the theater was fairly full, in spite of the blackout and the gas-mask nuisance. People wanted to relax and be entertained, and our show was just the sort of dim-witted piece of nonsense they were looking for. There was another theater in Birmingham, however, and that one sold out every night. No wonder, since the play was by Noël Coward, and three top stars of the London stage were appearing in it. They too were staying in our hotel, the only decent one that was still open. They too gulped still unrationed, but awful, supper in the hotel restaurant after the performance. One of those three stars from the rival play scrutinized me nightly and openly through his monocle. Finally, Leslie Banks, our leading actor, brought him to our table and introduced him to me: Rex Harrison.

I knew him by name, of course. Coincidence that he happened to

be on tour in Birmingham at that time, coincidence that he was
staying in the same hotel and eating supper in the same restaurant
at the same time—but no coincidence that he, too, visited Lord
Dudley's ancestral home outside Birmingham the very next day.

"By the way, what are you doing tomorrow morning?" he asked
as soon as we'd said how do you do.

"I'm going out to the country to see Dudley's animals."

"I'll come along," said Rex firmly.

I had met Lord Dudley the night before. He knew about my
passion for animals. I was a Fellow of the London Zoo and
privileged to visit outside regular visiting hours and on holidays. I
knew all the keepers, shook hands with the inmates, and was allowed
to hold one paw of the baby panda when he had a tooth pulled.

Dudley's dilapidated old ancestral home housed his animal collection, the biggest private zoo in Europe. Sea lions swam in the moat,
monkeys swung from the branches of ancient trees, and a few lions
sat morosely under the medieval walls, their manes soggy in the
rain. The young man with the monocle turned out to be an animal
lover who didn't care if his impeccable clothes got ruined. Even
when I draped a boa constrictor around his neck, he kept his eye-
glass firmly in place.

Standing in front of the cages, pretending to be interested in the
apes, we arranged to meet that night after our shows and walked
about the streets, talking theater talk. Nothing else. Rex wanted
to come to see my matinee the next day, and I planned to see his the
day after. Strange how lifeless the city seemed in the blackout. The
streets were empty and silent except for us and a few dogs. We
chatted about plays and roles and fellow actors, stood still from
time to time, looked around, and enjoyed being all alone in the
dark. Suddenly we were both hungry and went in search of a
restaurant, because we didn't want to go back to the hotel and to
our colleagues' curious, amused, knowing eyes.

Over a powdered-egg omelet, Rex told me that he was married
and had a son five years old, but that his marriage had always been
unhappy and full of trial separations. He didn't know, he said, what
it was like having a home.

Then it was my turn. I told him a little about Parsifal Road, Paris, and Berlin. He listened attentively. "But if it was so hard for you in Paris, why didn't you go back to Berlin?"

I stared at him in amazement, opened my mouth to answer— but thought better of it. He realized he had said the wrong thing, but he didn't know why. How could I begin to explain? I dropped the subject. Once and for all.

Next afternoon he showed up at our theater as he had promised, praised the show, and made some good suggestions about my part. That was obviously something he knew about and was passionately interested in. The following day, it was my turn to see him in *Design for Living.* I was overwhelmed. I had seen him in London in other plays, but now I watched with new eyes. No wonder that at the age of twenty-eight he was already the most sought-after comedy actor on the English stage. He was that rare combination: a born comedian who looked like a leading man.

I, on the other hand, had so far not aroused any storms of enthusiasm. All the films and plays I'd appeared in had been mediocre or worse, although thanks to Elsa my own reviews had always been good enough to ensure that when the final inglorious curtain fell on one show, I was ready to begin rehearsals on the next. From now on, said Rex, things were going to be different. As soon as we got back to London, we would find a really good play—for the two of us. We didn't find one, but it didn't matter anymore.

During that winter and all through the spring and summer of 1940, we drove daily into the country outside London, wandered through the woods and fields, and explored and discovered each other. I was so wrapped up in my own personal affairs that I took in the catastrophic, world-changing events around me as if filtered through several blissful layers of gauze. Though I can pinpoint a few salient moments of that first fateful year of the war: Rex and I standing in a field, craning our necks upward to watch a duel between the RAF and Goering's Luftwaffe, and feeling guilty as we drove back to London after our golden day in the country, confronted by headlines screaming RAF DOWNS 160 LUFTWAFFE PLANES—35 RAF PLANES LOST. Or having a drink at lunch in some small pub somewhere and listening to Churchill's first broadcast as prime minister, giving the British people an account of

a brief visit to France and acquainting them for the first time with
his special intonation and speech impediment: "Shank God for the
French army!" he said at the end. A couple of weeks later, Hitler
cut through that army like a knife through butter. Or June 17, the
day after the French armistice, driving in Rex's car through Piccadilly, lifeless in broad daylight, with hardly any vehicles or pedes-
trians about, the great wide avenue swept bare as though by some
global catastrophe.

Back in September '39, Rex had volunteered for military service,
but had been rejected because of his poor eyesight. (He could see
almost nothing with one eye, hence the monocle.) But after the
Dunkirk disaster in June, the Home Guard accepted him in one of
the local units that were being set up all over England. They had
no arms except ancient shotguns from the First World War, usually
without ammunition, but they assembled every day to drill. Rex
was elected CO. He never found out why—perhaps because they
knew his name. But it soon became apparent that he knew even
less about military matters than the middle-aged men grouped
around him who watched him expectantly—among them a couple
of World War I veterans.

"Well, now," he said finally, smiling amiably, "what are we going
to do? I'd like you to . . . sort of . . . line up . . . perhaps . . ." At
which a veteran barked, "Don't like us to. *Tell* us to!" Rex was
demoted in favor of the veteran. But he later succeeded in bypassing
his draft board and joining the RAF ground forces. By that time he
had got his divorce, and in January 1943 we were married and living
in the country outside London, not far from his RAF station.

Slowly, slowly, the war was creeping toward us; slowly, slowly,
every aspect of our daily life was affected. If all the regulations,
restrictions, and deprivations had fallen on us from one day to the
next, we would have found them unbearable. As it was, we were
hardly conscious of the total change; we only noticed every new
step and treated it as just another annoying inconvenience. Second
nature to pull the blackout curtains before switching on the light.
Absolute acceptance of all kinds of scarcities. A feeling of triumph
if you could get hold of "extras" like curtain linings—unrationed—
to be used for dresses, an occasional chicken or piece of pork from

a pig that had been "accidentally run over," forbidden gallons of gasoline. The war days, once they had really started, were far from dull for the civilian population. In many ways they were exhilarating and occasionally convulsing, like the memorable day when Rex bought a much needed overcoat for which we'd been saving up coupons for months. We had stroked the cloth, selected the cut, and all but kissed the finished product when it finally arrived. That night William, our Sealyham, got hold of it and lavished his affection on it in his own way. We collected the bits and pieces in the morning— and we cried.

I had tried in vain right at the beginning to contribute something by offering to drive ambulances, for I was automatically excluded from any of the active services. Aliens had special restrictions, any-way: they had to be home before midnight, were not allowed beyond a radius of thirty miles from their local police station without spe-cial permission, and couldn't own a radio. (This last was unen-forceable.) For non-Jewish aliens, things were tougher. They had to prove that they were loyal by support from somebody who was somebody and whose word meant something. If an alien had no estimable British citizen available, he or she was put into quarantine on the Isle of Man. Rolf was lucky. He not only had Prince Bern-hard of the Netherlands, a former classmate in Berlin, to vouch for him, but he was able to use his medical training for the first time, for doctors were at a premium. He packed away his easel and "practiced." As he tells it, he was more of a clearinghouse than a doctor, for when a patient showed up with symptoms of any kind, Rolf at once directed him to a specialist, thereby declining all re-sponsibility. (And keeping his easel and paints at hand in his "con-sulting room.")

It was May 1943. Total war, air raids at night, queues in the daytime. I didn't care, because I was pregnant. Unbelievable. What did it matter if I felt sick, if we didn't have a penny? Nothing mattered. I was stuck with morning sickness, but maybe I could do something about our shortage of money. Studios had opened up and movies were being made again, though a lot of time was lost because of air raids, and material, transportation, and labor were all in short

supply. I was offered a part in a film called *English Without Tears.*
I signed the contract hastily and confessed about my condition afterwards.

Ever since the Helen Hayes precedent in New York, pregnancy is
considered a *force majeure,* along with war, strikes, and pestilence,
and entitles both parties, employer and employee, to break the contract.
It was during the Helen Hayes controversy that Dorothy Parker had
sent her the famous telegram: "I always knew you had it in you."
In my case, there was no controversy: I knew I had it in me. The
producers, however, were worried about something else: would I
be able to hold out for the long months of shooting? The studio
and my agent argued back and forth. As a result of the suspense, I
spent most of my days in the bathroom. Rex's meager RAF pay
didn't even cover the rent, and we had no savings. How were we
going to live if I were handcuffed for nine months? Also, Rex's first
wife, Collette, and their eight-year-old son, Noel, had to be sup-
ported.

Telephone. I rushed out of the bathroom. The producers. They
wanted to see me and form their own impression. Good! It was
going to be a terrific impression. I put on my best dress—so far
nothing showed—extra rouge on my cheeks and confidence in
my eye. The confident eye was considerably dimmed when I had
to make an urgent stop behind a tree on the way. After dousing
myself with the cologne I had brought along for this purpose, I
drove on.

They probably couldn't find anyone else for the part, for they
gave a deep sigh and decided to try me. (I had lied an entire
month off my pregnancy.) Ecstatically, I rushed home. We were
saved.

Driving to the studio every morning—early morning was my
worst time—I would stop at "my" trees (always the same ones, out
of superstition) every mile or so. On the set they had grown used to
seeing me suddenly dash for the exit, sometimes in the middle of a
scene. But the worst of it was that I was playing a girl in uniform.
For the first two months of shooting, we got by by punching new
holes in my Sam Browne, but later on my entire uniform had to be

let out an inch or two every week. When the film was finally finished, I was in my sixth month.

Suddenly there came a bombshell. Retakes! The last part of a long, important scene had to be reshot. A new uniform was made up in which I looked like a khaki-colored sea cow. The end result was a unique performance on my part: I enter my parents' bedroom as a thin young girl, stand my ground in a heated dispute, and argue my case with such passionate dedication that when I leave the room I have not only tears in my eyes but twenty extra pounds on my belly.

The film didn't exactly make us rich, but it allowed us to sleep peacefully for the time being. I grew contentedly fatter and fatter, hadn't seen my knees for weeks, and when I went walking with our Sealyham and it began to rain, the clever animal would shelter under my belly.

One cloudy afternoon we were sitting in the living room with two friends, the director Harold French and Deborah Kerr. Everyone had a drink in his hand, a gin, that is, with some sticky sweet stuff in it instead of vermouth. The all clear had just sounded when Rex, who was standing by the window, suddenly shouted, "Get down!" I got down as fast as my size permitted; the others were already flat on the floor. Rex had watched a single plane break through the clouds and then—unforgettable sight—had seen the bomb leave the plane. There was a tremendous explosion, then silence, then an extraordinary soft crumbling and grinding sound. The walls of our house were slowly collapsing and falling in on us. The bomb had landed in the garden about fifty feet from our front door. After the grinding, there was silence once again, while we tried to free ourselves from the thick layer of rubble and plaster and broken tiles on top of us. Deborah was the first to sit up, and she dug me out. We blinked at each other with some difficulty, because our eyelids were caked with plaster dust. She scratched the debris off my head, but when I tried to do the same for her, I found that the gin had spilled into her hair and, mixing with the cement, had framed her head with a thick white crust like plaster of Paris. Rex and Harold were pinned down under beams, but the house was so jerrybuilt that it had collapsed without really injuring us. Most important of all, what was later to be my son was moving around inside me, knocking vigorously from within.

A few minutes later there was knocking from outside too, and a male voice shouted, "Anyone hurt in there?"

"No," we shouted back through the debris.

"Anyone like a cup of tea?" called a female voice.

"Yes!" yelled Harold, a true Englishman.

The air-raid warden quickly broke down the shattered door and waded toward us through the debris, followed by his female sidekick, armed with a friendly smile, a first-aid kit, and a thermos of hot tea.

During the last three months of my pregnancy, I woke up every morning vaguely worried. I suddenly knew what equanimity meant, for I seemed, inexplicably, to have lost it. I felt a need to conciliate something or somebody to avoid giving offense. Superstition? I had made fun of it all my life. What or whom did I want to bribe? Was somebody up there keeping track of me? All of a sudden I decided to stop being so cocksure and instead offer blanket atonement for previous arrogance to whatever or whomever it might concern. I now carefully walked around ladders instead of under them, avoided the number thirteen, and once even returned home, though deeply ashamed of myself, because a black cat had crossed my path from the left. Was it possible that my Old Testament ancestors were suddenly making themselves felt? The Jews have inevitably become pessimists in their two thousand years of Diaspora. Their version of "optimism" is: worse it cannot get. Gradually their doubts about the benevolence of fate crept even into their expressions of endearment. While other nations show their affection by adding special syllables to a name—Robert, Robbie; Jeanne, Jeannette; Mama, Mamita—the Jews thought this plain twaddle. They are only satisfied by adding an entire word, *Leben,* meaning "life," to the beloved name (Sarah, Sarahleben), because life, nothing else but naked life, was the tenderest expression of affection they could think of.

I finally confessed to my doctor. I was not at all certain that I was capable of giving anyone "naked life," not at all certain that I could hatch a normal child. I was terrified that I would be punished for having been so sure of succeeding in everything I had set out to do. Now I was going to find out what it was like to fail—fail in something any peasant woman can do without even trying, bringing a healthy child into the world.

"Nonsense!" said the doctor. "You're as sound as a bell. So is the child." I attempted to penetrate the very depth of his eyes, but they seemed to be hiding behind his glasses.

"Can you guarantee me a healthy baby?"

Angry flashes from behind the glasses. "What a question! You don't guarantee anything in medicine. Whatever would your father have said? You ought to be ashamed of yourself. Now get out of here."

I *was* ashamed of myself, but it didn't help. Secretly I began to pray. I remembered my childhood prayers: "O God in Heaven . . ." right down to the P.S., ". . . Bless my parents and sisters and Fräulein and me and let me find my left gym shoe, three times please, amen." Now I prayed in English: "and let me bring a healthy child into the world, three times please, amen."

When I went for an X ray in the eighth month, as prescribed, I sat shaking among other enormous mothers waiting for the verdict. In a minute the radiologist would appear and call my name, give me a searching look, take my hand, and say gently, "I'm sorry, Mrs. Harrison, but I have to tell you that your X ray shows something most peculiar—" The radiologist appeared in the doorway, called my name, casually said, "Everything's fine," and was about to go away again when I rushed over to him and kissed him passionately, tears streaming down my cheeks, right in front of everybody.

My "forebodings" finally got on my doctor's nerves to the point that he, too, was affected and gave strict instructions to the hospital that I was to be given no drugs that could conceivably harm the baby. Even the sensible, experienced nurse who, according to English custom, had been living with us in the country for the last couple of weeks, had kept an especially watchful eye on me. During the war the baby nurse often had to act as midwife if the doctor couldn't get there in time. I loved Sister Racle, her quiet ways and her dry sense of humor. On our daily hikes (a mile and a half a day, doctor's orders), she listened patiently to my nightmares and fears. Her only comment was "Piffle."

One day she asked me out of the blue, "How long has your cook been with you?"

"Mary? Three months. I know she's pretty awful, but out here in the country you have to take what you can get."

Sister Racle made no comment.

One evening—Rex had just come home—the three of us were listening to Edgar Bergen and Charlie McCarthy when my under-carriage was seized by such violent cramps that I thought there would be four of us any minute. The night of February 19, 1944, was particularly cold, and the roads were icy. The ambulance taking me to the hospital in London skidded wildly, and Rex skidded behind it in our little car. I screamed for all I was worth and heard Sister Racle ask the driver if there was a pan of some kind in the ambulance, because she didn't think I'd make it to the hospital.

I did make it, by the skin of my teeth. In my daily fantasies about "the day," I had seen myself arriving at the London Clinic, head high, smiling and waving gaily in all directions. Instead I lay face down on a stretcher and only realized that we'd arrived at the hospital by the sudden icy draft as I was carried across the sidewalk. I bit into the black leather mattress as hard as I could so as not to alarm the porter with my yelling, but the head nurse, who happened to be passing, heard my gurgles and ran to the telephone to call my doctor. Obstetricians usually arrive too early and wait about for hours, especially for first babies. Mine almost missed the big moment, although he got to the clinic within a few minutes. This baby was in such a hurry that less than two hours elapsed between Charlie McCarthy and its arrival.

Even before they handed me the bundle—wrapped in an old hospital towel, because my basket full of all I'd knitted had been left at home in the commotion—I heard a big bang outside. "Air raid?" I croaked. (I had bellowed so mightily that I was hoarse for days.) Yes, an air raid. The last series of air raids on London began that night. Many Londoners still remember February 19, 1944, as the night when they lost relatives or home. Incendiary bombs rained down on the hospital. The faces of everyone around me showed the strain. But amid the uproar and confusion arrived the moment that I had been conjuring up for months in every detail and variation, the moment when I would finally set eyes on what I had been carrying around with me for so long.

"Here's your big moment," said Sister Racle, and put the bundle on the pillow next to me. (It was her big moment too. It was she and nobody else who introduced mother and child.)

My son had his eyes tightly shut and was silently opening and closing his mouth like a fish. I knew, of course, that newborn babies are ugly, but I wasn't prepared for *that!* Rex sat down on the bed and said, "Darling, he's ours, and we'll love him. But don't let's show him to anybody, please!"

My first visitor arrived, beaming, at six o'clock the next morning, the woman from the birth registrar's office, wanting to know the child's name. "Oh dear, we haven't decided yet," I said sleepily. "You see, we were so sure that it was going to be a girl."

"I'll give you ten minutes while I register the others," she said severely. "There may be another air raid tonight, so it could be your last chance. You never know, do you?"

Ten minutes. I hadn't the heart to call Rex, who had been pacing the hall all night during the air raid. So I named the baby Rex Carey Alfred, to be called Carey, which was Rex's family name. (Alfred for my father.)

The woman from the registrar's office was right. The sirens sounded early in the evening, and nurses immediately wheeled all the mothers of newborn babies down to a windowless corridor in the basement. To pass the time, they handed the babies around, and I admired lots of little girls—mine was the only boy—with hair and dimples and asked if anyone wanted to exchange. Perhaps someone would like a son. Mine was available.

The next day we were all evacuated. The air raid had been too intense, and the incendiaries had done considerable damage to the hospital. An ambulance took me back home to the country, and there, in peace and quiet, I was able to unwrap my son and examine him properly for the first time. He hadn't a hair on his head, and no eyelashes, either. And those dear little hands they talk about were nothing but tiny gray claws. His skin hung in folds around him, as if he were wearing a suit several sizes too big. It took him three months to grow into it, and shortly after that he looked as if he would burst out of it, like a miniature Buddha. Nonetheless, even during that first moment of detached inventory-taking, I was ecstatic that he had all the essentials. Never before or since have I felt such an overwhelming sense of satisfaction.

I was allowed to stay in bed and watch Sister Racle handle the baby. On the fifth day she let me get up.

"But today is cook's day off," I said in surprise.

"Right," said Sister. "She's already gone. Have you a second key to her room?"

"Has she locked it?"

"We'll have to break the door open."

Before I could ask why, she had left the room and then the house.

Mary? What could Sister Racle have against our fat Mary? Half an hour later I knew. A workman broke open the door to the maid's room with a crowbar, while I watched from a chair in the hallway. Sister Racle stood by, holding the baby. The door was easily lifted off its hinges, and Sister was the first to look inside. "I thought so," she said, making way for me.

I stood in the doorway speechless with astonishment, turning my head from one side to the other. The room was chock-full of things strewn over the chair, the bed, the chest of drawers, the table, and the floor. Civilian clothes of Rex's, a suit, ties, shoes, and shirts that we thought were packed away in suitcases in the attic, dresses of mine that I hadn't worn for months because of my pregnancy, blouses, underwear—and an entire pantryful of food. A whole lot of nonrationed canned food I'd been able to buy was piled on the windowsill or under the bed. What upset me most was the sight of my personal weekly ration of apples, a "special treat" for expectant mothers, which, according to Mary, had been "discontinued." There they were, at least six pounds of red-cheeked beauties, neatly piled in Mary's gold-rimmed chamber pot.

Sister Racle put me back to bed. "Don't upset yourself. Leave it all to me."

"Who'll do the cooking?" I asked weakly.

"I will. It won't be the first time," she said grimly. "When the mistress gets pregnant, the mice make merry. I have the address of an agency that will send us someone decent. They know me."

I sank back on my pillows. How marvelous, I thought. Somebody cares, somebody's in charge, somebody's got the situation under control. I can lie here, weak and chickenhearted. How marvelous.

Towards evening, as it was getting dark, I heard Mary's key in the lock. Sister Racle was giving the baby his bottle. "Here," she said, handing me the bundle, and left the room. A minute later, over Carey's contented burps, I heard a piercing shriek. Mary had found her door wide open and Sister Racle standing in the middle of her room. Her only refuge was a series of shrill cries of despair. In between I could hear Sister's quiet voice. A few more earsplitting screams, the sound of feet running down the hall, the front door banging. I got up cautiously, balancing bundle and bottle, and walked over to the window.

Mary was running across the garden to the gate, still screaming, her arms held over her head as if to ward off blows. "Help! Help!" she screamed. "I'm in trouble! Help!" I watched her run down the road until there was only a glimpse of wildly gesticulating hands disappearing in the darkness.

It was just as well that my son had grown accustomed to bombs even before he was born, for he caught it again before he was four months old. This time it was the very latest weapon, a V-2.

Rex had been released from the Air Force, we were making our first movie together, *The Rake's Progress,* and our finances were looking up. We rented a house called "Brackenwood" close to Pinewood Film Studios in Buckinghamshire, bigger and more comfortable, surrounded by a large garden full of beautiful old trees.

At seven o'clock one morning, at my former home base, the Gaumont-British Studios in London, I was sitting in the makeup room under the dryer when Rex poked a worried face under it.

"Now, don't get into a flap," he said, "everything's all right—a V-2 has dropped near the house—the baby is absolutely okay, honest to God!" We dropped everything and drove back home, Rex without a coat, me with curlers in my hair.

"Everything's all right" was something of an exaggeration. Brackenwood had neither windows nor doors, and most of the tiles from the roof were lying on the ground. But the baby really was unhurt; he hadn't even awakened. Lying in his carriage on the terrace, he had been chewing on a soft piece of cloth, for he was teething. The V-2 had landed half a mile from the house with an explosion that made our former bomb look like a firecracker. The baby and the house were saved by a huge rhododendron in front of the entrance, at least twenty feet high and about thirty feet wide. Rhododendrons of that size are not uncommon in England. In Cornwall you can see them twice that high, in every color of the rainbow, white with red throats or yellow and orange. Ours was the common mauve variety, and since it was May, it was covered with thousands of blossoms. The blast had instantaneously stripped it bare. It stood there, stark naked, as I had never seen it before (rhododendrons keep their leaves even in winter), an enormous tangle of black, debris-strewn branches, pointing toward the sky. The lifesaver.

The carriage had overturned, but since the baby was strapped in, he had remained lying on his side, not very comfortable but asleep. They had found his teething rag half in his mouth, half covering his face, and full of glass splinters from one of the windows. But they didn't tell me that until the next day.

Thirty years later I drove every morning for weeks to the Pinewood Studios, where I was shooting an American television series. Nothing had changed on either side of the road I used to trudge along with Sister Racle. Every time the car came to a certain spot, I told the driver to drive slowly, please, because I wanted to see something. The something was the same old wooden gate with "Brackenwood" in white letters above it.

One day I couldn't bear it any longer and asked the chauffeur to drive right through the gates toward the house. "Do you know the people that's living there, miss?" he asked. "No," I said, "but I used to live in that house long ago. Drive slowly, please."

He drove at a snail's pace, and there, right in front of us, loomed the giant rhododendron bush, covered in lilac blossoms. "Where to, miss?" "Just . . . drive round that rhododendron . . . and now quickly out again."

From then on, I made him drive in and out a couple of times every week. Occasionally a car would be standing in front of the entrance, and I could see people behind the windows. "Miss," said my driver, "them people in there must think we're crazy or something." "Never mind, we're just looking." "But, miss, did you see them with their noses against the windows just now?" I had seen nothing except my rhododendron.

A German reporter showed up at the studio with the usual question: Wasn't there anything happening on the set? No, I said, nothing. The only happening happens to me every morning—and I told him the story of the rhododendron and my early morning pilgrimages. He got quite excited. "But we must take a picture of you next to it."

My chauffeur balked. "Good Lord, miss, they'll have us arrested for trespassing, they'll think we're spies or something, they'll take the number of me car . . ."

We drove in. The car stopped, I ran close to the rhododendron, trying to look easy and relaxed (as you can see in the photo), and the reporter's camera clicked. As I was jumping into the car, which made off at extraordinary speed, I saw through the back window a couple of people running out of the house, waving and shouting. I never dared drive in again.

From the first this child, awaited with so much fear and foreboding, was independent, cheerful, and intelligent. (Rex used to say, "He must have been here before.") This undoubtedly had something to do with the remarkable woman who was his nanny.

For the first six months I had to settle for somebody who was available. I knew she wasn't ideal, but there was little choice during the war years, when everybody who was at all capable was busy working either in the forces or in industry. Rex liked Janno because she could make a good cocktail out of gin and "orange juice." Gin was available all through the war; the only question was what to put in it. Janno quickly solved the problem. Every week the government filled thousands of bottles with a yellowish liquid that tasted vaguely of oranges, which we hadn't seen for years, and distributed them to expectant mothers. You presented yourself at the appropriate office every Tuesday with your doctor's certificate in your hand. These queues were the longest in England because of the size of the participants. An occasional husband would sometimes stand in line for his wife, looking thin and self-conscious. My ration was at once handed over to Janno, who presided at the bar and was better at mixing cocktails than baby formula. (There was another special ration for expectant mothers. From the third month on, you got a book of coupons printed with the message: "MOTHER: Do not share this extra piece of meat with your family. EAT IT YOURSELF." I ate mine myself, but Carey still only weighed five pounds.)

Janno came from Wales. They say all Welsh people have a screw loose. Janno was no exception. She was also occupationally handicapped. A bomb had exploded too close to her and damaged her eardrums, so she could hear a baby only if it was howling at the top of its lungs. She slept under the kitchen table at night and wore a tin hat all day, never taking it off, even to give the baby his bottle. Since she then had both hands full, the tin hat would slip down over her nose, leaving her sitting in the dark. She didn't seem to mind, but it also prevented her from noticing when the bottle was empty and my son was swallowing nothing but warm air. So I sent her away. Carey lost his first nanny and Rex his best bartender.

I was determined not to compromise a second time. The right person simply had to be found. While I was working, I often had to be away from home for weeks at a time, and the child would then be at the mercy of a stranger. I took my time and interviewed women and girls of all ages. One day an Irishwoman came to see me. She was in her late forties, with kinky yellow hair, intelligent eyes, and a mouth like a knife blade, touched up with lipstick; having no lips, she had painted the skin.

Toward the end of our conversation, she said, "Mrs. Harrison, there's something I must tell you, which may make you decide not to take me."

Aha, I thought, an illegitimate child. Okay, let her bring it along.

"I dye my hair."

"So do I," I said. "We can do it together."

She didn't smile. "I'm an albino. I'm ugly enough as it is. If I had white hair and white eyelashes as well, it would be too much. Children don't like ugly people. That's why I dye my hair."

I mustn't let this one get away, I thought.

That was Pat, Pat Jennings. She stayed with us for five years, the first five years of my son's life. I learned things from her that I'd never thought about before. "If you want to punish a child," she said, "never do it in anger. Never lose control. The child mustn't see that you're upset, because that gratifies him and he wants to make it happen again. If he talks back to you, the way he did just now, leave the room for a minute and cool off. If you still want to spank him, come back and do it quickly and calmly."

Every day she read to him for an hour out of his books, and before he was two he knew them all by heart. He remembered the exact word at which Pat turned the pages, and he loved to come into the living room and "read" to us. To the astonishment of any visitors who happened to be present, the tiny child would "read," moving his head to follow every line across the page and turning over at exactly the right place, sometimes in the middle of a word.

I kept a diary about him from the day of his birth to the middle of his sixth year. My mother did the same with her three children and gave each of us her diary on her twenty-first birthday. Such a record, written by somebody else, is an impartial, merciless document. It's a strange feeling to read about things that happened to you years ago, which you never knew before or remember only vaguely or quite differently. Yet—no quibbling, for there is the date of entry. Irrefutable.

On March 1, 1948, a week after Carey's fourth birthday, I wrote this: "Pat asked if she could give him a ten-minute lesson every day. He insists he must learn to read. I said yes, ten minutes but no more." Six months later he could read fluently. He read like a grown-up, without childish intonation, though he had a pronounced lisp. I gave him the *Children's Encyclopedia* for his fifth birthday, and from then on all was quiet in the nursery. He read.

Pat accompanied us from London to Hollywood without hesitation, but when we later moved to New York, she unexpectedly decided to stay behind. "He doesn't need me anymore," she said, staring out the window. Pat without Carey? Carey without Pat? Unthinkable. Had it been possible to analyze the child's feelings, his love might have gone to me, but his sense of security came without any doubt from Pat.

"If you're giving notice, Pat, I refuse to accept it. How are we going to live without you? I thought you were going to stay with us forever. You belong with us!"

"I belong with children," she said. "It's going to be very hard. I'll never have another like Carey." (Once she wouldn't speak to me for days because I'd said the child was—perhaps—not musical.) "But I'll find the strength."

I bought a "friendship ring," three intertwined bands of gold, silver, and platinum, so that she would know we were friends for life. She accepted it hesitantly and returned it a few days later.

"My father confessor doesn't want me to keep it."

"Why ever not, Pat? What objection can he possibly have? It's only a poor token of all we owe you."

She shook her head silently and gave me a look which said plainly that I wasn't capable of "understanding" anyway.

During the three months before we left for New York, she ate almost nothing, and her albino eyes were red-rimmed. Carey didn't notice. He was looking forward to New York, where he would at last be allowed to go to school. He had no idea that Pat wouldn't be coming along. We hoped that amid the upheaval of moving, his first visit to a big city, a new nursery, and a classroom full of playmates,

the separation would be easier for him than if it took place against
the familiar background of Pat's chair, Pat's teapot, Pat's sewing
basket.

She didn't say good-bye to him, just pressed our hands briefly
on her way out.

"Pat, your address! Where can I write to you?"

"Not now. I'll get in touch with you later."

"But Pat, suppose Carey should get sick—"

"Then you'll have to take care of him yourself. I mustn't come
back to him."

The child asked about her, was surprised rather than disturbed
for a time—and forgot. I had a hard time finding anyone for him in
New York. After many interviews, I finally engaged a girl. He
received her full of curiosity and excitement, and informed her the
next day that she was a dumbbell. Which was perfectly true. With
the next one, a vigorous young Swiss woman, strong-minded and
good-tempered, he got on well, but he never loved her. She immediately introduced a system he liked. Every Saturday she hung
a report card on the wall, showing his grades in every "subject" of
his nursery life: Honesty, Helpfulness, Cleanliness, Tidying up the
Nursery, Bathroom Manners, Manner toward Parents, Manner
toward Mademoiselle, Playground Behavior, and so on. Carey had
to determine his own grades, and it surprised me every time to see
how strict and finicky he was with himself.

"Playground Behavior: C-minus," I read. "Why only C-minus,
darling? Mademoiselle says you've been very good all week."

"I hit Juliet on the head with my shovel behind the litter bathket.
Mademoiselle didn't see it."

"Oh."

He never mentioned Pat again, and I didn't either. This conspiracy of silence was probably the only way to handle the separation.
A few years later we received our first Christmas card from her, and
then an occasional letter to me. She moved from one job to another
in Hollywood and preferred to take care of infants, because, she
wrote, in that first, animal stage she found it easiest to be fond
of them. She was highly paid and never out of work, and used

her wages to put an impecunious nephew through medical school in America.

When Carey was twenty, he visited his father in Hollywood, where Rex was making *My Fair Lady*. I wrote him to go and see Pat. "But I don't even know what she looked like," he wrote. "I can't remember her at all." (I had had no way of keeping her memory alive for him with photos, because she would never let herself be photographed.) Elsa Schreiber, who remembered Pat well from the old days, had kept in touch with her and invited her and Carey for coffee. Instead of the slight, fair-haired child, a tall, dark, bearded young man appeared in the doorway.

"She stared at him," Elsa wrote, "and her chin began to tremble violently. She couldn't even hold her cup and saucer. Carey sat down on the sofa beside her and took her hand. They didn't have much to say to each other. 'How's your mother? How's your father?' 'Are you taking care of a—a nice child just now?' 'Carey, do you remember the three little pigs on the windowsill?' 'Three little pigs—er, yes, I remember.' 'And the cottage cheese with mashed tomatoes that you wouldn't eat?' 'Mashed tomatoes with . . . no, I don't remember that.' After half an hour they stopped talking and just looked at each other."

It was their only meeting.

Not long ago I received a letter from Australia—unfamiliar handwriting, unfamiliar name, not a fan letter. Pat's nephew, the doctor she'd put through medical school, wrote that she had come to him in Sydney to die. Could I fulfill a last wish of hers? She knew she had cancer and hadn't long to live. Would Carey write to her? Otherwise she was resigned and content.

Carey wrote at once and sent pictures of his wedding, of himself and his young wife. Soon afterward we heard again from Sydney. Carey's letter had arrived just in time. They had to read it to her several times, and she had smiled. But it had been too late for her to look at the photographs.

9

Hollywood: Work

❀

O N NOVEMBER 21, 1945, the boat train had taken us from
London to board the *Queen Elizabeth*. Five days later, she
reduced speed. Land was in sight. From that moment on we never
moved from the deck, just stood there, watching. Rex had been in
New York once before, but I knew the famous skyline only from
the movies and stood as awestruck as any of the millions who had
sailed past the Statue of Liberty before me. A tug towed us in to the
dock, and the yelling of the troops aboard was matched by the
screaming of the thousands of relatives and friends thronging the
pier, drowning out the band set up to welcome the homecoming
veterans. Moved and involuntarily involved, we watched the demonstrations of happiness, from plain hysterical shrieking to silent
gazing upward.

We, too, were welcomed, though less emotionally. Leland Hayward greeted us in the name of Twentieth Century-Fox, and our
agent was on hand to help us get off the ship, collect our luggage,
and pass the customs. This last formality was a most important one,
judging by the thoroughness with which every single piece of
luggage was searched.

"Whatever are you looking for?" asked Rex of the official who was
just closing my suitcase.

"Arms, sir," replied the burly officer. "You have no idea how many of them fellows there try to smuggle their guns into the country."

"Dear, dear," mused Rex and helped the man with the lock on his suitcase. The lid flipped open and the customs man jumped. "Well, waddaya know!" he exclaimed, and pointed. Leland, the agent, Rex, and I all stared aghast, for there, right on top, neatly in the center, lay Rex's RAF pistol. "Good God," said Leland. Our agent retreated a couple of steps, I was struck dumb, and Rex said, amazed, "I say! I'd quite forgotten about the thing." It took several hours, plenty of talking and "explaining," and the good offices of several highly placed people in Leland's circle of acquaintances to get us off the hook and prevent them from shipping us back at once or sending us into quarantine on Ellis Island pending further inquiries.

We arrived at our hotel in the evening exhausted, worn to a frazzle, unable to do anything but sink into our beds. Next day we were already on the train to Hollywood. There had been some hurried interviews at the hotel, for there was a certain amount of interest from the press, not only in our future plans but also because our film, *The Rake's Progress,* was running successfully on Broadway. They had renamed it *The Notorious Gentleman* so that the American public, unfamiliar with Hogarth, would not mistake our war epic for a gardening manual.

During the three-day train trip, we were initiated into the Hollywood Way of Life—dos and don'ts, traditions and taboos. It all sounded fine to me, except for one thing: I would not be allowed to take charge of our bank account, as I had done in England in my good old Prussian way. I had taken on the job of underpaid secretary soon after we were married, when I found out that Rex was emotionally not up to filling out his check stubs. So I filled them out, argued with the tax people, and paid the insurance premiums. In this way we at least knew how much we had in the bank. Generally not much. Sometimes nothing at all.

Now, however, our Hollywood agents severely bade us turn over our affairs to a "business manager." He would pay everything—taxes, wages, the butcher and the hairdresser; we would only have to initial the bills. The business manager would "save" for us.

We would draw a weekly allowance of spending money. It would just take a little getting used to.

We got used to it in no time and plunged headlong into Hollywood life, buying clothes and cars. Even Pat learned to drive, when she finally arrived with Carey three months later. Nobody can live in Beverly Hills without a car. No streetcars or buses serve those interminable avenues. Parks and children's playgrounds don't exist; everybody plays in his own garden. You don't go for walks either. The "story" of the foreigner strolling along a street in Beverly Hills one evening and having a hard time explaining to a police officer what he was "doing" is true.

Pat, of course, obstinately walked Carey every day down the avenues of palm trees, as a British nanny should. Her life centered on Carey, God, and her driving lessons. Of the three, God gave me the most trouble, because every Sunday I had to drive her to early mass at the nearest Catholic church. Since we went to a party every single Saturday night, I had an awful time getting up after only a few hours' rest. The minute Pat disappeared through the church door, I was asleep over the steering wheel. When she woke me up three-quarters of an hour later, I would still be in a daze, while she radiated strength and happiness and was almost talkative on the way home.

The most important event by far, however, had been Rex's first encounter with the director and producer of his film, *Anna and the King of Siam*. Immediately after our arrival at the Beverly Hills Hotel, suitcases still unpacked, he was on the phone to Twentieth to "make contact." Apparently everything was ready, everybody on their toes, the red carpet rolled out. A car was on its way to take him to lunch at the studio commissary, where Buddy Lighton, the producer, and John Cromwell, the director, would be waiting.

Two months ago, in England, when he had read the script for the first time, he had said to me, "I would never have accepted this part if it had been an English production. Let's face it—I've always played roles that were more or less up my alley. But this fellow is way out of my ken. I mean, he even has a death scene, and a bloody long one, too! I've never had a role in which I died, ever! I don't have a clue how to play this sort of . . . primitive madman, and a Siamese one at that, who lived a hundred years ago! I've never played in a period piece. I don't have a natural feeling for costumes —like Larry Olivier, for instance. But I could learn pretty quickly. The marvelous thing about Hollywood is that they do have good directors for this sort of film over there. The dialogue is unspeakable sometimes, but all the details are first-class. I don't know the fellow who'll direct this film, his name's John Cromwell, but Zanuck wouldn't have chosen him if he didn't know his business. Can't wait to meet him and hear all he has to say!"

The moment had come.

"I might be a long time," said Rex, departing. "I'll really nail Cromwell down on all the details so that I can start working. Marvelous feeling, to be able to rely on your director!"

He was back at the hotel after barely an hour, white in the face. In the commissary, he reported, after the initial mutual expressions of enthusiasm, he had come down to brass tacks without further ado.

"Mr. Cromwell," he had started, while soup was being served, "how do you see this King Mongkut? I mean, how does he speak? What kind of accent does he have? How does he move?"

Pause. Everybody was busy with the soupspoons.

"You know, Rex," said Cromwell at last, "I wouldn't worry about any of those things if I were you. All that sort of stuff will come to you quite naturally, you know, when you're in your costume."

Rex turned pale and put his spoon down. There was no more to be gotten out of either director or producer.

"We'd better pack again and go back to London," he said to me. "It's obvious that Cromwell either doesn't have a clue or doesn't give a damn what Mongkut is like. I'd rather break my contract than make a fool of myself in a part like that."

Depressed and helpless, we stared out the window at palms and banana trees.

The rescue squad arrived at eight o'clock that evening.

My first Hollywood telephone call had naturally been to Elsa Schreiber. I hadn't seen her since before the war, when I had waved good-bye to her at the station in London. Of course I had tried to tell Rex all about her and our work together, but he had just shaken his head and said, "Don't talk to me about your witch doctor; I can't stand the idea of middle-European miracle-workers." Tonight of all nights, on this disastrous first day in sunny Hollywood, Elsa would be coming to dinner. Bad timing.

Her very entrance was unfortunate. She marched into the room straight as a ramrod, radiant with sun-tanned California health, while we sat there vinegary and wartime green. Both parties eyed each other warily, Elsa with her clear, penetrating gaze, Rex withdrawn behind narrowed, mistrustful eyelids. The conversation dragged, because Elsa and I didn't want to exclude Rex by reminiscing. She knew at once that something had shaken him to the core that day and decided to take the bull by the horns.

"It's certainly an interesting idea to cast you as the King of Siam."

"Why?" said Rex suspiciously. "Do you know the script?"

"I know the novel. It's always more exciting to cast against type, isn't it?"

"Is it?"

"Of course. Provided you thoroughly understand the other 'type' and his characteristics."

Pause. Rex gave Elsa a searching look.

"And what in your opinion are the characteristics of the King of Siam?"

"Several things. First, the way he speaks, his accent."

Rex cut in at once: "What kind of accent would he have?"

Elsa thought for a moment. "Have you ever talked to an Oriental? To our ears they sound staccato and high-pitched, a bit like birds twittering."

"Like birds twittering?"

"Yes."

"And . . . what other characteristics does he have?"

Elsa reflected for a moment. Then she said quietly, "I think his laugh is the most important thing."

"His laugh?"

"Yes. That man laughs almost inaudibly—and convulsively, in a way that's completely foreign to us."

"How?" asked Rex almost threateningly.

Elsa laughed briefly and jerkily in an uncanny, joyless way, almost like a hound yapping. At that moment she looked exactly like King Mongkut of Siam.

Rex got up. Without taking his eyes off her, he backed out of the room and returned with the script in his hand. "Here," he said, setting it down on her plate. "For instance, in this scene, right at the beginning—"

"No," said Elsa, pushing the script aside, "I have to read it before I can say anything."

"Can you read it tonight?"

"Yes."

"Come on. I'll drive you home."

"Can't she finish her dinner first?" I asked.

"No," said Rex, getting his coat.

"Never mind," said Elsa, "he's obsessed. I understand that."

Rex appeared at her front door first thing in the morning. A little while later he was back at the hotel, thoughtfully pulling at his nose.

"I'll work with her," he finally announced grandly. "It can't do any harm."

For the next three weeks, until shooting began, Rex was invisible. He worked with Elsa from early morning until late at night, until even she groaned, "I'm exhausted. That madman is killing me."

Finally the first day of shooting. Rex was made up to look extraordinarily like the old daguerreotype of the king taken in 1867. In the first take he sat cross-legged on his throne and spoke his opening lines in the Asiatic intonation in which Elsa had so carefully coached him. Before he had said more than a few words, John Cromwell interrupted him, horrified. "What in the world do you think you're doing, Rex? Why don't you speak normally?"

"I'm speaking," said Rex, "like King Mongkut of Siam."

"Out of the question. We hired Rex Harrison, not a bird imitator. Kindly speak in your normal voice."

But Rex wasn't going to budge an inch from his interpretation of the king, and the first day of shooting ended with gnashing of teeth on both sides. Darryl Zanuck, the head of the studio, was immediately informed by Cromwell and was waiting anxiously and with dire misgivings for the first day's rushes. Recasting was in the air. The rushes were hurriedly processed so that Zanuck could make up his mind without delay, and early in the morning of the second day Rex was summoned from his makeup table to the holiest of holies.

Darryl Zanuck's private office was the size of a ballroom. Six people could easily have sat behind his desk. He himself was small and at first glance insignificant-looking, with intelligent, restless eyes and a mouselike mustache above protruding teeth, the subject of numerous jokes in the industry.

"Well, now, Rex," he said, chewing on his perpetual cigar. "Well, now—we've certainly got a tough situation here. I've, uh . . . the fact is, I've just seen your rushes. They're extraordinary. You *are* the King of Siam, there's no doubt about it. But what are we going to do with John Cromwell? I'm going to have to side with the actor against the director. I can't remember ever doing a thing like that before. Are you prepared to go your own way, without any direction at all?"

"Yes," said Rex. He never spoke another word to his director during the shooting, except to wish him good morning and good evening.

When the picture was released in New York a few months later, the critics outdid one another in praising Rex's performance. With his first film, he had moved into the top rank of American stars. The morning after the premiere, he sent Elsa a telegram which she has kept to this day: "WONDERFUL PRESS THANKS TO YOU AND YOU ALONE LOVE REX."

In the evening we attended a dinner in his honor. We were seated next to Garson Kanin. "There's one thing I don't understand," said Garson. "John Cromwell's an old friend of mine and I've seen some pretty good things he's done, but the performance he got out of you is absolutely incredible."

"He didn't get anything out of me," said Rex. "After the first day of shooting we didn't exchange another word."

"What?" said Garson, amazed. "You played that part without any direction? But how did you find the accent, the intonation, the gestures, the laugh? It's unbelievable!"

The pause seemed too long to me. I broke in enthusiastically, "Of course Rex had direction, but not from John Cromwell."

"What on earth do you mean?" said Garson, completely at sea.

Rex was silent. I launched into a detailed and appreciative description of Elsa's personality and work. But Garson's reaction was not at all what I expected. He was neither impressed nor pleased; on the contrary, he seemed embarrassed and picked at his food without speaking. It dawned on me that as a director he identified with Cromwell, whatever the circumstances or the effect on the picture.

On the way home, Rex and I had our first big fight.

Many years later I told Binkie Beaumont, London's most famous theatrical producer, who had known us both for well over twenty years, about the incident.

"Rex was right," he said. "You should never have mentioned Elsa Schreiber. Rex is a star. He can't afford Boy Scout ideas about what's fair or unfair; his one and only concern has to be to give an outstanding performance. How he does it is nobody's business."

I was reminded of Shaw's words to the same effect: A great actor can have only one love—himself.

Hollywood. Letters to my family in England really did begin with the dateline Hollywood. We'd been there a whole month, but I still had to pinch myself several times a day. Since the era of "The Nibelungs" and my double role as Siegfried-cum-dragon, I had been stubbornly waiting for this, despite all detours. Hollywood, seventh heaven.

"The Nibelungs" had been my first obsession, at the age of ten. From then on, throughout my teenage years, I kept a careful record in a special diary of every single movie I was allowed to see: Title, Actors, and—the most important column—Comments. My comments bordered on insanity. "Super" followed by three exclamation points was the most negative verdict. "Fantastic" with five exclamation marks was my average. But for any movie featuring Gary Cooper, words failed me and I just filled the entire column from left to right with exclamation marks.

I saw him first opposite Marlene Dietrich in *Morocco*, children under eighteen not admitted. I was only fourteen, but thanks to my mother's high-heeled shoes and a hat with a veil, they let me in. In those days they were still strict about young people seeing "that sort" of picture. *Morocco* was that sort, for Cooper kissed Marlene several times on the mouth, to my entire satisfaction. From then on I loved him and him alone, and bent my girl friends' ears repeating to them time and again that someday I'd play opposite him, come what may. During the dark days in Paris my passion continued unabated, and I never missed a single one of his films. He also became a sort of best friend and father confessor. On my way home, I would "report" to him the day's events and all my hopes and disappointments. The conversation was one-sided; I did the talking, and he sat there and occasionally said "Yup." But I loved our "talks"; they comforted me.

Over the years, as I slowly got on my feet in London, our relationship came a bit unstuck, but even during the war years I saw every movie Cooper was in. With the uncritical love of the true fan, I watched him grow older, with circles under the eyes and a couple of lines around the mouth. In *For Whom the Bell Tolls*, the sight of him lying on the ground about to expire affected me so deeply that I had to grope my way out, despite vociferous protests from everybody else in the row. I was in my ninth month and didn't want to upset the baby. After Carey was born, Cooper's image began to fade, and I felt vaguely guilty about him, as if I hadn't written to a close friend for a long time.

Once in Hollywood, my first thought was, well, now you'll finally get to see him. And during the first few weeks, in strange houses, surrounded by strange faces, I often stared hopefully at the door. But he remained invisible.

While Rex struggled with King Mongkut every day in the Fox studios, I was busy with Carey, Pat, and the household. We had rented a little house in Bel Air, high above Beverly Hills with a view over all Los Angeles. It had all come true, including the orange trees and the swimming pool. Letters from England still talked about rationing, and we sent weekly food parcels, yet we often felt as if we had left England in the lurch.

Thank God that I was given no time to twiddle my thumbs. I had hardly settled in the new house when the phone rang. My agent. Warner Brothers were asking for their new acquisition. Screen test tomorrow.

"What for?" I asked curiously.

"For the lead in *Cloak and Dagger.*" Director: Fritz Lang. Star: Gary Cooper.

I had already been to the Warner Brothers studios a couple of times. After all, I was under contract and drawing a weekly salary. I had wandered about, taking in the immense size of the place, the enormous sets, the restaurants, the specialized departments—a small city full of people, driving in cars or walking fast, all with a purpose showing in their faces and no time to lose. Would I ever "belong?" My agent guided me like a pilot fish, talking cheerfully all the while. I'd even been received in the inner sanctum, the office of Jack Warner, the studio head. He had said hello quite cordially, though without that certain flicker in the eye I was watching for, the flicker that meant, well, well, aren't you something! Perhaps they didn't go in for that kind of flicker in Hollywood. Or just flickered inwardly. In any case, Jack Warner had said to come in for a screen test.

First they showed me my dressing room. Dressing room? A two-room apartment with bath and kitchen! My silence was misinterpreted. They hastily apologized: this was just a provisional dressing room; they would give me a proper one as soon as possible. Words failed me. I just nodded.

This first test, as I was told to my bitter disappointment, was only for lighting purposes. They wanted to see how I looked on the screen. No acting. No Gary Cooper. Just move your head from left to right. I was made up and driven to the set. The studios were so spread out that it would have taken me fifteen minutes to walk. One of the all-time famous German screen directors, Fritz Lang, was waiting for me. He made a point of speaking only English and was reasonably friendly, in a curt sort of way. Authoritarian, though. Even moving my head from left to right turned into a third degree.

Suddenly he said, "Take her blouse off and get her a vest."

"A what?"

"An old-fashioned undervest. What poor people wear to keep warm," he growled impatiently.

They got me a vest. The Warner Brothers wardrobe department, like that of all the other Hollywood studios, was a fully equipped department store where you could find anything, no matter how unusual. Modestly hidden by a screen, I exchanged my blouse for the undervest. Back in front of the camera, I felt naked and self-conscious. Lower down, I was still wearing my skirt, but above it, nothing but the awful woolen undervest. The lights blinded me; I could see nothing but silhouettes. Suddenly a tall silhouette, much taller than the others, materialized beside the camera, a silhouette I knew well. Cooper.

"More to the left," rasped Fritz Lang. I didn't care. There was Gary Cooper, looking at me. In my undervest. I squinted in his direction, boiling hot under my makeup, and thought I detected a slight grin. He said a word to Fritz Lang and left.

That was it. I was allowed to dress and was finally handed a few pages of script—a scene, *the* scene, that was to be my acid test. I had three days to work on it. Instead of going home, I went straight to Elsa's. I came home each night worn out, fell into bed, and was back at her house at eight the next morning. Tirelessly she kneaded me into shape until I was *à point*.

On the fourth day, bathed in cold sweat, I drove to the studio. The undervest was already laid out for me in my dressing room. Never mind. I would of course have preferred to float towards Cooper in something diaphanous, but that wouldn't have fitted the part, a penniless Italian guerrilla fighter. Decorously covered by a dressing gown, I was put into the studio car, ready for the great moment. The door to the set opened: zero hour. There was the camera, Fritz Lang on a chair underneath it, lights, a few shabby pieces of kitchen furniture to provide the right atmosphere—and a very tall man standing with his back to me. He turned around and smiled uncertainly. The assistant director introduced us: "Mr. Lex Barker. Mr. Barker is going to stand in for Mr. Cooper in this test, Miss P."

Miss P. came closer to fainting than ever before in her life. The shock was too brutal. I only just managed to shake the young man's moist hand. This was to be his screen test, too, his very first. A few weeks ago he'd been released from the navy and someone had "discovered" the tall, good-looking youngster. Perhaps some day he'd be a star. He had studied his lines with the studio's coach for beginners, that was all.

During our first rehearsal, when I suddenly had to hug him close as required by the script, he uttered a muffled gasp of alarm and his innocent blue eyes stared at me in such bewilderment that I forgot my lines. Fritz Lang's mood dropped to zero. But this scene was followed by a lengthy monologue of mine, which Elsa had hammered out with particular care. Mr. Lang stopped snarling and gave me an almost friendly look. That was the end of the test. "Good-bye, Mr. Barker, and thank you very much." The car took me back to my sumptuous dressing room, where I took my makeup off with shaking hands.

An entire week of tortured waiting had to be lived through. No use pestering my agent. He didn't know anything either, and could only drown me in a lot of phrases he'd been trained to use in situations of this sort: distraught-client-awaiting-studio-decision. He had started taking care of me from the moment we arrived, and I liked him, though he handled me warily. I had insisted on inserting a clause in my contract allowing me to break it if for any reason my husband should be released from his contract with Fox. I held out for this clause, even though it cost me considerable financial concessions. Ever since, the agent thought me a little soft in the head.

The telephone was kind and reduced my seven days of suspense to five. My agent's confidence-inspiring voice requested me to report to the studios. Mr. Lang was waiting for me. He even managed a genuine smile as he congratulated me.

And that afternoon finally brought the long-awaited screen test with Gary Cooper. No acting; it was just to find out how we looked together. Ludicrous, that's how we looked together, for I only came up to his belt and they had to bring me a box to stand on. (All through the film.)

"How do you do?" I managed to say.

"Hi, kid," he said with a friendly wink.

Naturally I never took my eyes off him during the first few weeks of shooting. He was the ideal movie actor. There are two different types, both equally effective on the screen. One is the superb, highly trained actor, such as Laurence Olivier, Spencer Tracy, or Humphrey Bogart. The other is the nonactor, the personality, such as Gary Cooper, Cary Grant, or Clark Gable. Trained actors work out their screen roles down to the last detail, sentence by sentence, word by word, just as they do their stage roles. The personality actor doesn't work out anything. He knows his lines, and that's it; for everything else he relies on personal magnetism and improvisation. This type has no nerves, while the trained actor strains his to the limit. Cooper could deliver a long speech on camera while rummaging in his pocket for a cigarette, continue talking while he fussed with the matches, pause for a moment of what looked like intense concentration, pick up where he left off, put the matches away, rub his nose, and go on talking as if the camera didn't exist. Charles Laughton, who used to work out his part down to the minutest details and knew on which particular word he was going to raise his eyebrows, once made a film with him. The story goes that Laughton burst into tears as he watched Gary innocently indulging in his usual "behavior" in front of the camera, that he embraced him and called him a genius.

Cooper shrugged it all off and never wanted to listen to my hymns of praise for his various roles, such as Sergeant York (for which he had received an Oscar). "It's a cinch," he said. "I just learn my lines and try not to bump into the furniture."

He was exactly as I'd always imagined him, only older, with iron gray hair. He moved slowly, spoke deliberately, tired quickly, and would then pull his hat down over his face and fall asleep wherever he happened to be sitting. There was something unassailable about him, a dignity which he never lost even in the most commonplace pictures.

I never mentioned the role he'd played in my life. What could he possibly have answered? But it seemed quite natural that he should gradually fall into the habit of spending the lengthy intervals between takes in my trailer, his endless legs propped up on the furniture. After all, he had been a friend of mine since I was fourteen! Like most Hollywood stars, he loved talking about old times and how the place had looked when the only decent road led to Pickfair, the Fairbanks-Pickford home. It seemed to me only fair that *he* should now be telling *me* his life story, after having listened to mine all those years. The fact that he never asked me to tell him anything about myself also fitted the picture. Why should I have repeated myself? So I just said "Yup" now and again, and we were even.

Right from the start, before the first week of our three-month shooting schedule had passed, I noticed that I was feeling more nervous and less confident every day. Usually, the opposite happens. You grope your way around for the first few days, learn the names and faces of the stage crew, make friends with fellow actors over lunch, and try to get rid of the inevitable self-consciousness as quickly as possible. For it is really odd to find yourself in the arms of a man you've never laid eyes on before because that's what the script calls for. Not to mention that a dozen other strangers are watching your every move with interest because, as cameramen or electricians or prop men, they're being paid to do so.

Passionate love scenes in front of the camera are anything but passionate, particularly in close-up. There you're lying, mouth to mouth, eyes closed, apparently transported by your ardor, while the cameraman complains, "I can see nothing but noses. Miss Palmer, can't you move yours a bit to the right?"

The director is the key to everything. He creates—dictates—the climate on the set, putting everyone at ease or making them shake with nerves. And when it comes to the moment of truth and the camera is rolling, he alone represents the audience, only to him can you turn for the feedback a stage actor gets instantly and unmistakably from a live audience in the theater. When that audience isn't with you, you'll get it as clear as the handwriting on the wall of Belshazzar's palace. And if, in the studio, a film director sits under the camera with his arms crossed and a fishy stare, it deflates you, takes the stuffing out of you, bursts your "inner bubble," as Rex called it.

Laurence Olivier, who directed us later in New York in Christopher Fry's *Venus Observed,* told me once that he always tried quite deliberately to "break down the barriers" on the first day of rehearsals, to save time. "I force myself to ham it up, I howl, I giggle, I make faces so outrageously in front of the cast that I make them feel quite sick. But I achieve what I'm after: they can't help thinking, well, if Olivier can make a fool of himself, I can let go too. And letting go, breaking down the last bit of resistance, in fact, total surrender—that's the essential thing."

I quickly made friends with my fellow actors and the stage crew. Cooper, the star, didn't behave like one. He sat around with us and listened, said "Yup" now and again, and fell asleep several times a day, a sign that he felt comfortable.

Not so Fritz Lang. He never ate with us and became more unapproachable every day. Any attempt to talk to him and "break down the barriers" was greeted with an icy look and a curt reply. One day during a break, my chair happened to be next to his, so I tried German on him. I told him of the unforgettable impression his film *The Nibelungs* had made on me and my classmates and of my first role as Siegfried and the dragon.

He looked at me without a word. Perhaps he didn't believe me. To prove it, I sang the still unforgotten Siegfried motif from the silent film and, when he still didn't react, the Hagen motif. Delighted at this sudden discovery of an unsuspected musical archive in my memory, I began the Volker motif.

That was too much for him. He got up and brusquely interrupted me, in English. "None of that interests me anymore."

In England I had worked several times with famous directors, including Hitchcock, David Lean, and Carol Reed. Every one of them, though occasionally strict, was anxious to have a relaxed, friendly climate in the studio. Fritz Lang was anxious to have the opposite. He was one of the few German refugee directors who were able to continue their illustrious careers without a break in a new country and a new language, a tribute to the quality of his direction.

Perhaps he needed tension and an electrically charged atmosphere. I certainly didn't. The moment the clapperboard announced the first take and I heard him bark "Action!" my heart dropped into my boots. What's more, I had the feeling that he wasn't quite so gruff with the other actors and spoke to Cooper in quite a civilized tone. Only when I was alone on camera was he on the warpath.

At the end of the first week of shooting, we went to a party at the house of Walter Wanger, the producer. His wife, Joan Bennett, had made two pictures under Fritz Lang's direction. She drew me off into a quiet corner.

"Well, how are you making out on Fritz's drill ground?"

"All right," I said cautiously, because I didn't know her.

"Oh, come on! Don't give me that. I've already heard. Fritz is up to his old tricks. Are you the only girl in the picture?"

"Yes."

"My sympathy," said Joan and laughed. "Do you know how I used to greet him, loud and clear, every morning while we were shooting? 'Good morning, Fritz, you old son-of-a-bitch,' right in front of everybody. That took the wind out of his sails, and everything went swimmingly afterwards. You've got to get it in first—you know what I mean?"

I knew. I also knew that you had to be able to do that kind of thing instinctively and not deliberately.

At night, driving home from the studio, I would "talk" to Mr. Lang and make mincemeat of him in front of the whole crew. But in the morning, as soon as I caught sight of him scowling under the camera, my throat went dry and my knees turned to water. Perhaps as time went by, he'd become aware of my desperate endeavors to please, perhaps he'd get better . . .

He got worse every day. Sometimes he screamed. But only at me. With the others he was curt, though he remained polite with Cooper, probably because he'd once spoken to him impatiently and Gary had just turned his head and looked at him as if he was hard of hearing. Which he actually was, in one ear. When he missed something, you never knew whether it was because he hadn't heard or hadn't wanted to. Since then Lang had treated him with a certain amount of care, and as Cooper was in most of my scenes, Mr. Lang kept himself under control. Only when I was alone on camera did things get dicey.

I had no one to ask for advice. The studio was like a town, where everyone lived and worked in a different neighborhood. If you wanted to visit another set where another Warner film was being made, you got into your car and drove down studio "streets" and finally met up with a whole bunch of people you'd never seen before.

Perhaps I should have gone to our producer, Milton Sperling. But he never set foot on the set, ran everything from his office, just looked at the rushes every evening with the director. What could I have said to him? Complain about the director? On my first picture?

That left only my agent, to whom I took my troubles more than once. He folded his hands tightly over his stomach, nodded sympathetically, and said, yes, Herr Lang had a reputation for needing a whipping boy on every picture he made—generally a female one. Whatever happened, I shouldn't lose patience. Not to worry. The main thing was to be sure that I got plenty of close-ups.

At the end of the first month, the boil burst. I looked at the schedule one morning and saw with alarm that Cooper was off and I was working alone with two supporting actors. We were shooting a scene in a tavern which I, the doughty girl guerrilla, was defending, with the help of the two supporting actors, against a whole mob of Fascist villains. The prop man handed me a live machine gun and showed me how to work it. The course lasted ten minutes, after which Mr. Lang decided that I ought to handle it like a veteran. It fired blanks, not live cartridges, but they burned very effectively if they hit you on bare skin. The script required me to race across the room—"I said *left* foot first," yelled Fritz Lang—smash the window with my machine gun and start shooting.

Once again I took off on the wrong foot, ruining the scene for Lang before we'd even begun. I then slammed the gun against the window too timidly—I was afraid of the glass splinters—so that it didn't break at the first blow. And then, though I managed to pull the trigger, the blanks hit me on the legs, burning through my nylons, and I must have let out an anguished yelp. In any case Lang bellowed, "Cut!" There then descended on my head such a torrent of abuse that from one minute to the next I became completely calm. Tense silence, while Mr. Lang awaited my apology. I put down my machine gun without haste and examined my burned stockings. Then I straightened my skirt, shook the glass splinters out of my beret, and walked past Lang and the camera to the exit.

It was June. The Warner Brothers studio is located in the hot San Fernando Valley. The temperature in the air-conditioned studio was always bearable, but as soon as you stepped outside, the heat hit you in the face as though you had stuck your head in an oven. The stars' trailers, all air-conditioned, stood directly opposite the exit door, but even those few steps left me panting. "Safe but not saved," I thought as I wrenched the door open. Inside, the curtains were drawn and it was delightfully cool. I locked the door and fell on the sofa.

That was it, all right. No doubt about it. My first Hollywood movie, the fulfillment of my childhood dream, co-starring with Gary Cooper—over! I wept into my pillow. What now? They would get somebody else for my role. That sort of thing happened in Hollywood. All my scenes would be reshot. With someone else.

A knock at the door. An unfamiliar voice. "Miss Palmer?"

"Yes?"

"May we come in?"

"Who's we?"

"Stage crew. Open the door. We're frying out here."

Three sweating men in shirt-sleeves crowded through the door, representatives of the electricians', property men's, and cameramen's unions.

"How're those burns doing? Need ointment? The nurse is on the way. Now you listen a minute. You're new here, right? Well, get this straight: we don't do no yelling in this place! Maybe they still do in the old country, but not here, see? Are you a member of the Screen Actors' Guild? Okay. Let that agent of yours earn his ten percent and tell him what's what. We just wanted to let you know we've quit work. 'Bye."

They left and were replaced by my agent, whom they'd run to earth somewhere on the lot (I wasn't his only horse in the Warner

Brothers stable). For the first time, he seemed at a loss and put out, as if the whole thing were his fault. What a mess! Who ever would have expected anything like this? Well, the union men were on their way to the executive office. The set was dark. Better go home and wait.

A third knock on the door, and the studio nurse appeared. She put Band-Aids on my (superficial) burns, while my agent shook his head and said tsk-tsk-tsk. Then I drove home. At ten o'clock in the morning.

The telephone stayed silent all day. But a large bouquet of flowers arrived with best wishes from the producer's office. A farewell present? That evening we went to a party. Everybody knew already. How? At eight o'clock the radio had announced news of a walkout at the Warner Brothers studio in protest against a director. The guests knew all the details, and my Band-Aids were examined.

Tyrone Power drew me aside. "What about Coop?" he said. "What did Coop do?"

"He was off today."

"So what?" said Ty. "This guy's been shouting at you for weeks, hasn't he? I'd never put up with that in my pictures."

"He doesn't shout when Coop's there," I said lamely, unhappily aware that my hero needed defending.

The walkout lasted three days. The upshot was a compromise: Fritz Lang was to continue as director, but during every scene in which I took part, a special representative of the management would sit by the camera to ensure a "suitable" working atmosphere. Was this acceptable to me? Yes. When I appeared on the set once again, I saw a gray-haired man in a slouch hat sitting unobtrusively beside the camera. For the next two months, until we finished shooting, he sat there watching. Sometimes he fell asleep and snored gently while we were rehearsing. The sound man woke him up before takes. Mr. Lang never addressed another word to me except the briefest instructions. It didn't matter anymore whether I took off on my left or my right foot.

Last day of shooting, final scene. Cooper has heroically accomplished his mission and must now return to America. The little airplane's engines are revving up. We are standing in a field of artificial wheat, and I tearfully promise to wait for him until the war is over and he can come back to me. Cooper cries too (this was one of his specialities, very affecting in such a tall man). We both cry; a last embrace; the engines roar; he runs toward the plane—will he make it? He makes it and climbs aboard at the last minute. I wave; the wheat billows around me, courtesy of the wind machine; the plane taxis slowly away (it can't take off, because we're in the studio, but it looks as though it will); I wave, I wave—"Cut!" The clapperboard snaps shut for the last time. The film is finished.

Cooper climbs out of the airplane. Stagehands run about clearing away the wheat. I turn around and walk toward the exit. Suddenly Fritz Lang is standing in front of me. I stop. Silence. Then he puts out his hand, shakes mine, and says in German, "Yes . . . well, goodbye. I'll do my best for you in the cutting room." And leaves.

He did do his best, too. Even in my scenes with Cooper, he used as many takes of mine as he possibly could.

Gary was waiting outside my dressing room, absorbed in a game of imaginary golf, practicing his swing. "Hey, kid," he said, hitting a splendid drive, "say, that business with Lang, you know—I probably should have . . . uh, but you see, I'm . . . not much good at that sort of thing, I never seem to find the right words. I need a script. Know what I mean?"

I knew what he meant. Words weren't exactly his strongest suit, and he was economical with them. Silence was his most eloquent weapon. Coop and I remained friends.

Years later we met by chance on a construction site where mutual friends were building a house. I'd just arrived from Germany. We hadn't seen each other for ages. Joyous reunion. Then he pulled me through an empty window frame and outside.

"Hey, kid," he said, peering at me with his black-fringed blue eyes, "how goes it?"

"Everything's fine, Gary," I said, hoping he hadn't read the shock in my eyes. I found him extraordinarily changed, almost transparent.

He continued to give me a searching look. "Honest, kid?"

"Honest, Gary."

Satisfied, he nodded and we climbed back into the house. I didn't know that he had only a few more months to live.

I received a letter with a Hungarian stamp addressed to "Lilli Palmer, Warner Brothers, Hollywood" and signed Miriam. Miriam! Of all my girl friends, she'd been my favorite. I knew that she had married a Hungarian doctor shortly before the war and lived in Budapest. That was all. This letter was our first contact in eight years. Thrilled and happy, I read how she'd survived the war and the Russian occupation. Completely cut off from the outside world, she now painted dolls' eyes in a Russian toy factory. How had she found out that I was under contract to Warner Brothers?

One evening, tired out after a long day's work, she was standing in line at her usual bus stop outside a suburban movie theater, where a poster advertised the coming attraction. A very tall man with a gun in each hand and determination on his face was carrying a very small girl in his arms, protecting her against all comers. Underneath it said "Gary Cooper and Lilli Palmer in . . ." whatever the Hungarian title was. Miriam stood outside the theater for half an hour. Buses came and went, but she couldn't tear herself away. Finally she got back in line, but as she boarded the bus, she turned back one last time and, overwhelmed, said aloud to her astonished fellow passengers, "There *is* a God after all!"

Cloak and Dagger should have been a success: Gary Cooper, directed by Fritz Lang, a decent script. It wasn't. The critics were lukewarm about the picture and Cooper. They praised me, the newcomer, all right, but without the exuberance I'd been hoping for.

Nonetheless, I had played opposite Gary Cooper, so I was immediately given a part in something called *My Girl Tisa*. I was Tisa, but not even Elsa could make anything of the role, in which, as a barefoot immigrant, I had a long, heartrending conversation with the Statue of Liberty in New York harbor.

Third time lucky, I thought, and waited. I might have waited for a good long time if they hadn't been looking for someone to play the lead in an already scheduled picture. The script was finished, but no female star had shown any enthusiasm for playing the nondescript heroine of an otherwise excellent story called *Body and Soul*. They finally thought of me and made the necessary changes in the script, turning a girl from Brooklyn into a young French painter, which immediately made the part more interesting. Elsa did the rest. John Garfield, the male lead, the prototype of American working-class youth, falls in love with the "classy old-world dame." Our contrasting personalities added something quite interesting to the relationship. When *Body and Soul* was released in New York, it was an immediate success, became one of the all-time standbys, and is still being shown on television. It was my first winner.

10

Hollywood: Play

❀

IN THOSE DAYS there was a party in Hollywood every night. The pretext, if your business manager demanded one, was usually somebody's return from overseas service. And in those days they were still around—the stars, the real superstars, a species now extinct, like certain wild animals. They needed an audience, today equally defunct, content to worship from afar. The studios would never have consented to "undress" their stars, because they knew that mystery is a most attractive quality. And a durable one. Erotic scenes were suggested, not acted out, putting the imagination to work. Explicitness would have been a mortal sin. The audience was supposed to cry for more and never get its fill.

We spent every evening at some star's house, hospitably opened to newcomers provided they played leading roles. Europeans were much in demand. Total strangers that we were, we felt touched and honored by the avalanche of invitations and accepted every one. What a feeling to sit on somebody's sofa and watch the door open on a cornucopia of famous faces we had known from childhood on the screen. Ernst Lubitsch called Hollywood "a village full of professionals lacking an audience." During those first few months, we served as audience and were duly fed. After dinner we listened to Hoagy Carmichael or Eddy Duchin at the piano, to Judy Garland singing "Over the Rainbow," to Bing Crosby or Sinatra or Walter

Huston doing his "September Song." Danny Kaye would try out his new act; Charlie Chaplin would reminisce. Once, Basil and Ouida Rathbone gave a party where the walls were covered with thousands of gardenias. I touched and smelled my way all along the walls; there wasn't a single paper flower.

This was the swan song of the fabulous Hollywood party. It had been the regular thing before the war, but now, in the sober postwar climate, it was dying out.

However, for a few more years the magnificent houses, brightly lit for the occasion, would still be thrown open to thirty, forty, fifty guests at a time, for butlers, cooks, and maids were still to be had at reasonable salaries. The small son of a famous director had to write an essay in class about "a poor family." He wrote: "Once upon a time there was a poor family. The father was poor, the mother was poor, the children were poor, the butler and the cook were poor and the maid and the gardener were poor."

Hollywood had its own social hierarchy, a rigorously observed caste system. It wasn't noticeable in the daytime, when stars and extras worked side by side in the studios. But at night, social life was rigidly structured according to the weekly salary checks. Stars invited stars, or producers, directors, and writers. Ticket of admission: success. Now and again you ran into a guest whose name had never appeared above the title. He was usually a bachelor. Bachelors were in short supply in Hollywood, and were sought after whenever a marriage broke up and a woman suddenly needed an escort to take her to a party. A female star never appeared unaccompanied.

There were also nationality cliques. Ours was, naturally, the English one. It was not restricted to stars; anybody qualified as long as he was British. (Patent of nobility.) We moved almost exclusively in that circle, which was affiliated to the French one, duplicating the wartime alliance.

Looking back, I ask myself how I could possibly have missed joining—on my own, of course—the colony of German refugees of a very different order—not actors, but writers and musicians. Did I never hear that Thomas Mann, Feuchtwanger, Werfel, Schönberg, Bruno Walter, to name just a few, were living in Hollywood at that time? Though even had I known, I doubt if I would have attempted to join. I was engrossed and immersed in the British world, convinced that I had made it mine, that I belonged, blind to the fact that I didn't and never would. Americans, far more easygoing and less discerning about remnants of accents or mentality, lumped me in with the British as a matter of course.

Paradoxically, Doug Fairbanks, Jr., an American, had made his house the central point of the English colony, probably due to his splendid war record and his numberless British friends, from the exalted to the unknown, who crowded his pool on Sunday afternoons. They usually appeared shyly with a war-green face and a letter of introduction and left suntanned and full of confidence. Young Doug was also whispered to be in correspondence with King George VI, whom he occasionally supplied with American camera equipment as yet unavailable in England. The story goes that he once sent him what was then the newest thing, the so-called stereo camera, which took color pictures in three-dimensional depth. The negatives had to be processed in the States, and Young Doug took the royal snapshots to a special camera shop in Beverly Hills to have them developed and mounted and returned to England.

One day, Ronald Colman, senior monarch of the British contingent and also the happy owner of a stereo camera, was wrapping up his snapshots at the same place when the owner beckoned him into the inner sanctum.

"Have a look at these," he said. "The King sure knows what he's doing." And he treated Ronny to the latest batch of views of the Edinburgh Tattoo, the Trooping of the Colour, and Balmoral Castle.

"I've got a treat for His Majesty," said the owner. "We've just received our first indoor film for the stereo. Only needs a minor adjustment in the camera. Maybe he'd like to have it. I'm enclosing a sample for him to see." And he handed Ronny a three-dimensional color shot of a fine specimen of American womanhood, nude to the waist and proud of her endowment.

"You're going to send this with the King's pictures?"

"It's the best I have," said the man. "You can really appreciate the flesh tones." And he put the picture into a carton, sealed it, and wrote in bold letters: To His Majesty King George VI, Buckingham Palace, London, England. Ronny closed his British eyelids and visualized the moment when the King would open the package and hand his latest artistic products to the Queen, and there, right among the shots of Queen Mary's garden party . . .

Ronald Colman, almost the last great actor from the silent days, also kept open house to visiting or resident British actors, who liked to hang around his bar or eat his sumptuous meals. This was largely due to his wife, Benita, a woman of irresistible charm and rare wit. Her friendship was a special award, and her letters were treasured by every one of the lucky recipients, Noël Coward among them. I have kept one she wrote me in 1968, long after we had both left Hollywood. Ronny had died, and she was at that time already married to George Sanders, and very happily so. It was a very special letter telling me in equable, detached, and totally unsentimental language the story of her mastectomy—in those days still a deep and deedy secret. She described the long and lonely walk after the doctor had "informed" her, and her collapse into George's arms when she told him that both her breasts would have to be removed. "Is that all?" George had said, relieved. "Who needs them?" The letter went on to describe the actual operation and the "fascinating experiences" that followed, for instance her first shopping expedition to get "the" special bra. The saleswoman had wasted no words or facial expression of sympathy ("You're the fifth lady this morning"), but had rapidly produced various well-rounded specimens, accompanied by matter-of-fact comment.

"We recommend this model here," she intoned, "it's the most pliable and natural-looking one, filled with birdseed. The only thing is, you can't wear it under your swimsuit."

"Because of the sea gulls?"

"Sea gulls?" repeated the saleswoman, outraged. "Good gracious, no. Because it swells up in the water, that's why."

But when I first met Benita in 1946, there was no need for her to use her wonderful debunking wit on anything more serious than entertaining the British colony at her husband's palatial home, a role she definitely enjoyed after a few lean years in the film capital.

She had been a leading London actress during the early thirties, but when she decided to try her luck in Hollywood, she found herself stuck with the first edition of the original Tarzan movies. These were dull where acting was concerned but rewarding in other ways, for there were always plenty of animals on the set who behaved in their own unorthodox fashion in front of the camera. Of them all, said Benita, the chimp gave by far the most trouble, for he was a large male specimen, passionately in love with Johnny Weissmuller. Whenever Weissmuller came on the set, the chimp not only sat on his haunches and howled with delight, he also showed other unmistakable signs of his homosexual affection, and you couldn't shoot on him until his ardor cooled off. "Okay," the director would sigh, "lights out. Everybody sit down and wait, please."

And wait they did, sometimes a full hour. One day the director's patience gave out. He turned to the prop man, pointed at the ape in his usual state of ecstasy, and ordered peremptorily, "Paint it black, please!"

Benita was released from her Tarzan chores by marrying Ronny Colman, and thus became the first lady of the Hollywood British colony before the war. Now, in 1946, when we first met them both, Ronny was at a low point of his career. Financially this made no difference, for he was well-off, having made his money before the great tax clampdown. But he was bored. What was there to do in Hollywood when one was not working? Even his adored child could not permanently entertain him. Perhaps it had arrived too late in his life. He was fifty-two when Benita, herself already forty, informed him of the forthcoming happy event. Ronny got up from his armchair, stood speechless, then paced the room in silence. Finally he stopped in front of his wife and said, "We'll be the laughingstock of the neighborhood!"

Any change in his daily routine, however insignificant, was a blessing, even a trip to the dentist. Being the lucky possessor of teeth without cavities, he only needed two checkups a year. On those occasions there was a special entry in the diary on his desk. Scrawled in large red letters across the entire day, it said: DENTIST.

Occasionally he read scripts. I found him one day in his magnificent garden, reclining under one of the red-flowering jacaranda trees, turning the pages.

"Good script?" I asked. He nodded.

"Good part for you?"

"Excellent."

"You're going to do it?"

"No."

"Why not?"

"Have a look," he said, handing me the manuscript. "Here, first scene: the captain—that's me—is standing on the bridge. Heavy seas. It's beginning to rain. Now turn to my second appearance: the captain in his waterproof coat and hood. There's a storm raging. And here, this is my third scene: captain enters, drenched from head to foot. *IT RAINS TOO MUCH IN THIS PICTURE!*"

Every Sunday evening was reserved for the younger members of the Anglo-French clique. We would get together for early supper at the home of Tyrone Power and his French wife, Annabella, so that we could start playing without wasting any time. The older generation had been more reluctant to recognize that now one didn't just drink, dance, and gossip at parties: one played. At first they had been afraid of making fools of themselves or of ruining their evening clothes, but in the end they too joined in and soon played as hard as we did. What we played was The Game.

The Game consisted of two teams competing in a kind of charade, the sort of thing you do in kindergarten. The only difference was the complicated rules. Each member of the team was given three minutes (timed with a stopwatch) to act out in dumb show a proverb, quotation, trademark, or slogan. Stars like Gable, Bogart, Jennifer Jones, James Stewart, and Henry Fonda, whose talents earned them thousands of dollars during the day, gave their all in those nightly sessions for free. In the studio, before the camera, they were sometimes mean or bad-tempered, but at night in The Game they blossomed, hopped around on one foot, cooed or whimpered or raved—docile children, eager to please.

With time The Game grew more and more sophisticated. There were dozens of hand signals meaning "it rhymes with" or "I'm cutting and acting the first or the second syllable" or "I'm going to act the sense of the whole thing," and so on. During those three minutes, the "mime" was deluged with questions from his own team, bullied, shouted at, and cursed, while the stopwatch ticked on. The professional actors weren't necessarily the best. Big stars were often washouts, like Clark Gable, who used up his precious three minutes counting the syllables in his phrase. Or Jennifer Jones, who had to act out "chili con carne" and could think of nothing except shivering with "chili"-ness. Surprisingly, the best players were often the obscure conjugal partners, male or female, who ordinarily stayed in the background, shoved aside in the crush around the famous other half. Amazing, how ready they were to leap around, how eager to crawl on the floor on all fours. At long last their hour had come.

No one played more fanatically than the twenty-five of us who used to meet regularly at the Tyrone Powers' house. Everybody pressed for an invitation, but Tyrone and Annabella couldn't feed more than twenty-five, so we remained a closed group, exclusive and envied. Until it all came to a sudden end one Sunday night in May 1946. No one ever played The Game in that house again.

One of the members of the standing teams was David Niven, the British star of many a prewar Hollywood movie. His twenty-five-year-old wife, Primmie, had just arrived from England, their new baby in her arms and their three-year-old son holding her hand. She had been a WAC during the war, doing a soldier's duties, lying in trenches, and driving ambulances during air raids. That's when she had met David, then a major in the army. Love at first sight. All the Hollywood glamour girls in his memory were eclipsed by Primmie's eyes and Primmie's smile.

That Sunday she made her first visit to Tyrone's house to be formally initiated as a new member of one of the teams. It had been a sunny, mild day, and Primmie and I walked about the garden alone for a few minutes. She picked an orange from a tree, sniffed it, turned it around in her hands, plucked an orange blossom, and marvelled that a tree should bear fruit and blossom at the same time. "I still can't believe it," she said. "It's too much."

"You get used to it pretty quickly, Primmie." Too quickly, I thought. We'd been in Hollywood only six months, and I remembered that I too had once been completely bowled over by the sight of an orange tree.

"But you haven't heard the great news. David has found a house

for us! I saw it yesterday. It's called the Pink House, and it's absolutely . . . I can't describe it. You can see the ocean and Catalina
Island! We're going to live there for ever and ever. David and the
babies and I, in peace for the first time. Imagine! Lil, will you paint
the nursery for me with Disney animals, like yours?"

"Okay. My housewarming present to you."

We went inside, because The Game was about to begin. Suddenly Cesar Romero, a permanent member of the Sunday club,
called out, "Listen, kids, let's play something else for a change. Just
for half an hour. As an hors d'oeuvre."

What?

"Sardines."

What was that?

Cesar explained. You turn the lights out all over the house.
Everybody hides, except one person, who has to find the others.
The last one to be found is the winner and gets the title "Sardine."

Idiotic. Just an excuse for necking in the dark, people grumbled.
Others laughed, not wanting to be spoilsports. Okay, just one round.
Tyrone turned off all the lights, and we hid. I crept under the
piano. Suppressed giggling and shushing from all directions. Then
suddenly, someone shouted, "Lights! Somebody's fallen down the
cellar stairs!"

Lights. Blinded for a moment, we were still asking who, where,
how, when they carried Primmie in, unconscious. She had wanted
to hide in a coat closet and had opened a door next to it. Not being
used to Hollywood houses, she didn't know that the door leading
to the basement is often right next to the coat closet. She had
plunged head first onto the stone floor of the cellar.

They laid her on the carpet, her head in my lap. The others
stood in an anxious circle around us. David examined her cautiously
but found nothing, no blood, no abrasions, nothing. Then he
jumped in his car and rushed off to fetch a doctor.

"Come on," said Tyrone. "There's no sense standing around. You
can't do anything for her. It will only frighten her when she wakes
up. Let's start playing."

They all went into the next room. Annabella brought a bowl of
ice water for compresses. Slowly Primmie opened her eyes, tried to

look around, but didn't move. "Primmie," I said, smoothing her wet hair back from her forehead, "don't worry. You fell down the cellar stairs, that's all."

It was a while before she spoke. "Lil, I feel so . . . strange . . . even when I had the babies I never felt so . . ." She closed her eyes again.

Tyrone opened the door and asked in a whisper if she had come to. We applied more compresses. She opened her eyes again and looked at me questioningly. "David's gone to get the doctor, Primmie. Just in case, you know." She nodded and tried to smile. "We'll never be invited again," she said, hardly audible, and closed her eyes again.

David returned with a doctor, and Annabella and I left the room. A little while later we watched through the window as they carried Primmie to the car. "Now, then," said Tyrone, "don't sit there like weeping willows. We'll carry on until David gets back. Annabella and Lil, back to your teams."

We played, but our eyes and ears were glued to the open window. Two hours later we heard the car. Tyrone ran to the front door, and we all stood up. David appeared, beaming, and hugged everyone in turn.

"It's nothing!" he cried. "Nothing. A mild concussion. They X-rayed her—no fracture, no bone injury. She'll have to stay in the hospital for a week, then she can come home. Now, for God's sake, give me a drink!" And he collapsed in a chair.

No one wanted to go on playing. We sat around for a few minutes and drank to Primmie's narrow escape. Then we all went home.

I was in the middle of my picture with Gary Cooper and had to get up early the next morning. I called David's house from the studio. Had they heard anything from the hospital? Nothing new; Mr. Niven had gone there to be with her. Everything was okay. During the lunch break I called again. Mr. Niven was still at the hospital. Everything okay. That evening I got David on the telephone. Nothing new. She was lying perfectly still and sleeping most of the time.

That was at eight o'clock in the evening. At ten the hospital called and asked him to come at once. A blood clot had formed on the brain; they would have to operate. David sat outside the operating room for an hour. Then the door opened. Two doctors came out. One of them raised both hands—and let them fall again. Primmie was dead.

I spent every Sunday afternoon on a ladder in the nursery of the Pink House, painting Donald Duck, Mickey Mouse, and Dumbo the elephant on the walls and watching David through the window sitting on the terrace steps, gazing at the ocean. I knew exactly what he was thinking. Dozens of times during the war Primmie had been in mortal danger and come through without a scratch. And at her first Hollywood party . . .

After a time we began to accept invitations again. Nearly every day we received a telegram inviting us to a party in honor of somebody. Rex loved seeing crowds of people at night. For me, though, once the novelty had worn off, the evenings began to sag.

"That's because you can't drink," said Rex. "Believe me, when you've got a scotch in your hand, even the dumbest conversation becomes fascinating."

I had tried, of course. Many times. But I couldn't stand the taste of whiskey, and gin was only slightly better. Neither "did" anything to me except make me sleepy. I practiced by holding my nose and pouring the stuff down my throat to get my stomach used to it. Dismal failure. Still, I refused to give up until I had final proof.

Rex had never spoken of his first wife in especially fond terms except when he described their hilarious evenings with friends in prewar England. Apparently Collette had distinguished herself not only as a wonderful hostess but by drinking everybody under the table while keeping a clear head herself. Now, why couldn't I do the same? What was wrong with me? Why did I have to be a spoilsport by sitting there with my sober face oozing silent disapproval? No good protesting that what I was oozing was silent envy. Fact remained that I didn't join in! My failure was more visible than ever now, in Hollywood, where I had to hold out for hours every night, cold sober, a dreary Teutonic wet blanket.

One day Rex brandished a letter from England in front of my sunbathing face. I had just finished the Gary Cooper picture and was enjoying my leisure and the lazy ease of California life. The letter was from Collette, who announced her forthcoming arrival, accompanied by Rex's son Noel, now aged thirteen, who, she felt, ought to see his father again. What to do? I wasn't enthusiastic about the idea—I had only met her briefly a couple of times—but who could stop her coming and staying at the Beverly Hills Hotel?

Shortly afterwards they arrived and visited us forthwith in our new home in Bel Air. Carey and his half brother, ten years older, swam companionably in the pool while Collette and I watched, equally companionably. A bit later, problems arose when they were bidden to leave the hotel after two weeks, which was the limit for hotel reservations in the summer of 1946. Now what? Collette and Noel knew there was a guest room in our house . . .

They moved in. That day a telegram from Norma Shearer invited us to a party at her beach house in Santa Monica. Could we just go and leave our guests in the guest room? We couldn't. I called Norma and announced that we had a house guest. "Bring him along," said Norma, "what is his name?" "Uh—Mrs. Harrison." "Really?" said Norma. "Rex's mother?" "No," I said, "Rex's wife. I mean his first wife." Pregnant silence. "Listen," said Norma, quite a friend of mine, "are you sure you want to bring her along? Things are complicated enough in this place. Don't you think you're being a bit too . . . well . . . broadminded?" I explained about the hotel and about Noel visiting his father. "I see," said Norma. "Well . . . see you all tonight."

By that night she had recovered enough to introduce the three of us on our entry as "the King of Siam and his harem." Yet after initial guffaws, the other guests made no bones about their feelings: marriage was dicey enough in Hollywood. Why voluntarily give fodder to the gossip columnists? "Broad-mindedness" was not appreciated in this community.

So what. We weren't doing anybody any harm. Collette and Noel spent one more week with us without anybody being any the wiser. Except me. I certainly was wiser after one unforgettable evening.

Rex had a radio play to do, and Collette and I were alone in the house. About six in the afternoon, she usually emerged from her room beautifully dressed and groomed and made straight for the bar. As I watched her gaily shaking bottles and filling her glass, I suddenly made a decision. "Collette, give me a drink, too. Whatever it is you're having." "Are you sure?" said Collette. "This is a dry martini. Pretty dry, you know."

She had three. I had three. Which made me propose that we go out and have dinner at a restaurant. At Romanoff's we ordered a splendid meal with two bottles of wine, white and red. I was feeling no pain. Loved Collette with all my heart. She suggested we should all live together. I agreed enthusiastically. The children needed each other. *We* needed each other. Coffee. And two "stingers," brandy and benedictine. They stung all right. But I made it to the car and we drove home into our garage without mishap. (Except that it cost $120 to get the car out again. I had wrapped it neatly around the center pillar, which had to be dismantled.) I staggered into the house, supported by my best friend's strong arm. We both felt like admiring our children, and stood by Carey's bed sobbing and then by Noel's, who woke up and said a few unkind words. And then Collette left me in our bedroom.

I must have passed clean out, for Rex found me later, fully dressed and face downward, lying diagonally across the double bed. He couldn't rouse me and, frightened, ran to wake up Collette. "It's nothing," she said soothingly. "She's a bit pissed." In the end he had to get into Collette's bed for the rest of the night, for Collette had her work cut out to undress me, hold my head, and change basins. Toward morning, exhausted, she passed out on the other side of the big double bed, and when the maid appeared carrying the breakfast tray, she found the two Mrs. Harrisons fast asleep, side by side, and Mr. H. in the guest room. I had acute alcohol poisoning and couldn't get up for days. I never tried again.

One night, just as it was getting light, I found myself sitting on somebody's sofa in somebody's house next to Lauren Bacall. The Bogarts had towed us away from another party to this one, whose hosts were strangers to us.

"Do you really enjoy this?" I asked her.

Betty Bacall looked at me in amazement. "Well . . . I don't really know. Maybe not. But Bogey does."

We looked at our respective husbands, who, fondling their ump-teenth scotches, were having a wonderful time. I suddenly felt the urge to get up immediately and drive home. Strange . . . I was used to it, after all. I had attended hundreds of parties and become resigned to the fact that I hardly ever enjoyed them.

Rex had one principle he held to firmly: he would not go home as long as both host and hostess were still about. Not until one of them disappeared for good would he get his coat, satisfied. This usually happened about 5:00 A.M. I never lasted that long with my one gin and tonic. By about 2:00 A.M. I had had enough and went looking for a sofa, generally to be found in the den. Most Holly-wood houses were built on a similar plan, with similar furniture and similar paintings on the walls. According to the owner's cultural aspirations, there were a number of French oils—impressionist, expressionist, and abstract. At the lowest level, you could count on a Utrillo (postcard period), maybe a Dufy (Riviera scene), or a Renoir (small nude). More ambitious types went as far as Rouault and Modigliani, and occasionally one ran across a high-prestige Picasso. In the den there was inevitably an American primitive, a Grandma Moses or perhaps a painting from the frontier days. Under these early American scenes I would lie, fast asleep. From time to time I woke up, tried to remember whose house I was in, and made a quick reconnaissance of the living room. If both host and hostess were still in evidence, I tiptoed back to the den, until the time came when I could drive Rex home.

At first he had insisted on driving himself. Not without certain hazards. He failed to notice, for instance, that Sam Goldwyn's entrance gate was already closed as we sailed through. So we drove through the streets with the gate draped symmetrically across our hood. The wrought-iron bars didn't exactly improve visibility, but somehow we got home. Another time he gave himself an even greater handicap by declaring that he was an Englishman and would drive on the left only. This he did faithfully, taking great care to keep to the wrong side of the road all the way home. Fortunately, there wasn't much traffic at that time of the morning. After a few less amusing and more terrifying episodes, he was persuaded that his place in the car was next to the driver, and I did night duty at the wheel.

Until suddenly, that early morning, as I sat next to Lauren Bacall on somebody's sofa, a bell rang in my head and the revolutionary idea occurred to me that this wasn't really my line at all and that life might perhaps hold something else. It hadn't come to a head yet. The bell had just rung once, though unforgettably.

11

Hollywood: Death

❀

T HERE'S A WHOLE LITERATURE on the rotten state of morality in
Hollywood. Dozens of picture magazines and other publica-
tions in all languages thrived on it. Innumerable people made their
living by observing the legal and illegal love life of the stars, spread-
ing rumors, casting suspicion, distorting, and sometimes even de-
scribing it quite truthfully. It was their daily bread, their chosen field,
and it paid their children's tuition. It started more than fifty years
ago and reached its height in the thirties and forties. Since then the
gossip business has been declining, gradually at first, now steeply,
because adultery is no longer the moral outrage it used to be, and
also because the star system doesn't exist anymore and the press
bureaus have collapsed with the big studios. There are still a few
gossip columns, but all they offer is mild titillation compared with
the earthquakes they were once able to cause.

When we went to Hollywood late in 1945, a star's private life was
still "supervised" by his studio according to conservative principles.
At least outwardly. Nearly all stars were married; most had children.
Nearly all of them were unfaithful to their spouses, but all, without
exception, tried to keep their escapades secret. Those notorious
American women's organizations that once could make or break a
person still existed, though they were less powerful than they were
in silent movie days. Take the case of poor Fatty Arbuckle. During

a party he gave in a hotel in San Francisco, a girl was assaulted and eventually died. The trial was quite sensational, and Arbuckle was acquitted. But he was never allowed to appear on the screen again. Many years later, Jack Warner still had to assemble a whole battery of defense witnesses to save Errol Flynn from certain ruin. A girl under sixteen claimed that one evening Flynn had lured her aboard his yacht, moored in the harbor, and had assaulted her as she stood by the window in his cabin. A famous criminal lawyer got Flynn off by asking the girl—who appeared in the courtroom in bobby socks and pigtails—whether she had seen the moon from the window. "Of course," answered the "child" with conviction, "quite clearly." That clinched it, because it could be proved beyond doubt that the moon was not visible from Flynn's cabin window. The public knew, of course, that Flynn had indeed had an affair with the girl, but it couldn't be legally proved, so he was judged innocent and allowed to go on making movies representing the ideal American male: six feet tall, upright, frank, and fearless, with gleaming white teeth.

For that was the crux of the matter: the image. The heads of the big studios were convinced that it was their damned duty and responsibility to tell the world how to live, love, and die. And a star's private life had to mirror his screen image, at least to some extent. The studio heads succeeded for decades, as long as the world was still innocent and movie-mad. The famous Johnston Office code of morality had the force of unwritten but unbreakable law. "Suggestive sex" was its specialty, and some of its rules were fascinating. When Rex and I were making *The Four Poster*, a lily white story, dripping with bourgeois morality, we were warned in advance to be very careful never to be seen in the double bed together, with or without benefit of wedding rings. If one of us was in bed, the camera had to make it clear that the other "had one foot on the floor." What the first foot was doing was nobody's business.

The Johnston Office code was not exclusively concerned with the erotic. In that same picture, they cut several lines that had become famous in the stage play. Situation: wedding night. After a lot of coy fiddling around, the virginal, eighteen-year-old bride is finally installed in the four poster, while the bridegroom sits on a stool, taking off his slippers.

> *Nervous Bride:* You know, I've never seen a man . . . uh, completely . . .
> *Bridegroom* (dead-pan): Well, you haven't missed much.

This brought the house down every night. In the film script it was out. Full of indignation, we went to see Mr. Johnston himself. "There's nothing immoral about that!" we protested.

"You're right," said Mr. Johnston, a most charming fellow. "On moral grounds we wouldn't have touched it. But we had to cut it on religious grounds, because man is made in the Lord's image, you understand?" This gave us a completely new conception of the Lord.

Such were the concerns of the Johnston Office. The public was much more interested in what went on in the private lives of Hollywood stars, so that they could live out their own dreams vicariously while maintaining a facade of righteous indignation. But suppose you had suddenly abducted one of those respectable housewives or upright fathers of families to Hollywood and set them down in a film star's shoes. What would they have done when they found the most glamorous people falling into their arms every day, and never the same twice? Would they have said no thanks?

It was difficult, almost impossible, to maintain a happy and monogamous marriage in Hollywood; the handicaps were too great. Actors who had come together late, having previously sown plenty of wild oats, seemed to have the best chance. Perhaps they were already satisfied. Or tired.

One evening a popular star of an earlier generation gave a party honoring all the couples "who had been married for more than ten years." We qualified, so we were invited. About fifty couples celebrated at the Beverly Hills Hotel. I looked around and recognized most of them. And all the ones I knew had either been or were at present unfaithful to their spouses. The host came to the microphone and made a cute speech. "Good examples" were called to the platform and vigorously applauded. They held hands, laughed, and hugged each other—and everybody silently remembered the times when they had been neither laughing nor hugging each other. The main thing was that they had come through in the end. Finally our host proposed a toast to marriage. He himself had been married for twenty years and had grown children, though there was a young woman on the horizon whom he later married. He was in the best of spirits. He was lucky, for he had never been caught.

Rex was unlucky. He was caught. And when the beans were spilled, it caused such a to-do that some nervous stars were said to have ditched their mistresses in a hurry.

When we first arrived, in November 1945, there was still a shortage of males. Many of the younger American actors hadn't yet been released from military service. In addition, Rex was English, which meant "class." Right at the beginning, at one of the first parties we attended, as I entered the ballroom at his side in my brand-new evening gown, I was pushed aside by a stunning girl. "Come on," she said to Rex, before they could even be introduced. "I'll show you how we dance the rumba over here." She dragged him over to the dance floor, put both arms around his neck, and began to "dance."

Suddenly somebody I knew was standing next to me—Mary Lee Fairbanks, wife of Douglas Fairbanks, Jr. "Don't worry," she said in her soft Southern accent. "It's just the way they behave here. It doesn't mean a thing. You just have to get used to it."

I got used to it.

Usually it really didn't mean anything. You gave it a try and had a bit of fun because you didn't want to miss anything, that was all. But from time to time, somebody got involved, and then it became a problem. The girl who got involved with Rex was called Carole Landis. Her father, a railroad switchman, had abandoned the family when she was three. Before she was sixteen, Carole married a policeman. Perhaps she thought he would protect her from the world. A year later she was unprotected again. A Hollywood contract followed, and three more marriages in rapid succession. She was blond, magnificently built, the prototype of the Hollywood star, universally known and universally popular. When she met Rex, she was twenty-nine years old and at the end of her fourth marriage.

From then on, things took their inevitable course. Rex spent a lot of time away from home, but his explanations were always plausible. We didn't take the *Hollywood Reporter,* or I might have learned that people were keeping an eye on the carryings-on of the English star "whose name begins with H" with the local glamour girl "whose name begins with L." Close friends knew but didn't let on. Finally Rex told me himself. I did the best thing one can do in such a situation: I withdrew from the battlefield and flew to New York. My sister Hilde had married there, and I discovered for the first time that she was no longer my kid sister but a friend and a help. I was in sore need of both.

Instead of relieving the tension and providing a cooling-off period for all parties, my exit only complicated matters. Rex lost his best excuse—"I've got to go home"—while Carole's hopes were crushed because, even though I wasn't there, he still "had to go home," where Pat and Carey were following their daily routine. Rex called Hilde's apartment in New York every day to make sure that the umbilical cord wouldn't wither. Two weeks passed. Then came a day when he called a second time: could I take the next plane—the girl whose name began with L had killed herself.

I packed and stood by at the airport for the next flight to Los Angeles. I got one at midnight. They turned out the lights so the passengers could sleep. I couldn't sleep, so I sat by a window, looking out into the night. At 3:00 A.M. we made a stopover in Chicago, and I wandered about the empty airport. At the newspaper stand, they were just setting out the morning papers. Something caught my eye, something nobody could fail to see. Every single paper had a huge red headline four inches high: CAROLE LANDIS SUICIDE. Underneath was a black headline, not much smaller: "Rex Harrison Finds Body in Bathroom." There was also a picture of the girl lying on the floor in a kind of dirndl dress. I hastily bought a paper, glancing around as though I might be arrested any minute. Nobody recognized me, although on an inside page there were lots of pictures of Carey and me, as well as of Rex. "Los Angeles flight now boarding," droned the loudspeaker, and I crept unobserved into line with the other passengers. Most of them had also bought morning papers, and were reading intently, without looking up, as the line moved ahead. Nobody looked at me; the story was too exciting. Once aboard, I kept my face hidden behind the paper until it was dark again. Then I turned on my light and read.

I already knew most of it; Rex had told me on the phone. He had had a lunch date with Carole but had tried to break it, because he wanted to meet Maxwell Anderson and Leland Hayward, who were preparing Anderson's new play for the next Broadway season. Getting no answer at Carole's, he went ahead and had lunch with Anderson and Hayward. After that, around three o'clock, he drove to her house and found her in the bathroom, dead. He called the police and a doctor and waited until they came. On her bedside table were two empty sleeping pill containers, one marked "Fast Acting" and the other "Slow Acting." Beside them was an empty whiskey bottle. The doctor pronounced her dead; the police made a note of Rex's address. Then he "had to go home." And called me.

The story in the paper was roughly the same, embroidered with biographical details about the victim and the 'involved" survivors— us. The tone was sympathetic toward Carole, a poor, beautiful, unhappy American girl, and vindictive toward Rex, an arrogant, callous foreigner.

Slowly it grew light. The dark blue of the sky was touched with red, and from one minute to the next the cabin was flooded with light. The passengers woke up, stretched, and gratefully accepted the coffee offered by the stewardess. None more gratefully than I. Then the captain's voice came over the intercom: "Ladies and gentlemen, we've got a tail wind, so we're a few minutes ahead of schedule. I'd like to give you a view of the Grand Canyon that you've probably never seen before." Then he turned sharply south and we could see in the distance the gigantic, naked blocks of rock. For a moment the sun hung on the horizon like a big red tomato; then it suddenly exploded. From one moment to the next, the dull gray wings of the airplane blazed as if on fire. As we approached the Grand Canyon, the red morning light fell on its stark, massive stone faces, which flamed as though someone had dropped an incendiary bomb. The passengers crowded to the windows. The captain banked and flew slowly and appreciatively along the rim of the giant ravine. Not only the sides but the fallen rocks at the bottom and the stony landscape all around were flooded with blood red light. The passengers shouted aloud with excitement. I shouted, too—and then clutched my throat. I was suddenly deathly sick, perhaps from the coffee—I hadn't eaten anything since lunch the day before—perhaps from the sharp turn the captain was making to get the plane back on course, perhaps from all that red below me. But perhaps also from the thought of the sleeping pills she'd choked down with the whiskey, one by one, until the bottles were empty. The plane was flying quite steadily now, and the passengers were startled when I pushed past them and made for the toilet. I wanted to get rid of what was cramped up inside me, get rid of it. Get rid of everything.

We landed at 6:00 A.M. The airport was deserted. In the dim, early morning light, one lonely figure was waiting. I recognized him and fell on his neck. Leland Hayward looked at me, decided I needed a cognac, and led me to the airport bar. He was up so early because he hadn't been to bed. He not only wanted to produce Maxwell Anderson's play with Rex in the leading role, he was also an old friend. Rex had called him immediately, and Leland had spent the evening and half the night with him. As I sipped my cognac, little by little, he brought me up to date on the situation. Little by little.

"Have you any idea what's in store for you right now?" was his first question.

"What do you mean, what's in store for me?"

Whereupon he ordered a cognac for himself. To begin with, he said, about fifty reporters and photographers were waiting for me.

"For me?"

"Yes, for you."

"Where?"

"In front of your house."

Fortunately, they didn't know where I was, or my arrival at the airport would have looked very different. Rex, said Leland cautiously, was all right. He'd had to barricade himself inside the house at first, but—

"Barricade himself?"

But in the evening the police had arrived and prevented them from breaking in.

"Who was trying to break in?"

The press. After all, it was their job to get an interview with Rex and me for their papers, no matter how they went about it. The paper would gladly pay any fines they might incur for trespassing. And for broken windows, too. No, no need to worry about Pat and Carey; they were okay. But there was one problem. How was I to get into the house? Would I perhaps rather go to friends? Though of course they wouldn't be able to keep it secret forever, and then the friends' houses would be besieged and . . .

"I want to go home," I said.

That was what he'd expected, said Leland. Well, he'd stick close to me, and I'd have to be prepared for some pushing and shoving, but as long as I kept my head and didn't utter a word, they'd have to let me through in the end.

"Can't the police keep a path open?"

Well . . . it wasn't quite that simple with the police. To begin with, they were certainly mad that he hadn't told them when and where I was arriving.

"Why didn't you tell them?"

Because you couldn't trust them. They might have leaked the information to the press.

The cognac glasses were empty. It was seven o'clock—a good time to go home. Maybe the reporters would be sleepy after their long, fruitless vigil. But Leland shook his head. "They come and go in shifts," he said. "They're used to waiting."

During the long ride home, he found the courage to explain the real danger, the one that threatened our entire existence. Suicide was a very shocking thing in Hollywood, he said, much more shocking than in any other part of the world. And since the community couldn't attack the person who had died, the object of its violent and irrational wrath was the person who was thought to have the "suicide" on his conscience. There had been occasional suicides in Hollywood (amazingly few, considering the hysteria and lack of self-control that were constantly crashing against each other in that place), but in every case it had meant the end of the "guilty" survivor's career. Suicide was a slap in the face to Hollywood's image as the world's serene, utopian paradise. It was played up rather than hushed up. And never forgiven.

"So Rex loses his contract with Fox?"

"Probably," said Leland gloomily. "Although I think Zanuck will fight for him. They haven't released his last picture yet, so he stands to lose a lot of money. I had a long talk with him yesterday, and with Harry Brand too, the head of the press bureau. By the way, Brand sent over one of his legal advisers this morning for Rex, and Warners are sending one for you. They'll come over every day."

"For how long?"

"Until the funeral. Don't make a move without discussing it with them. And don't talk to anyone. Even on the phone."

Our house was in Mandeville Canyon, not far from the ocean. We had bought it only a short while ago. A typical California house, all on one floor, white with white shutters, surrounded by a partly wild garden with tall old trees. You drove through a wooden gate and up a short driveway into the garage, opposite the house. At the back of the garden were stables and a riding ring overgrown with weeds because it was never used. The stables housed half a dozen palominos with long white manes. The former owner had asked us to board them, and we used to watch them grazing, fenced in but quite close. You couldn't make friends with them. They showed their yellow teeth and snorted with rage if you set foot in the stable, so they served as scenery only.

The entrance gate was wide open, and Leland drove slowly through. He stopped for a minute to think—I couldn't see anyone and thought maybe they'd all left—then he suddenly stepped hard on the gas and roared toward the house. An instant later the car was surrounded by some fifty men. "Get out," said Leland between his teeth, but my door was already blocked. He forced his open and tried to fight his way around to my side. Flashbulbs went off all around me like fireworks. Somebody wrenched my door open.

"Here!—No, over here!—Look this way, Lilli!—Look over here!—Look at me!—Over here!—Now look at me!—" I couldn't see anybody or anything in the dazzling light of the flashes. "Let her get out!—No, stay at the window!—Over here! This way!—Get out—"

Someone dragged me out, but the crush was so overpowering that those in front were pressed too close to me to be able to take pictures. Cameras were held high, low, directly under my nose; flashbulbs popped. I kept my eyes tightly shut. Then came the questions. "Are you going to make a statement? What's your reaction? Did you know Carole Landis? Had you left your husband? Are you going back to him? Where were you? Will you attend the funeral?" They all shouted at once. The noise was deafening. The cameras were still clicking. I was pushed this way and that.

Suddenly there was a lull, because Leland was approaching with two police officers in tow. "Break it up, boys," they yelled. "Get back. Get back. Let her through."

Cursing, they gave up on me. The policemen spread their arms, and I found myself at the front door. It opened a crack, and Leland pushed me inside.

It's surprising what you can bring yourself to do, despite emotional turmoil and a threatening situation. Eat breakfast, for instance. It doesn't really stick in your throat, as they say. We both ate our usual huge meal, with a double portion of coffee. Then I went into the nursery, where Carey, excited, was standing at the window watching all those men with cameras outside our front door.

Pat stood beside him, glowering. "What kind of people are they anyway?" she asked, holding a *Los Angeles Times* under my nose. "They talk about Mr. Harrison and his *mate*. I suppose they mean you. Are we dealing with gorillas?"

"Gorillas!" exclaimed Carey radiantly, and ran to fetch one of his picture books. He opened it at a group of photogenic apes. "That's you. That's the female," he said, pointing to an unmistakably female specimen with pendulous breasts.

"How do you know?" I asked in surprise.

"It's got a kinder face," he said firmly.

In view of the gorillas outside, he was right. None of them looked the least bit kind. They were all mad at us. We weren't playing fair. They weren't here for fun.

"Pat," I said, "you won't be able to go for a walk today."

"Why not?"

"They won't let you through."

"Me?" All Ireland, five hundred years of rebellion, lay behind the contempt in her voice. "No one can stop *me*. And just let anyone touch Carey! Look at this!" She brought out her big black English umbrella. "I'll give them one on the head with this."

"Pat, they'll try to question you!"

"Me?"

At the murderous look in her eye, I turned tail.

A little while later she flung open the front door with all her might—the uproar outside made me jump—and disappeared in the crowd. But only for a moment. Then I caught sight of her umbrella high in the air—and a relative silence fell and a path was cleared, through which she marched, head high, holding the child by the hand, in the direction of the garden gate.

At some point the promised lawyers showed up, escorted by police and by studio bodyguards. We were glad to see them, even those legal-eagle faces. The telephone rang incessantly, but Leland had advised us not to answer it. Probably right, but hard on the nerves. Now the lawyers lifted the receiver, calmed our friends, and gave vague information to the press. Luckily we had an unlisted number; otherwise the anonymous abuse would already have begun. (In Hollywood, some people make nuisance calls as a hobby, if they can discover a star's private number. For years, a deep female voice used to call me, both at home and at the studio, shouting "You bitch" before I could hang up.)

In the intervals between telephone calls, they explained the legal situation. Someone had stated that the handwriting on the pill bottles—"Fast Acting" and "Slow Acting"—was Rex's. Pure invention, but enough to make the coroner refuse permission for immediate burial. (A suicide is a criminal act.) Not to worry: it would all be cleared up in the course of the day. By the way, the autopsy had shown that the alcohol content of the blood was very high.

The real difficulty was something else again. At that time the Hearst press was anti-British and not inclined to let this run its normal course. In the first place, they could sell a lot of papers, and in the second, make bad blood against the British. We'd have to be prepared to put up with the situation for a few days.

A few days? Like rats in a trap, held prisoner by those guys outside?

Well, we *could* get rid of the reporters if we could bring ourselves to give them an interview. Both of us together. Step outside, give them five or ten minutes, pose for pictures, and answer questions. Were we prepared to do that?

We went into the den by ourselves and discussed it. There was nothing for it; we'd have to face the music. Okay, let's get it over and done with. Both lawyers stepped outside. They had their pictures taken; then they bargained. Result: withdrawal of all reporters and photographers in return for one extensive interview. Time: in ten minutes.

I combed my hair and made up my face. No reason to look like a piece of cheese in the pictures. Then we stepped out the door.

They maintained a distance of about twelve feet, standing in a semicircle, taking their time. Why should they hurry? Their prey was right in front of them, not moving. They gave their instructions and took their pictures. "Look at each other. Look at us. Hold hands. Smile. Smile at us. Put your arm round your wife. Put your arm round your husband. Kiss." Other positions didn't occur to them.

Next came the questions. Where and when had we first met Carole? Was it a love affair?

No, a friendship.

Do you love your husband?

Yes.

Do you love your wife?

Yes.

Was I a friend of Carole's too?

Yes.

How do you feel about her death?

Sad.

Why did she kill herself?

No idea.

Was she unhappy?

No idea.

Did you find her attractive?

Of course.

Where had I been yesterday?

In New York.

What for?

To visit my sister.

Were you jealous?

No.

Would you both go over to the swimming pool and point to the water?

All right. (Photographs at swimming pool.)

Would you pet the horses?

They don't like to be petted.

Would we go to the mortuary so they could get a picture of us with the body?

NO!

Then they actually went away. All of them. Only the police stayed. And the lawyers. Leland said good-bye too. He wanted to get some sleep.

I stood at the window watching the palominos grazing. They snorted and stamped and shook their splendid manes. How beautiful they were. And how peaceful on this blue summer day. From the window I saw Pat and Carey returning from their walk, Carey disappointed that all the gorillas had left. He ran to the fence and held a lump of sugar flat on his palm for the horses, Pat right behind him, her umbrella poised to give the horses one on the nose if necessary.

A lawyer came to tell us that a Mrs. Haymes from New York was on the telephone. Rex went to take the call and was gone a long time. When he returned, he looked better. Mrs. Haymes, mother of the pop singer Dick Haymes, had been Carole's best friend. She wanted to tell him that Carole had made several suicide attempts before she ever met Rex. That is, she'd often taken an overdose of sleeping pills. Then she would call Mrs. Haymes, who would have time to summon a doctor with a stomach pump. The night before last, Mrs. Haymes had come home late and found a message that there had been a call from Los Angeles. But she hadn't called back, because it was so late.

Gambling with death. *Va banque* with sleeping pills. Maybe, maybe not. Painless Russian roulette. A test of nerve, a dare, an adventure, a calculated risk, an act of revenge ("You'll stand by my corpse and cry!")—all mixed up, muddled and blurred by alcohol. Usually it was April Fools' Day, but sometimes, in spite of the rules, the trap was baited.

Carole hadn't only called Mrs. Haymes; she had taken other measures too. She had packed two suitcases with photograph albums and things she wanted to "give away" and left them, at night, at the back door of friends who lived nearby. It was to be expected that the friends, or their maid, would open the back door to take in the milk the next morning and find the suitcases and the farewell note. There would still have been time, because she must have been alive in the morning. The curtains in her room were drawn back, and no lights were burning in the house. What she had forgotten was the date: July 4. Holiday. The friends slept late; the maid didn't come; the suitcases, along with the milk, remained undiscovered until the afternoon. The trap door fell shut.

In the evening, the lawyers left too. Exhausted, we slept without sleeping pills, as if dead. Next morning the lawyers were back, looking worried. The burial permit had still not been issued, although it had turned out that the writing on the pill bottles was Carole's doctor's. The coroner was "unavailable." Obviously the Hearst press was behind all this; they wanted to keep the case going for a few more days. The lawyers showed us a copy of the *Los Angeles Examiner*, the local Hearst paper. WHY DID CAROLE KILL HERSELF? read the headline on the front page. Underneath were yesterday's photographs of us, smiling pleasantly and apparently indifferently at the camera (the arrogant Englishman and his cold-hearted wife), as well as one of Carey with Pat brandishing her umbrella. The accompanying article was chiefly concerned with speculation about motives for the suicide. The obvious one, disappointed hopes cum alcohol, would have allowed the case to peter out, and that had to be prevented at all cost. Everyone would just have to play along, from the coroner, to the studio, to us. No good trying to cut and run. The lawyers had been instructed to get us to "do what the situation required."

We didn't understand. Weren't our studios on our side? Of course they were. Only the game was lost anyway, and there was no point kicking over the traces. The most sensible course would be to give the Hearst press its head for another couple of days—let them have a bit of "material," understand?

We still didn't understand. Material? What kind of material? Just then a call came through which would explain it all. Harry Brand, head of Fox press bureau, was on the line in person, asking to speak to me—not to Rex, to me.

"Hi, Lil," said Mr. Brand. I didn't know him personally, but his tone was most cordial. And how was I?

"Okay."

"That's fine," he said. Then he came to the point. He had just learned—he had his own sources—that the headline on the front page of tomorrow's *Los Angeles Examiner* would read: "Motive for Landis Suicide: Lilli Palmer Pregnant."

"But that's completely untrue!" I said, outraged.

"That's not the point," said Mr. Brand soothingly. "They can always say next day it turned out to be a false alarm. But it gives the paper two profitable editions, after which they're willing to drop the whole thing. So do them a favor, and play ball."

"I'm not going to play ball," I shouted. "Tell the *Los Angeles Examiner* that I'll sue if they print it!"

"Keep your shirt on," said Harry Brand. "I'm calling you to do you a favor and warn you, so you won't get too much of a shock tomorrow. That's what I get for my trouble."

I shouted some more, furious, incoherent. He hung up.

We didn't play ball with the Hearst press. Our cup was about to run over. In the afternoon we were sitting in the garden watching the palominos. Two of them were embracing; one would put its neck over the other's neck and nuzzle it. Maybe they were in love.

The lawyers came out of the house and joined us. Instead of looking worried, as they usually did, they looked embarrassed. We steeled ourselves. They sat down and hung their heads. Then they came out with it: a policeman was here. He said a note had been found in Carole's clenched hand.

Who had found it?

Well . . . the policeman himself had found it as they were taking her to the hospital. And kept it. It contained something highly compromising. So he'd rather turn it over to us than to . . . than to the authorities . . . or, well, the press. Of course it would cost something.

How much?

Five hundred dollars.

Just a minute, please. We'll have to think that over. We went into the abandoned riding ring, bolted the wooden gate, and sat down among the weeds. Five hundred dollars was a lot of money in those days, especially for us, whose contracts were about to be cancelled. On the other hand, what could the note contain? An indictment? A cry of despair? We went back to the lawyers and said we'd chance it. The policeman could do what he liked with the note. They looked dubiously at us and at each other, shrugged their shoulders, and went away. We remained, watching the horses.

A little while later they were back with an envelope. The note was supposed to be inside. They'd been able to make the man see reason. We opened the envelope, and a small piece of crumpled paper fell out. On it, a few almost illegible words: "The cat has a sore paw. She must go to the vet."

Next day permission was finally given to bury the girl. The coroner probably thought things had gone far enough. It was explained to us that the funeral would be another free-for-all. For one thing, a man had shown up who claimed to be Carole's father (the railroad switchman?). He had come to attend her funeral—and claim his inheritance. Was he really her father? Instead of PALMER PREGNANT, the *Los Angeles Examiner* carried the headline CAROLE'S FATHER THREATENS TO BEAT UP REX HARRISON. We must be prepared for anything: rocks thrown at us, a brawl, abuse—a good time for all. Wouldn't it be better not to go to the funeral in person? A beautiful wreath with a ribbon—"In deepest sympathy, Rex and Lilli"—would do nicely. No? You really want to go? All right. Special detachment of police.

There were minor problems, too. What should I wear? I called Mary Lee Fairbanks; she'd know. "Mary Lee, what does the well-dressed woman wear to the funeral of her husband's mistress? Black?"

Mary Lee hesitated. "Well, dear," she said finally, "that might be going a bit far. Have you anything in navy?"

It was a bad day for Rex. He was very pale and didn't say a word. Two friends sat with us in the limousine on the long ride to Forest Lawn. Two bodyguards were crowded into the front seat beside the chauffeur. Now that all was said and done, now that she was lying in her coffin and the earth would soon fall—now she really was dead. Senselessly dead. At twenty-nine.

We had never attended a Hollywood funeral, but we had a rough idea of what was in store for us. Thousands of people outside the church. The usual army of reporters and photographers, stationed where they could take pictures of the stars as they drove up in their limousines, as if it were a premiere. The only difference was that this took place in daylight, without klieg lights, and the stars were not in evening dress and diamonds but in street clothes and dark glasses, which they took off for a moment for the benefit of the photographers. And instead of laughing and waving, they nodded with dignified restraint in all directions. An amazing number of stars were there, even though some of them had not been very close to Carole. The newspaper photos the next day testified to the solidarity the profession had shown in mourning one of its own who had come to grief in, and through, Hollywood.

We also knew what was in store for us inside the church. In America the dead are dressed and made up to look as though they are "only sleeping." The coffin is open; you file slowly past and proceed to a numbered seat, as if you were at the theater. Sometimes props are added to emphasize the departed's personality. If he had been gregarious, he might be holding a cocktail glass in his hand, and his face might be massaged into a smile. A businessman might repose in his casket in a gray flannel suit, his glasses on his nose and a telephone receiver at his ear. This is more comforting to millions of bereaved families than the sight of a closed coffin and the thought of the dead person inside with a white shroud and gray face.

We got out of the car a little way from the church in order to avoid the red carpet leading up to the door, which exposed every new arrival to the crowd and the photographers. Perhaps we could manage to slip up the steps behind someone else—Rex and I in the

Aged three,
with décolleté.

My father,
during the
First World War.

With my mother.

Juanita Sujo

Rolf

"Les Soeurs
Viennoises"
in green
taffeta . . .

Sweet (fat)
seventeen .

and in raincoats.

With Rex,
pre-Hollywood.

With Carey.
"Let's not show him
to anyone—
please!"

"Brackenwood" (England)
in 1973.
Left, the rhododendron
that saved Carey's life.

Elsa Schreiber,
Hollywood, 1960.

Dolling me up
at Gaumont-British—
still fairly fat
and friendly,
in 1936.

Minus ten pounds—
first film,
Crime Unlimited,
with Esmond Knight.

First play
in London:
*The Road
to Gandahar,*
at the
Garrick Theatre.

Second stage appearance
in London:
The Tree of Eden.

Trying (in vain)
to look like Marlene.

Rex and Irene Dunne in *Anna and the King of Siam*.

With Gary Cooper in *Cloak and Dagger*.

Rex, Carey and I,
Hollywood, 1946.

With Carey,
Hollywood, 1946.

Cleopatra
on Broadway,
1950.

With "Pye" in
Bell, Book and Candle
on Broadway,
1951.

With Rex in *Venus Observed*,
1952. (THE THEATRE GUILD ARCHIVE IN
THE COLLECTION OF AMERICAN LITERATURE,
THE BEINECKE RARE BOOK AND MANUSCRIPT
LIBRARY, YALE UNIVERSITY)

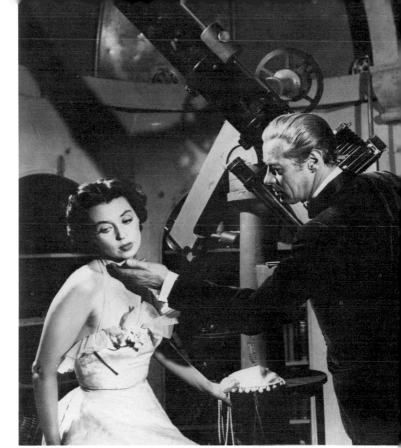

With Leueen McGrath,
Theresa Helburn, Lawrence
Langner, and Rex Harrison,
looking over the script for the
Theatre Guild production of
Love of Four Colonels, 1953.
(THE THEATRE GUILD ARCHIVE IN THE
COLLECTION OF AMERICAN LITERATURE,
THE BEINECKE RARE BOOK AND MANUSCRIPT
LIBRARY, YALE UNIVERSITY)

With Clark Gable
in *But Not for Me,*
Hollywood,
1959.

middle, the bodyguards before and behind us, and friends on either side. Not a chance. We were recognized immediately, and photographers pounced on us from all sides. Flashbulbs popped so wildly that I couldn't see the steps and stumbled. A bodyguard quickly picked me up. The crowd pushed forward, but the mounted police formed a solid phalanx. We climbed up the steps leading to the church without hurry, looking neither left nor right. No rocks, no abuse. Silence.

Organ music came booming through the wide-open doors: Schubert's "Ave Maria." Of course. Twice through. Our tickets were taken, and we joined the line filing slowly past the "stage." The dais was decorated with wreaths. The coffin stood in the center, slightly tilted to give you a better view. Carole had her hair beautifully done in long blond curls, her face made up as if for a movie take. She was dressed in something white and shiny, with long sleeves; impossible to say whether it was a nightgown or an evening dress. No props, just white roses in her hands. She looked very beautiful, and was smiling peacefully. I couldn't help thinking of all those sleeping pills. There was a strong smell of gardenias and tuberoses and incense. I was afraid my stomach might turn over, as it had done in the plane, but we were quickly past the dais and shown to our places, somewhere discreetly on the side aisle. When the church was full, the minister entered the pulpit. He said that in her short life Carole had made many people happy, and that they had all loved her.

Not I. I hadn't loved her. She hadn't made me happy. I thought of all the "conversations" I had had with her when I woke up in the middle of the night or when I was driving alone in the car. I liked "talking" to her in the car. Then I could shout. I had asked my friends never to tell me where she lived. I knew it was somewhere very close to us. I didn't want to be tempted to pick up a kitchen knife some night . . .

I looked over at the white coffin and made my peace with her.

A fellow actor—I don't remember who it was—came up to the dais and read a passage from the Bible. The organ boomed again, and we all rose. It was over.

12

A Home in New York

❀

REX BOUGHT HIMSELF out of his Fox contract. We wanted to move to New York so that he could go back to the legitimate theater. His first Broadway play was to be Maxwell Anderson's *Anne of the Thousand Days,* the play Max was discussing with him at lunch while Carole lay dead in the bathroom. Zanuck didn't stand in his way. He had done all he could to save Rex's Hollywood career, but he was powerless in the face of a unanimously hostile press.

When we were finally dropped from the headlines, the gossip columnists took us up, voracious, snarling, and untruthful. One columnist went too far: she wrote—purely on spec—that we had left Hollywood with a number of unpaid bills, i.e., the butcher's, the grocer's, and so on. I yelped with outrage and, through our lawyer, forced the lady to retract. She must have wondered why we let so many other libels and aspersions pass and only jumped at that one. But then, she didn't know my father.

On the whole we acted as if we couldn't read, saw no one except a few friends, and tried to sell the house with the palominos.

I dealt with the mail, which left me numb with depression because of all the filthy anonymous letters. One specimen stuck in my throat, and I remember it to this day. *The Loved One,* Evelyn Waugh's satire on California burial rites, had recently appeared. Waugh had devoted a special chapter to the Hollywood pet cemetery and its quaint custom of sending owners of dead pets a yearly reminder card on the anniversary of the burial. The card read, "Your little Fifi [or Muggsie or whatever the pet's name had been] is thinking of you in heaven today and wagging his tail." The anonymous letter read, "Your little Carole is thinking of you in heaven today and wagging her tail."

Rex was bidden to leave for New York without delay to get ready for his play. I flew east with him to find an apartment, in case the play turned out to be a hit and run for at least a year. Leland called a press conference at our hotel to introduce us to New York reporters. And suddenly, during this first official interview, we burst and "talked."

New York had not been nearly so worked up about Carole's death. She was hardly known there, and anyway New York didn't go in much for muckraking in actors' private lives. The reporters' questions were chiefly about the play, Rex's role, the start of rehearsals—sensible questions of fact. Right at the end, however, one of the reporters asked, "What's your reaction to the Hollywood press campaign against you?" Rex replied that he didn't give a damn what alcoholic illiterates like Louella Parsons and her ilk wrote about us.

That appeared in the papers verbatim.

For Hollywood it was the last straw. Never, the *Hollywood Reporter* declared in an editorial, had the motion picture capital been so insulted by a foreigner whom it had received with open arms. Never again, wrote Mr. Wilkerson, the editor-in-chief, should this foreigner presume to set foot in the sacred studios. (Or words to that effect.) Other "defenders of Hollywood morals" followed suit, headed by the two chief oracles, Louella Parsons and Hedda Hopper.

When we cursed them collectively, we referred to them as Lulu Popper. Louella looked like a very old tadpole. At parties she would sit in the corner of a sofa all evening, and no one could say for sure whether she was loaded or just addled. Nonetheless, she collected an astounding amount of garbage, which she poured out, with a sugar coating of moral indignation, in her daily column. She also had a Sunday night radio program with an audience of millions, which was worth listening to because it was occasionally hilarious.

The Sunday after the release of the sensational news that Ingrid Bergman was expecting a child out of wedlock by Roberto Rossellini, Louella moaned on the radio, "Ingrid, Ingrid! Whatever got into you?"

The other one, Hedda Hopper, fancied that her column ought to be not merely malicious—an irate actor once mailed her a dead skunk, gift-wrapped—but also "significant." Once, when Tyrone Power changed girl friends, she headlined the event in her column with: "TY LEAVES LANA TO FIGHT COMMUNISM." Where Rex was concerned, she didn't even take the trouble to hide her poison. She published a diatribe devoted exclusively to him, ending with the prophecy, "Rex Harrison's career is as dead as a mackerel."

The mackerel started rehearsals in New York. He was playing Henry the Eighth, a demanding part, and he wrestled with it day and night. So much the better. It left him no time to think.

I flew back to Hollywood alone to wind things up. First, I was formally released from my contract with Warner Brothers, thanks to the clause about my husband's change of domicile. Then I put an ad in the paper (giving just our address, no name) in the hope of selling the house. The people who came to look at it, and who immediately recognized me, were put off either by the memory of recent events or by the palominos. No one even made an offer. Nevertheless I obstinately began to pack. Pat was packing too—she wasn't coming to New York with us, a bitter blow at this moment— and Carey was packing his toys. At night, alone in the quiet house, I wandered through the empty rooms, wrangling with fate, myself, my marriage. I wrangled with Carole, too, breaking my pact with her. After all, she'd lived in Hollywood; she must have known that Rex would find her and what that would do to his life.

Pat and I were packing kitchen equipment when a big woman with a hat and a red nose, dressed in a skirt and an old jacket, appeared in the doorway. She had seen in the paper that the house was for sale.

"Yes, it is," I said hopefully.

Well, she didn't like it, she said. She'd been expecting something else. What? Well, something else. It didn't look homey.

"No house looks homey when there's no furniture in it and it's full of packing cases."

Maybe, she said. Still, she didn't like it.

I nodded and kept on packing. No point showing her the bedrooms. She left.

Suddenly she was back at the kitchen door. "I looked around anyhow," she said, "and I don't like it. But there's a picture in the library that I like. I'll buy it."

I went into the den with her. Set into the panelling above the fireplace was a painting of a boy, David Copperfield-style, sitting on a chest drinking out of a cup. Kitsch but quite decently painted. It had cost $500.

"I want that," said the woman, in a voice that brooked no contradiction. "Get it down for me."

"I can't," I said, "it's set into the woodwork."

"What? Does that mean I've got to buy the damn house to get the picture?"

Pause. For a second I thought I was dealing with a madwoman. Then I caught on. "That's right," I said. "No house, no picture."

She bought the house. Out of her shabby handbag she took a checkbook and wrote a check for $85,000. Then she climbed into her old station wagon and rattled off. I rattled off, too, to the bank. They telephoned and inquired. Her check was good. I drove home, singing at the top of my voice.

I stopped singing the next day. Our Hollywood business manager, our "friendly neighborhood savings bank," calmly informed us that though we had sold the house, we didn't have a penny, because, first, the mortgage would have to be paid off, and second, we owed a large sum in back taxes.

"How come?" I said, aghast, "they've been deducting regularly for taxes."

"Yes, but only on an estimated basis. What you actually owe in taxes is worked out and collected two years later."

Why didn't they warn us? To this day I don't know. Perhaps it was a way to prevent actors from leaving Hollywood. Now we would have to work doubly hard to earn the tax money, and that would be the first link in an endless chain. In our case it amounted to $35,000 in California taxes, to be paid in weekly installments. The two of us together, because I too had just received an offer to appear for the first time on the New York stage. A French play. Author: Jean-Pierre Aumont, one of our closest friends. Probably it was at his urging that I'd been given the part. Rehearsals and their day-to-day problems were supposed to keep me, like Rex, from having time to think. We would start in a month. By then we had to find an apartment (difficult because of our financial situation), a replacement for Pat (fat chance!), and a school for Carey (no problem, I thought).

Rex's rehearsals were over; the out-of-town tryouts began. No novelty to us, for in England, too, a new play is tried out in the provinces. What was new to us, and quite extraordinary, was the number of "play doctors" who arrived from New York, writers and directors who had nothing whatever to do with the play. They came to help, like so many midwives at a difficult birth, free of charge, out of loyalty to the suffering author or director or out of devotion to the theater. This is one of America's most admirable qualities: an ungrudging generosity, unmatched anywhere else. In no other country have I heard actors speak of their colleagues as American actors do, with wholehearted recognition of a rival's achievements and genuine pleasure at the success of another star, director, or producer. In America we found a completely original attitude to a competitor's success. "If someone has a good time at my rival's show, he'll feel like going to the theater again, and next time he may choose my play." We had never heard that kind of language before. Perhaps America could afford to be generous, being more affluent and less insular.

Rex, immersed in the chaos of daily rewriting and nightly confusion on the road, was relieved to hear that I had at last found a suitable little apartment and was on the track of a replacement for Pat. The only outstanding question was the best school for Carey. For weeks now, the boy had been on tenterhooks every time the subject was mentioned. For his sake, too, I was glad we'd moved to New York. At that time there wasn't a school in Los Angeles that came up to our ideas of discipline and curriculum. In the postwar years American schools, particularly those in California, were experimenting with the concept that "the child knows best." Later they dropped this notion—and it was perhaps no coincidence that they did so after the first Russian sputnik was launched.

Hunter College Elementary School, I had been told, would be the best school for Carey, the most demanding as well as the most progressive. As soon as we moved into the new apartment, I took Carey to the principal's office. He sat next to me, breathless with excitement. The principal welcomed us and asked for some information. I told him what little there is to tell about a child: that he was just five, healthy and intelligent. He had never attended school, but he could read.

"You can read? Okay, read to me." He picked up a book from his desk and opened it at random. Without hesitation, Carey began at the top of the page, in the middle of a sentence, and read the complicated scientific article fluently and with growing interest. The principal watched, speechless, and finally interrupted almost rudely. "All right, fine, that's enough. Go and wait outside a minute. Hey, leave the book here!"

Carey left with a long face, and the principal turned to me. "I can't possibly take this child. I'd have to put him with the twelve-year-olds, and they'd only beat him up. Try the Lycée Français. In French he won't know any more than the others, so he'll be pretty much on their level."

So Carey was sent to the Lycée Français and was angry with us because he couldn't understand or speak a word, since French was the language of instruction. The only compensation was that, like all the other children, he was addressed as "monsieur." There were also "mademoiselles" in the class, and he liked that, too. Six months later, he opened his mouth one day and spoke French, though still with a strong lisp.

He was a schoolboy now, being "schooled" every day, something he had longed for. His character, temperament, and essential quality were established. He was gravely serene, thoughtful, and, from the first, independent. He never complained, rarely cried, and gave no one any trouble. But I felt a twinge of envy when a friend said regretfully that she had to go home because her child wouldn't eat if she wasn't there. Carey ate whether I was there or not.

He had very few toys and didn't ask for more. Once Rex took him to F.A.O. Schwarz, the biggest toy shop in the world, seven floors crammed with playthings, a children's paradise. He was to choose a toy as a reward for something or other—anything he liked. Right at the entrance, Carey saw a little red car. "That's what I'd like!" he said.

"Now, hold on, old boy," said Rex, "look at all the other things first."

Reluctantly the child allowed himself to be dragged through all seven floors, past all the magnificent shiny playthings, some of which Rex wouldn't have minded getting his own hands on. "The little red car, please," Carey said when they'd seen everything, and bore it home in triumph.

His first visit to the theater was to see his father as Henry the Eighth in *Anne of the Thousand Days*. He had just turned five, and sat on my lap in a box, fascinated by the auditorium. "People in layerth!" he exclaimed, looking up at the balcony seats. Earlier he had watched his father in his dressing room put on his costume and makeup, so he wasn't unduly surprised when Rex made his entrance as Henry, complete with padding, beard, and plumed hat. He followed the medieval dialogue without much interest until one of the courtiers pointed toward a window and spoke of "a clump of red deer, grazing within view," a line that no one had ever paid the slightest attention to before. But Carey almost fell out of the box, because he wanted to see the red deer too.

Then Anne Boleyn entered in her sixteenth-century dress with long, flowing sleeves, her hair hidden beneath her three-cornered headdress. I could see from Carey's puzzled face that he was trying to figure out what species she could possibly belong to. His encyclopedia had no pictures of any creature resembling this one. In the first scene between the king and his recalcitrant beloved, Henry angrily knocks her down—whereupon the child hid his head on my shoulder and demanded to be taken home. Then he brooded gloomily over his supper. Finally he unburdened himself to Mademoiselle. "You know," he said, without taking his eyes off his plate, "This afternoon, Daddy was very rude to this—this perthon."

One afternoon he was lying beside me on the sofa, telling me, as he liked to do from time to time, whatever happened to occupy his mind at the moment. That day he had just read an article in his encyclopedia on the Diaspora.

"And after the Emperor Titus had dethtroyed the holy temple of Jerusalem," he intoned, "the Jews dithappeared and nobody ever heard of them again."

"Oh, but you're wrong there," I interrupted, "they have been heard of again."

"Really? Are there any left?"

"Yes," I said. "A whole lot."

"Do you know any?"

"Yes, I do. So do you."

He sat up straight and looked at me. "I do?" he repeated incredulously. "I know some? Who?"

"Me," I said.

An unforgettable moment. I looked into my son's wide-open, intelligent, innocent eyes and could read every single thought. Stupefaction, at first, then doubt, then surprise, and finally respect. I observed it all in silence and with appreciation. The silence lasted quite a while, because he was looking at me as though he were seeing me for the first time.

"How absolutely fathinating," he said at last.

He stayed at the Lycée until he was ten. Then he was sent to a prep school in England. Englishmen have to go to an English boarding school, said Rex, otherwise they're not Englishmen. But from the British point of view, he started out with one strike against him anyway: his mother was a foreigner. Suspicious and irremediable. A second strike (remediable) was his early years of schooling at the Lycée Français. I remembered how important it is to "belong" and resigned myself.

The school was at Sunningdale, not far from London, a magnificent eighteenth-century estate, once privately owned. Lovely gardens and grounds, a panelled dining hall, no central heating. Rex and I drove him down, dressed in his new light gray uniform. I'd spent days sewing on name tapes or painting his initials on every item of his belongings, sniffling and sighing away. Our first real separation. The child was neither sniffling nor sighing, but was all eyes and rapture.

We handed him over to his house master, who took him to join the other new boys. In the billiard room, the new boys, and only the new boys, were allowed to play billiards. Parents were politely dismissed. While Rex had a sherry with the headmaster in his study, I sneaked out to find Matron, asking her to take special care . . . "All mothers come sneaking and asking," she said. Ashamed, I sneaked out again.

We were allowed to visit the billiard room to say good-bye. Twenty small heads were bent over the green table, absorbed in the new game, oblivious of their parents. Which one was Carey? Impossible to tell. They were all the same height, wore the same uniform, had the same blond, trimmed English haircut. "Carey-boy!" I called. A head was raised for an instant, a small hand waved good-bye, then the head merged again with the others. I cried all the way back to London.

Within a year he was completely at home there, had new friends, liked his teachers, and joined enthusiastically in every school tradition. One Sunday, on visiting day, he informed me that today was Blub Sunday.

Blub Sunday? Who blubbed?

"The new boys," he announced happily. "Today all the new boys blub, because it's the first Sunday that they're away from their mothers. And we wallop them."

"You what?"

"We wallop them. They hide, but we find them, and anyone who's blubbed gets walloped."

I gave him a long look. Not a sign of remorse; purest pleasure in his blue eyes. "Well," I said, "I hope you choose the right boy. A real small one who couldn't hit back."

He caught on. "I've been walloped too," he said. "I hid under that rhododendron bush, but they found me."

"So today you looked under the rhododendron bush."

He nodded. Couldn't quite conceal a note of sly triumph. "I knew somebody would be sitting under there, like me last year . . ." The essence of the democratic British system of education: first you get walloped, then you're allowed to wallop somebody else.

Carey had had only one real spanking in his life, while he was still at the Lycée. For some unknown reason, he had forged his governess's signature on his weekly report card and obstinately refused to admit it. The evidence was there, no possibility of error. We gave him time to think it over, "until after the matinee." If he owned up, he wouldn't be punished.

Before the performance, we asked the other actors if they had ever been beaten by their parents. Nearly all of them had. But only once, and, as they all hastened to add, it was richly deserved. Some of them maintained that it had done them good. Their eyes shone as they spoke of it, as though it marked a milestone in their lives.

All right. We'd mark a milestone for Carey. Rex was offered all kinds of advice about the best way to go about it. Unanimous opinion: across your knee, with a leather belt. "Otherwise he won't feel it."

In the taxi home we were nervous. Impossible to back out now.

Carey was eating supper with Mademoiselle in the nursery. When we entered, she raised her eyebrows significantly. Asked whether he was now ready to tell the truth, the child maintained a stubborn silence. He had gone beyond the point where we could build what my mother called a "golden bridge" for him.

We left the room. "All right," I said, "let's get it over with."

"Just a minute," said Rex. "I'm going to walk once around the block; then I'll be able to do it." He put his coat on, left the apartment, returned ten minutes later, looking determined, took off his belt, and entered the nursery. I chickened out and hid in the kitchen.

That night in the bathtub Carey proudly showed Mademoiselle his red bottom. "And you know," he said triumphantly, "it hurt Daddy more than it hurt me."

Rex's Henry the Eighth was a tremendous success when, after a difficult pregnancy, the play was finally delivered on Broadway. The serious critics didn't care—perhaps didn't even know—what had happened in Hollywood. Hollywood was three thousand miles away, another world. They devoted whole paragraphs to Rex's performance, overjoyed at having another great actor on the New York stage. Rex was overjoyed too. The wounds were beginning to heal.

We had an apartment; Carey was going to school every day and liked his new governess; Rex loved his performances. I looked around me like God on the seventh day of Creation, found it good, and rested. For three days. Then rehearsals began for Jean-Pierre's play *My Name Is Aquilon.*

Right from the start it was clear that we had problems. French plays, like local wines, don't travel well. Even outstanding contemporary French playwrights like Anouilh, Camus, Sartre, and Roussin are more successful with American critics than with the public. Puritanical American theater audiences feel uneasy and patronized by traditional French sophistication; they suspect that they're not really "getting" everything. In our play, for instance, the characters were listed in the program as Monsieur X; Madame X, his wife; and Mademoiselle X, his mistress. To an American, this meant a triangle; to a Frenchman it was just a list of characters. Jean-Pierre's play had been a hit in Paris, where they had no trouble understanding it. In America, the lack of understanding started with the translation.

I struggled through my part, got no help from the director, and was plain bad. When we opened in Philadelphia to terrible reviews, I screamed for help. Elsa flew in from Hollywood, took a look at the whole dismal business, and shook her head. The "midwives" arrived from New York, wrote new scenes every day, and turned the play inside out, but it didn't help much. Luckily no major changes had to be made in my part, and Elsa went to work without delay. The result was amazing. When we opened in New York two weeks later, the play was pulled to pieces, but the critics outdid one another in praise of my performance. The *New York Times* wrote, "Miss Palmer is the finest thing that has happened to the Gotham stage for quite a long time. If our housing commission is a really enterprising organization, it will find permanent quarters for Miss

Palmer and her husband, Rex Harrison, and see that they never get out of town."

My play closed after four weeks. Rex's ran and ran. The Tony awards were to be handed out early in the year. Rex received a written invitation to appear at midnight at the theater where the celebration was taking place, which meant that he'd been nominated for an award. This year's emcee, we read to our dismay, would be his arch-enemy, Hedda Hopper.

We were seated in the first row of the packed theater. The rostrum was surrounded with television cameras and microphones. First we endured several comedians and singers, then a musical interlude—and finally the lady everybody was waiting for appeared on stage in rose pink chiffon and golden hair, smiling radiantly, arms outstretched: Miss Hedda Hopper, former actress in silent films, still pretty, though a bit on the plump side. Behind her was somebody with a glass bowl full of sealed envelopes, which was set down on a table before she made a little speech. Great to be in New York (applause). So exciting for a poor little reporter from the California sticks (laughter). Cultural level of American theater unique (applause). A great honor to present its elite with their well-deserved awards. A red-letter day in her life (prolonged applause).

We looked at the pink bundle of charm on the platform and remembered the column in the *Los Angeles Times* that the poor little reporter had devoted to Rex, comparing him to a dead mackerel. That was only six months ago. It seemed like six years.

There was a flourish of trumpets and a roll of drums. The television cameras moved in on the glass bowl. Hedda showed her pearly teeth and reached for the first of the sealed envelopes. As with the Oscar presentations, the distribution of awards begins with those for supporting roles, female and male; then come the leading roles in musicals; and finally, the high point of the evening, the nominations for the outstanding starring performances in straight plays. Hedda paused dramatically; there was another roll of drums; then, with becoming dignity, she announced the name of the best actress: Martita Hunt, an English actress, who had scored a personal triumph in Giraudoux's *The Madwoman of Chaillot*. Martita, who was sitting near us, uttered a little gasp of delight and stumbled up the steps to the platform. Applause. Television close-up of Hedda embracing Martita and handing her the Tony medallion.

Now came the great moment. "The year's best leading actor is . . ." I steeled myself for disappointment and tried to look as indifferent as possible. Rex's hand on my knee was trembling. For the last time, Hedda reached into the glass bowl and tore open the envelope. Flourish of drums. Pause. She looked up and announced hoarsely, "Mr. Rex Harrison." Calls from the audience: "Who? Who? Louder, please." Tonelessly, she repeated, "Mr. Rex Harrison."

In one bound Rex was on stage, his back turned to Miss Hopper, bowing in response to the thunderous applause. He had to take bow after bow and ended by stretching out his arms as if to embrace the whole audience. Then he calmly turned toward Miss Hopper. She had had time to recover herself and to remember that she was still on camera, in close-up. "Congratulations, Rex," she said, and handed him his medallion. He nodded to her and bounded down the stairs to the orchestra.

We went out afterwards and celebrated with Martita. We celebrated so abundantly that Martita left her Tony in the taxi that brought us home.

My play had died a quiet death, but my reviews were remembered, and I was offered something new. And old. George Bernard Shaw's *Caesar and Cleopatra*.

13

GBS

❀

WHEN I MET George Bernard Shaw, he was ninety-two. During Shaw's lifetime, any actor who possibly could went to see him to ask formal permission to appear in his plays. Since he was too old to go to the theater—he was hard of hearing and too vain to wear a hearing aid—he liked actors and actresses to visit him occasionally. Especially actresses.

Rex had met him when he was making *Major Barbara* during the war, and the old man had said that he was his favorite of all contemporary actors. He said Rex could act in any of his plays, because he reminded him of himself as a young man. In all Shaw's plays, the male characters—and sometimes the female—are portraits of the author in different disguises. When Rex later played Professor Higgins in *My Fair Lady*, he was a perfect replica, because Higgins is the quintessence of Shaw.

There were four of us on the long drive to Shaw's country house: Gertrude Lawrence (whose husband, Richard Aldrich, would produce *Caesar and Cleopatra*); her friend Radie Harris, the journalist; Miss Patch, Shaw's secretary for forty years; and me. Miss Patch looked exactly the way an elderly English lady is supposed to look. She was so thin that she barely cast a shadow. Her face looked like two profiles stuck together. Piercing blue eyes, a nose like a knife blade, lipless mouth, tweed suit (despite the warm weather), sweater, and pearls. She had decided at the last minute to come along so that she could "prepare" me. There were a few elementary rules: "Don't get rattled. Talk back if necessary. Above all, don't cry." I waited in vain for one more piece of advice: don't step out alone on the balcony with him unless you want to get your bottom pinched. I'd been given that tip by Vivien Leigh, who knew what she was talking about. Maybe this was—perhaps always had been—Shaw's only sexual activity. But Miss Patch didn't seem to know anything about GBS's outdoor exercises.

I looked at her sideways. She was looking out the window with relaxed English calm, without making the least effort at conversation.

"Miss Patch," I said, "did you type Shaw's manuscripts?"
She nodded.
"Then you were the first person to read them?"
She nodded again, blushing slightly.
"What was it like? Do tell me."
"Well, he wrote his quota every day, and when he finished a scene, he gave it to me in the evening. He wanted to see it typed before making the final revision. He's very finicky. Every semicolon is important."
"In other words, you got home and read the scene and typed it right away?"
"Sometimes I typed right through the night, when I knew he wanted to see a complete act."
"Miss Patch, you've had a splendid life!"
Pause.
"Perhaps," she said, "but it would have been even more splendid if just once in those forty years he'd said thank you."

Shaw's house, Ayot St. Lawrence, is a nondescript, medium-sized Victorian abode, surrounded by flower borders, lawns, and a large kitchen garden that provided him with his daily food, for he took his vegetarianism seriously. The only exception in his meatless diet was the daily spoonful of liver extract, which he referred to as "those chemicals."

We waited in the living room crammed with upholstered furniture, chests of drawers, photographs, knickknacks, and a wide selection of portraits and busts of the owner. You could have followed the story of Shaw's life from the names of the artists who had painted and sculpted him, from Sargent and Augustus John (still with a flaming red beard) to Topolski (white beard), from Rodin (smooth, crafty face) to Epstein (thin and furrowed). I looked at the miniatures and photographs, reading the names on the dedications, awed and overwhelmed by this repository of enduring fame. These were not portraits and photographs of celebrities, but of immortals. Marie Curie, Einstein, Anna Pavlova, Eleanora Duse, Sarah Bernhardt, Diaghilev, Lenin, Churchill, Clemenceau, d'Annunzio, Ibsen, Strindberg, Gerhart Hauptmann, Yvette Guilbert, Toulouse-Lautrec, Renoir, Tolstoy, Gorki . . . it would have seemed perfectly natural to find a miniature inscribed "To my dear GBS—thy humble servant, W. Shakespeare."

This life had already spanned almost a century, more than half of it spent in intimate contact with the great of his time. In intimate contact? Oscar Wilde had said, "An excellent fellow, Shaw. He has no enemies, and none of his friends can stand him."

The manservant opened the door to the study, and there, with his back to us, sat bolt upright a skinny old man, dressed in old-fashioned clothes: knickerbockers, dark green puttees, and a lavender-colored jacket buttoned up to the knot of his tie. He made no effort to get up or turn around to welcome us, but waited until we came into his field of vision. Gertie, who knew him of old, kissed him, which he tolerated; then he nodded to Radie, whom Gertie introduced—he was always affable to "the press"—and then he turned a cold stare on me: "Rex didn't come?"

"Rex has a son from his first marriage, Mr. Shaw, and he has to go and see him today." The bushy white eyebrows shot up. "The boy's at public school, you see, and Rex hasn't seen him for three years, and today is visiting day."

"So he'd rather visit his son, eh? Great mistake. He still has plenty of time to see his son. But not me." (He was right. Rex never had another chance to see him again.)

"As for you!" His high, old man's voice rose to a furious cackle. "I'm told that you and Cedric [Sir Cedric Hardwicke] have agreed to a cut in your salaries to help the producer, otherwise there's no way of financing the production. I'm told that everyone involved is going to tighten his belt and muck in. I won't have it!" He pounded his knees with both fists, screeching at the top of his voice. "My plays weren't written so that actors should make a financial sacrifice to perform them. My plays aren't artistic ventures. My plays are commercial enterprises. I'll withdraw my permission immediately unless you can prove to me that you're asking exactly the same kind of money you'd get for appearing in some half-witted Broadway-frippery . . ."

I had made a few polite interrupting noises and even raised my right forefinger, to no avail. Now, however, he had to pause for a split second to catch his breath, and I quickly cut in. "Mr. Shaw, do you know what I'm getting for Cleopatra?"

He looked at me sharply, leaned forward and cupped his hand behind his ear.

"How much?"

"Seven and a half percent of the gross."

"What? Too much."

At that he sank back in his chair and bade us sit down at last. Gertie and Radie retired somewhat to the back, for they wanted me to have my interview with the old man "unaided." Miss Patch had dissolved before we entered the room.

I sat and had a good look at him. Redheads in old age often grow the most beautiful white hair. Shaw's narrow skull was still fully thatched, although the scalp showed through. He had goat's eyebrows, probably helped by a bit of daily twirling into those Mephistophelian triangles above the wintry blue eyes, which reminded me of a dead chicken. His face was narrow, his skin, as with most redheads, delicate and not much wrinkled. The mouth was ungenerous with thin purple lips, but not unhumorous. I knew that face by heart. During the war I'd bought a little portrait of Shaw by Felix Topolski as a birthday present for Rex, and it went with us wherever we set up house. Shaw had signed it for him in red ink on the canvas: "GBS, who is only eighty-six, looks ten years younger and much tidier."

There was a moment's silence. Just as I was about to launch one of my icebreakers, he pointed imperiously at his desk.

"Go over there and take a look, young woman. You won't believe it."

I got up and gingerly approached the desk.

"Well," he insisted, "what do you see?"

I saw nothing except a tidy desk, an inkwell, old-fashioned penholders and pencils, carefully stacked letters, a couple of books, and a blotter. On the blotter was a loose check, from which I hastily averted my eyes because I was sure it wasn't meant for them.

"Come now," said the old man impatiently. "Don't you see it?"

"No," I said feebly.

"The paper," he croaked. "That scrap of paper."

"The check?" I stammered, aghast.

"What else? Look at it. What does it say?"

"To the Board of Inland Revenue . . ."

"Well? Go on young woman, go on."

"The sum of fifteen thousand pounds. George Bernard Shaw."

"What about that? I just wrote it. The ink's not dry yet. Fifteen thousand pounds for one year's taxes! What do you say to that?"

"Well," I piped up, "I say that you must have made a lot of money last year, Mr. Shaw."

He gave me a look that wasn't a hundred percent amused and snorted that that was one way of looking at it.

Another pause. Time for an icebreaker. Let's try a down-to-earth one.

"Mr. Shaw," I warbled, "I came to ask your permission to be your Cleopatra on Broadway. I can't tell you how thrilled I am at the prospect . . . I mean . . ." Under the cold stare of those chicken eyes, I began to bog down. "I . . . I don't know whether you've ever seen me on the stage or read anything about me. Or if . . . you've probably never even heard my name . . ."

He let me run on to the bitter end and took his time about answering. "Anyone can play Cleopatra. The role plays itself."

So much for my opening gambit. I couldn't remember the follow-up. My head was a vacuum with one important piece of advice floating about in it: above all, don't cry.

Luckily Shaw had a question: Were we going to do his seldom-performed prologue or not? I rallied and managed to reply that we were. That seemed to please him, and he asked about Cedric, whom he had once directed as Caesar in that very play at the Royal Court Theatre in London. I recovered still further and remembered another of my standbys for difficult sacred cows. It was always a wise ploy to ask about the good old days, a surefire topic for lengthy conversation. In Hollywood it had been very useful when I found myself sitting at dinner next to a famous star of an earlier generation. I would ask him how it was back in the time when the only paved street in Hollywood led to Douglas Fairbanks Senior's house. That usually kept us going until coffee.

Shaw was no exception. I asked him about the first performance of *Caesar and Cleopatra,* and he blossomed like a thistle (which has a beautiful flower). He recalled details of the staging down to the leading actress's makeup, and treated me to a whole series of anecdotes about the original Caesar, Sir Johnston Forbes-Robertson, not a single one of which was flattering. He enthusiastically described the shortcomings of this performance—for instance, the unsatisfactory manner in which the traitor Pothinus met his end. Pothinus is killed offstage, stabbed by Cleopatra's nurse, Ftatateeta, at her mistress's command, and the audience hears only his death cry. But as GBS rightly pointed out, unless that scream rang out in all its fear and agony, shaking the audience to the very marrow, the following confrontation between a guilty Cleopatra and a grim Caesar loses its dramatic impact. As Shaw described it, the original Pothinus's last howl left a lot to be desired, so the author himself felt obliged to put his shoulder to the wheel.

"One night I went backstage," he said, and suddenly there was a joyful sparkle in those foggy old eyes, "and told that chap Pothinus to hold his tongue when the cue came. And then *I* gave such a cry! Such a cry!" He pounded his bony old knees with his fist in ecstatic memory.

"It was such a splendid cry that Forbes-Robertson said to me in the interval, 'My dear Bernard, if we were to ask the actor to yell the way you do, he'd be hoarse and we'd have to engage a different man every night just for that yell. That would mean ten shillings extra, and that's simply beyond our budget.' " He cackled and hit himself on the knees again.

I decided to squeeze a bit more juice out of the subject of dramatic cries, and asked him whether he had ever heard one of the most famous ones, uttered by Laurence Olivier as Oedipus when he realizes that he is married to his own mother.

"No," said the old man, cupping his hand behind his ear again. "What's that? What's that?"

I embarked on what I hoped would be a compelling description of Olivier's long-drawn-out animal moan in all its scale and variety. When I got through, Shaw gave a short derisive snort, leaned back and said, "Hm. I think that's a lot of nonsense."

"Nonsense?" I yelped, crestfallen.

"I'll tell you what," he said, "I've never liked Sophocles. Has no sense of humor. Give me Euripides any time. As a matter of fact, I always wanted to rewrite the *Oedipus*." He paused and looked at me slyly. "Now then, tell me, why should that fellow Oedipus get into such a state when he finds out that he's married to his mother? It should have added to his affection!"

(Exit Freud.)

More delighted cackling and knee-pounding. I took heart and tried a few more icebreakers, but with little success. They were all too commonplace and edifying and positive, and that kind of thing bored him. He wasn't inclined to waste his precious time talking about "nice" people. But he immediately came to life when I mentioned Gabriel Pascal, the Hungarian actor-director-adventurer, who had arrived in England penniless but determined to film Shaw's *Pygmalion* and who had bamboozled Shaw into virtually making him a gift of an option on it at their first meeting.

There are several versions of that remarkable encounter, all of them good. My favorite is the one Gaby told himself: how he called the famous Whitehall number and happened to get Shaw at the other end of the line, and how he got an appointment because the old man was so enchanted by Gaby's incredible accent, unique even in the annals of Hungarian emigration. At their meeting, Shaw listened with delight to Gaby's account of his life, which was fantastic in the true sense of the word. Finally Gaby asked for an option on *Pygmalion*—something that many far more eminent producers had already done without success. Shaw stroked his beard, smiled in his cagey way, and asked, "How much can you pay for a six months' option?" "One pound," answered Gaby promptly. "Done," said the old man, laughed, and held out his hand for the money, whereupon Gaby fished ten shillings out of his pocket and asked, "Can you lend me ten shillings, sir?"

No wonder that in Shaw's eyes, Gaby could do no wrong. Moreover, *Pygmalion*, his first motion picture, was a great success, and GBS loved him more than ever. The next one, *Major Barbara*, wasn't nearly so good, and the third, *Caesar and Cleopatra*, was a disaster. Still his credit held good with the old man, who decreed that Gaby, and no one else, was to film all his plays. The most remarkable thing was that Gaby had managed to persuade Shaw that he didn't understand "finance" and was a babe in the woods as far as his own interests were concerned.

"I have to write the contracts for Gaby," Shaw told me. "Everybody takes advantage of him if I don't stick up for him. He's just a child. A child of nature."

I had my doubts about that. My mind went back to the time shortly before the end of the war when Rex and I had visited Gaby on his magnificent farm not far from us. I was eight months pregnant, and Gaby looked at me fondly and called me "ta littal muttah." Suddenly his eyes lit up—always very effective, because he had a lot of very white teeth in a dark, grayish brown face and deep set, coal black eyes under a mop of black hair. ("Ven I vas young and cavalry officer in Hongarian Guards regiment, I vas beautiful like Greek god," he used to recall modestly.)

"Little mother must have good milk," he declared. "I make you present of good cow. I pick out finest cow in my barn. You will have best milk in England." He accepted graciously our vociferous thanks. In the last year of the war good milk was scarce, and we were deeply touched by his concern.

The next day the telephone rang. Gaby.

"About cow," he said in his deep, guttural voice.

"Yes, Gaby. Thank you again so much—"

"I think I keep cow in my barn. Better for cow. You get ten percent of milk and you send me check for sixty pounds. Okay?" I stammered that the doctor thought I shouldn't drink quite so much rich milk right now and thanked him again for his "present."

Shaw was delighted with this story, and as long as he didn't need to discuss Cleopatra or other professional matters, he seemed to be enjoying himself. But I was keeping an eye on the clock. Miss Patch had said, "Don't tire him. Don't stay more than an hour or he'll become tetchy from one minute to the next." So I stood up and made some valedictory noises. Shaw looked surprised. "Must you go already?"

Delighted, I sat down again. "Would you like me to stay a little longer, Mr. Shaw?"

He considered. "No," he said. "I'm always glad when people go." (Miss Patch had told me that when King George VI came to visit him and stayed a long time, Shaw had taken his gold watch out of his pocket and had given it a long, attentive look.)

We stood up. Suddenly he grabbed his hat. "I'll show you the garden," he said.

In the hall he picked up a walking stick, but he hardly used it. Gertie complimented him on his health.

"Yes," he said smugly. "I keep well. And I intend to go on keeping well. I live sensibly"—he pointed toward the rows of vegetables— "so why not? To live is normal; to die is abnormal. I intend to go on living well over a hundred years."

He probably would have, too, if he hadn't fallen two years later and broken his thigh. He had to stay in bed and have a nurse take care of him, and suddenly he stopped enjoying life and decided it wasn't worth it anymore. A few days later he was dead.

As we walked through the little woods, he turned to me and said, "You know, I'm the only author who's ever had a new play performed after his ninetieth birthday."

I was suitably impressed.

"I'm not saying that it's a good play, mind you, but it was performed." (*In Good King Charles's Golden Days*, at the Malvern Festival.)

I thought I detected a small wave of friendly feeling coming my way. Encouraged, I pointed to a big bed of peas we were passing.

They were just ripe, thousands of green pods swinging in the breeze.

"May I have one, Mr. Shaw?" (One!)

"No," he replied firmly and walked on. After a while we stopped outside a little hut that looked like a chicken coop on wheels. Two steps led up to the door. One window: that was all.

"Go on in," said the old man, "go on up and have a look. This is where I've written all my plays for the last forty years. I come here at eight o'clock every morning and write until one. I had it specially built so that it wouldn't be too heavy. I can turn it to face the sun when it's cold and push it in the shade when it's too hot. Go on in."

I opened the flimsy door and looked inside. There was just enough room for a desk under the window, and one chair. The table was meticulously tidy, with a stack of paper, a few pencils and pens, and, on a blotter, a pair of mittens. Apparently the old knuckles got cold, even in summer. So this was where he'd written *Saint Joan, Heartbreak House, Don Juan in Hell, Back to Methuselah,* and all the rest. I stood in awe, as if in church.

We walked slowly back to the car. As I thanked him and said good-bye out the car window, he suddenly bent forward and said, "Well, did I give a good performance?"

"If mine's as good as yours, Mr. Shaw," I said, "the play will run a year on Broadway."

He cackled contentedly and waved after the car.

Although we hadn't mentioned Cleopatra again, I assumed that Shaw had no objection to my playing her on Broadway. I realized that this was going to be my acid test. Not because Cleopatra is one of Shaw's few female characters with passion and exotic color, but because this would be the first time I'd worked in America without Elsa. (She was tied up in Hollywood during my rehearsal period.) At every difficult passage, I asked myself: what would Elsa say? Think, think, that's what she'd say, turn the sentence around, approach it from the opposite angle, start again. Think of the character. What is the meaning of this scene? What is she thinking? Why does she talk like this?, etc., etc.

Since this was a new production of an old play, we dispensed with out-of-town tryouts and opened cold in New York. During the dress rehearsal our Caesar, Cedric Hardwicke, who had played the role almost thirty years earlier under Shaw's own direction, lost his voice. Acute laryngitis. He refused to give up and consulted specialists, who gave him injections and painted his throat. He made it through opening night, but he was inaudible beyond the first few rows. Two weeks later, long after he had recovered, he received a postcard from Shaw, which had arrived by boat. (Shaw liked to write postcards. Less postage. He never used air mail.) "Dear Cedric," it said, "gargle every night with salt water. Yours sincerely, GBS."

As far as I was concerned, I remember standing at 12:30 at night under the lamppost in front of Sardi's reading, rereading, and rereading once again the review that Brooks Atkinson had given me in the *New York Times*. After briefly and regretfully mentioning Cedric's laryngitis, he wrote: "But Lilli Palmer is not only in good health but in radiant spirit, and her Cleopatra is nothing short of ideal. Miss Palmer has personal beauty that is notable on its own account. But her limpid, girlish, roguish Cleopatra is also a superb exposition of character that would delight the old man of English letters if he could see it . . ."

14

Portofino: The Party

❀

DURING THE FIFTIES, Portofino became the favorite resort of the international sun-seekers. Depending on their bank accounts, they stayed either at the Hotel Splendido, which dangled perilously and "splendidly" from the mountain high over the bay, or at the cheap and noisy hotels down below in the ancient little harbor town. They arrived by train from Genoa or by car, winding their way carefully along the narrow road between rocks and sea. Some turned up in their-own yachts, white and aloof, and tied up inside the tiny port.

But in 1949, when Rex and I built a house there, even higher up than the Splendido, we were still pioneers. Few foreigners lived there—a couple of writers, painters, and eccentrics—and about eight hundred locals. The place was still essentially Italian. It consisted of a toy harbor with a few dozen toy houses around it, a church, and a peninsula crowned by an old fortress, all of it jealously guarded by the Ministry for the Preservation of Picturesque Localities. Building of any kind was strictly prohibited. No new roads, hotels, private houses or cowsheds without special permission, which was never granted.

We had the extraordinary luck to get a building permit, but only because an old house had stood on the site before the war. The German occupation troops had torn it down and erected a gun emplacement on the spot because it commanded a unique view, not only of Portofino harbor and the bay of Paraggi, but of the entire coastline as far as La Spezia. We blew up the concrete gun platform—I lit the first fuse—set our house with its back close to the rock, and planted a little vineyard around it. The view from the terrace was breathtaking.

The other nonnatives in the vicinity didn't mind if they had to climb steep paths to reach their houses, or had to do without electricity or running water. The view of the aquamarine bay with its cliffs, grottoes, cypresses, and olive groves got into your blood. Our guests used to spend their first few days on the terrace, silently staring down at the panorama and the ever-changing color of the sea.

The German commander who had chosen the old fortress over-looking the harbor as his headquarters must have felt the same way. In 1944, when he received the order to retreat, he couldn't bear the idea that from now on other people were going to enjoy this view. He ordered the entire town, including the castle, blown up and gave the inhabitants forty-eight hours to leave. Every little street was separately mined. There was nothing the desperate villagers could do but pack their few possessions.

Directly below the castle, at the farthest end of the harbor, stands a large house, San Giorgio, built around the turn of the century, the only "modern" house in Portofino. In it lived an old lady, Signora von Mumm, English by birth, German by marriage, who had not been seen for several years. She was said to be so deaf that one could communicate with her only by ear trumpet. But elderly people in the village liked to reminisce, remembering the red-letter day in the history of the town, shortly before the First World War, when the young and beautiful Signora Baroness von Mumm had stood with her husband on the dock to receive Wilhelm II, Emperor of Germany, as her house guest. At that time there was no way to get to Portofino except by mule or, as Kaiser Wilhelm did, by private yacht. His big black sailing vessel rode pompously and regally in the harbor.

The imperial yacht never came again. The beautiful signora was rarely seen, and when she became deaf in her old age, she remained invisible inside her house.

At the time of the German occupation, she was over eighty. The mayor of Portofino, who was the cook at the harbor restaurant, took it upon himself to inform the old lady that she must vacate her house immediately. Since she either couldn't or wouldn't understand a word he said, he wrote it down for her in a note which she read very slowly. Then she nodded and simply asked when the mines would explode. The mayor wrote, "8:00 A.M.: Withdrawal of Occupation Forces. 10:00 A.M.: Explosion." All the inhabitants were to vacate their houses by 8:00 A.M., with or without their possessions.

The old baroness, however, gave orders that nothing was to be packed. Her servants wrung their hands and wept all around her, but she went quietly and early to bed. At seven o'clock the next morning, she had her gardener help her up the steep path to the castle, slowly, step by step, leaning on her stick. The gardener carried the ear trumpet. At the castle entrance she ordered him to leave her, sat down on a rock, and waited.

At ten minutes to eight the commanding officer appeared with his staff. The old woman struggled to her feet, stepped into his path, and spoke to him. Perhaps it was her fluent German that took him unawares; at any rate he answered her relatively politely—he was very agitated—that he had no time to spare, that he was expected in the harbor and had to embark at once. He set off. But Frau von Mumm limped along beside him and started to talk. Like it or not, he had to slow down while she pushed her ear trumpet toward his mouth and he obediently shouted into it.

Nobody knows what she said to him. Eyewitnesses report that they walked more and more slowly and that the man finally stood still and stared down at the harbor. She too was silent and just stood there by his side. He kissed her hand, she hobbled away, and without further explanation he ordered all the mines removed. He then jumped into his jeep and drove off at top speed without looking back.

When we arrived there five years later, Signora von Mumm, honorary citizen of Portofino, had just died. But I often looked down at her house from our terrace and thought of her.

That terrace was the focal point of our daily lives. We ate our meals there and, in fact, lived there. In one corner was a big telescope, which reputedly had come from a Japanese warship. I used to train it on the bay of Paraggi to watch Carey swimming fifteen hundred feet below. His swimsuit was easily picked out, and I could even see his legs moving under water. A telescope of that kind was a must among Portofino property owners. Everyone who had a terrace overlooking the bay played the same game. The telescope would be trained on any ship as it slowly entered the harbor, with its passengers hanging over the rail believing themselves unobserved. That was the point of the game. Hundreds of eyes followed every gesture, every inaudible word as in a silent movie. Once a neighbor in our mountain aerie, Giovanni Falck, trained his telescope on a friend who happened to be eating lunch on deck as they were tying up. Falck telephoned the harbor master and watched his friend being called to the phone. "Look at your left lapel," said Giovanni, "I thought you might like to know, there's a spot of tomato sauce on it."

The vital question was always, Whose yacht is it? Friends? Enemies? Strangers? Even before the anchor chains had rattled down, one knew. The same yachts came year after year, carrying the same passengers. In those days there was no great selection of boats to rent for a Mediterranean cruise. Very few people owned one. Onassis did, of course. (His was the only yacht too big for the Portofino harbor.) Even people like the Duke of Windsor used to rent a fairly battered old tub, built, like all the others, before the war. The *Sister Ann* used to show up punctually every year at Portofino, with Windsor, his duchess, and some friends on board.

We had met the Windsors in New York. In the middle of boisterous parties, he would seek out a quiet corner to recite German poetry with me. After all, his mother, Queen Mary, had been a German princess, Mary of Teck, and had spoken English with a slight Teutonic accent all her life. Windsor had learned to speak fluent German from her as a child, although he was obliged to forget it all during World War I. But he liked to excavate it whenever he had a chance. Once we even made a recording of our recitation. In the background you can hear lively jazz and over it Windsor declaiming, "*Was hör ich draussen vor dem Tor, was auf der Brücke schallen. . . .*"

For a few days every year, he liked to tie up at Portofino "for his

German lesson." When he came up to the house to dine with us, it was certainly an honor but not an unmixed pleasure. Although it was twenty years since he had abdicated, he liked to see protocol observed, only you had to guess when to observe it and when to ignore it. Naturally you had to be punctual to the minute and stand up whenever he stood up; even if he was only going to the toilet, respectful attention was drawn to a function that common people prefer to attend to as inconspicuously as possible. When you greeted him, a little bob or rudimentary curtsey was appreciated. I only bobbed to him. His duchess got a firm handshake. (Benita Colman, our house guest, refused to bob to the Duke. "I only curtsey to what sits on thrones!" she said firmly.) He also had to preside at the head of the table, something Rex only reluctantly conceded. Before dinner, however, the Duke surprised me by gallantly relieving me of the tray of hors d'oeuvres I was passing and handed it around himself. This spoiled Rex's appetite. "I just don't like seeing my former king passing the sandwiches," he said.

The first time he came to dinner, I had told Carey, then eight years old, all about him. How he had once been the golden Prince of Wales and then King of England, but only for eight months, because he had given it all up, as he said on the radio in his famous abdication speech, "for the woman I love," Wallis Simpson, a twice-divorced American whom the Empire would never have accepted as queen. "Take a good look at her," I said. "Some day, when you have children of your own, they'll want to know what she was like, the woman for whom he gave up the throne." But as they walked slowly up the garden steps, Carey had eyes only for the man. He stared and stared—and all for nothing, as he told me later. Windsor wasn't wearing a crown!

He was a small, elegant man, hardly taller than I. From the back he looked like a boy. Facing you, he looked his age, fifty-five, although his blond hair was touched up. The face was still handsome, crisscrossed with tiny wrinkles, the nose sharp and pointed like a hunting dog's. His duchess wore a perfectly plain blue linen dress without pleats, pockets, or collar. Its cut alone made her look almost beautiful. Wallis Windsor, however, was anything but beautiful. Many people have puzzled over what it could possibly have been that so irresistibly attracted the King of England. I believe it was her defiant independence ("I'm at my best with enemies!"), her marvelous carriage, and her voracious vitality. If she had happened to be hungry, she might have taken a bite out of you. Whenever I looked at her, I was reminded of the nutcracker we used for cracking walnuts when we were children. It was made of polished wood in the form of a woman's head, it could open its mouth very wide and—c-rr-ack! The nut disintegrated.

One of their "courtiers" at that time was Jimmy Donahue, a Woolworth heir, who escorted them both everywhere. The Windsors were never alone, but always surrounded by a few people who had nothing better to do at the moment. Jimmy Donahue was a cheerful playboy who never did a stroke of work, never had a thought in his head, but knew everyone, remembered the first names of the *maîtres d'hôtel* of all the best restaurants, was good company, and amused the Duchess.

But how did one amuse the Duke? That was more difficult. His sense of humor on the subject was disturbing. "You know," he once said to me with a smile, "I've got a low IQ."

"But, sir," I protested loyally, "just think of your book, *A King's Story*. That's a fascinating tale and very well written."

"Didn't write it myself," he said. "Anyway, that's all I know."

Since I wasn't born in England and therefore had not been indoctrinated from the cradle with veneration of the royal family in general and the Prince of Wales in particular, I had no latent feelings of allegiance. To me he was no more than a romantic and odd relic, and we talked, always in German, about subjects that might usually have been taboo.

"Are you never homesick for England, sir?"

"No," he said dryly. "Never."

"Not even at Christmas?"

"No. You see, my trouble is that I never really felt at home in England. When I first set foot on American soil as a very young man, it came to me like a flash: this is what I like. Here I'd like to stay. And when I married an American, I hoped we would live in America. But as fate would have it, my wife hates America and only wants to live in France. That's the way it goes."

"But your friends, sir. One misses one's friends."

"My mother was the only person I missed. Since she died, there's really nothing to tempt me across the Channel." Pause. "Do you know my brother Gloucester?"

"No, sir, I've never had the pleasure."

"Pleasure!" he said, rolling his eyes heavenward. "Did you know my brother Kent?" (It sounded like Shakespeare: my brother Gloucester, my brother Kent.)

"Unfortunately not," I said and meant it. The Duke of Kent, his youngest brother, who was killed in an airplane crash during the war, had been the universal favorite.

"Pity," he said. "He was a fine chap."

Our conversations usually dealt with heads of state he had known and about whom he liked to tell anecdotes. "Uncle-an-ecdotes." The old Emperor Franz Josef of Austria, like most heads of European ruling houses, was an uncle. He apparently had difficulty finding manservants to give him his bath at four o'clock in the morning, for at that time they were either asleep or drunk. Franz Josef's day began at 4:00 A.M. and his first audience at six. Windsor sometimes had to pay his respects to him at that ungodly hour, which didn't endear the old gentleman to him.

Another "uncle" was the King of Württemberg, a fat gentleman with a fat wife, whom Windsor had to visit when he was a young man. "After luncheon every day they would drive through Stuttgart, their capital, in the open state carriage, showing themselves to their subjects. I would sit on the jump seat opposite. Uncle kept falling asleep and snoring loudly with his head on the shoulder of his better half. Whenever we passed an officer saluting, my aunt would poke him in the ribs with her elbow, and Uncle would automatically raise his hand to his forehead, snoring away."

One evening, while Windsor, his wife, and Jimmy Donahue were having dinner with us, there was a telephone call. Greta Garbo and her longtime companion, George Schlee, were in the harbor and wanted to know if they could come up. I told the Duke, and to my surprise he became quite animated. "Yes, tell them to come up," he said enthusiastically, "I've always wanted to meet her." The Duchess was equally delighted; she had never met Garbo in person either. Rex jumped into the jeep and drove downhill to pick them up.

It was a historic moment. The two women sat face to face and sized each other up from head to toe. Both knew they were legends of the twentieth century. Looking at them, I thought that life casts people in roles that a good scenario would never assign them. The woman for whom a man would be willing to give up his throne should obviously have been Greta Garbo, forever the world's most beautiful woman, unique and unattainable.

There's no need to have beautiful features in order to be beautiful. It is the overall arrangement and its particular harmony that gives the impression of beauty. But in Greta's case every single feature was not only boldly designed but perfect by itself. Nothing was small in her face. A broad, high forehead, a strong, chiselled nose, a wide mouth, and most impressive of all, enormous dark blue eyes set under eyebrows curved like butterfly wings. When we swam together, she would dive and reappear on the surface with drops of water clinging separately to eyelashes that looked as if they had been purchased at the drugstore. To me, though, the unique quality of her face showed at its best when she was displeased. In Greta's face, even her frown was a thing of beauty.

Yet, there she sat in old blue slacks and a faded blouse, a lonely woman. ("Why haven't I got a husband and children?" she once said, during one of our long walks through the olive groves. "Are you serious?" I asked. "A million men would have been happy to crawl on all fours to the marriage license bureau." "No," she said, "I never met a man I could marry.") And there, next to her, Wallis Windsor in something white and exquisite, with what were probably fabulous jewels around her neck. Greta's brown hair hung straight and shapeless, matted from seawater, around her face. Wallis, of course, traveled with her own hairdresser. The Duchess's voice was decisive and metallic. Greta's was husky, barely audible. Sweden's Queen Christina against America's splendid Nutcracker.

"I'd like to give a party for you aboard the *Sister Ann*," said Wallis benevolently.

"I have no dress," murmured Greta.

"Then it will be an informal party," said Wallis with a glance at her husband, who nodded eagerly. "All right. Tomorrow at eight in the harbor."

The general conversation languished. Greta never contributed much anyway, Schlee did his Russian best, Jimmy wasn't in form. And yet Wallis had brought up a subject that ought to have interested all actors and actresses.

"Who will portray us on the screen when the time comes?" she asked. "Because there certainly will be a film about us, won't there?"

No doubt.

"Well, then, who will play us? What do you think?"

We didn't know; we hesitated. This was slippery ground.

"My part is easy to cast," said Wallis, "because they won't show me as I was, forty years old and God knows no beauty. They'll choose some curly blond mooncalf or a vamp à la Theda Bara with a long cigarette holder, to make our story plausible."

One of us said, "Whom would you choose, if it were up to you?"

"Katharine Hepburn," said the Duchess without hesitation.

"And to play the Duke?"

Wallis didn't answer. But Windsor nodded politely in Rex's direction and said: "I think perhaps you would be the best choice."

Rex pulled hard at his nose and muttered something gratified, if inaudible.

That subject having been laid to rest, what next? I had something in reserve in case the silence threatened to become deafening.

"Duchess, who was the most fascinating man you ever met? Present company excepted."

Wallis thought for a few seconds, then broke the expectant silence during which Windsor, too, had been watching his wife with curiosity.

"Kemal Ataturk," she said firmly.

We looked at her in awe. We didn't move in the same circles as the father of the modern Republic of Turkey. Windsor smiled.

"Now just in case anyone might get the wrong impression, I met Ataturk for the first and last time on the Mediterranean cruise the

Duke and I took in 1935," said Wallis slowly. "They called him 'the Gray Wolf.' His hair was gray and so were his eyes, and he always dressed in gray. He was certainly a wolf, wasn't he, David?"

Windsor nodded affectionately. "A dangerous man."

"Yes," said Wallis, and I had the feeling she meant something else.

That evening, too, drew to a close. George and Greta wanted to walk down to the harbor. Rex helped the Windsors into our dirty old jeep.

"Don't you ever have the seats recovered?" said Wallis reproachfully to me, settling gingerly in her white dress on the lumpy back seat as if she were about to sit on a raw egg. After a little encouragement, the motor started. Windsor, next to Rex, held on to the windshield, and the jeep tottered in fits and starts down the hill and through the olive grove toward the harbor.

Next day we collected Greta and Schlee from their yacht, which was tied up at night at the farthest, stinkingest end of the harbor, where they hoped, in vain as usual, to escape notice. Her entire life was devoted to finding some way to spend her days unrecognized and anonymous, as other people do. The harder she tried, the more persistently the press and the general public pursued her. Garbo hadn't made a picture in twenty years, but people still felt the urge to stare as closely as possible into her face. The rented yacht could dock only at night. During the day it drifted half a mile or so from shore, the deck shielded by canvas awnings, as though they were expecting a cloudburst. Photographers and reporters circled the yacht in rowboats and dinghies.

We went out to Greta's yacht in our small Cris-Craft, the *Lilli-Maria*, and quickly climbed aboard by the ladder their sailors lowered for us. Greta and Schlee were sitting, somewhat cramped, under the awnings. "Maybe if you'd pose just once for the photographers," I said, "give them five minutes, perhaps they'll leave you alone."

A cross Swedish frown appeared between Greta's eyebrows. "No use," she said. "They won't go away. I've tried everything." So we all sat under the canvas and sweated. From time to time I peeped through a crack to see whether the boats had finally given up. There were only a few left, their occupants green in the face, because the sea was rising. "Won't be long now," said Schlee, the voice of experience.

We waited. I wanted to wash my hands and climbed down the narrow stairs to the cabin. Looking for Greta's bathroom, I went into the first one on the right, attracted by all kinds of pleasant smells. The glass shelves were loaded with bottles of cologne and perfume, and there were soaps of all colors, bath salts, and oil beside the tub—and an electric razor. Wrong one, I thought, this is George's bathroom. I tried the opposite one. This was Greta's all right; her swimsuit was hanging on a hook. Otherwise the room was practically bare: a toothbrush, a comb with a couple of teeth missing, half a bar of Lux soap.

When I got back on deck, the last dinghy had disappeared. We all climbed into our motorboat and dashed back to the dock at top speed, trying in vain to tie up between two strange yachts without being recognized. The photographers were triumphantly waiting for us, surrounded by a crowd of people. Greta realized that it was hopeless, and climbed stony-faced behind me up the steps to the dock. At the top the crowd was waiting.

For the first time in my life, I was physically afraid. I thought that any minute I would be crushed, smothered, or at best thrown into the water. The furious jostling of the people at the back thrust those in front hard up against us, and we couldn't give way, for there was nothing behind us, just boats and water a few feet below. Fortunately the photographers at the front of the crowd were as badly off as we were; they were being pushed into us and thus couldn't take any pictures. They had a hard enough time protecting their cameras. "*La Divina!*" yelled the frenzied crowd, surging forward. A minute more and we'd have all been in the water, with the photographers and the fans on top of us. Schlee had his arm around Greta, Rex was punching anyone within reach—but the rescue came from the photographers, who hit out at the crowd with their tripods, yelling wildly in Italian. Finally we made an opening and fought our way through to the jeep, kicking anyone who got in the way. For once, the jeep started immediately and we roared off, panting and completely unnerved.

It was much worse than I had imagined it. "I only know the rear entrances of the hotels I stay in," Greta had once said to me. "I always have to climb over garbage cans and hampers full of dirty linen and sneak up to my room on foot or in the service elevator." She had tried everything to be able to spend at least her holidays in peace. When Garbo-hunting was at its height and she was travelling in Italy for the first time with Leopold Stokowski, she was advised to come to a gentleman's agreement with the press: she would meet them for an hour, be interviewed, and pose without dark glasses, in return for a few days' peace in Venice. The reporters enthusiastically accepted, both sides gave their word of honor, and Greta patiently answered questions and posed for pictures. When she said good-bye to them an hour later and left the hotel, on foot, the laughing, howling horde of photographers pursued her just as before.

When the news leaked out that she was coming to visit us in Portofino, the post office engaged extra mail carriers to stagger up the steep path to our house with hampers of letters and packages. "What shall I do with them?" I asked her.

She didn't even glance at the pile of baskets in the entrance hall. "Throw them in the sea," she said.

"But the packages. They're marked 'Gift' and they've all got return addresses."

"Throw them in the sea."

Up at our house she was safe. Only the jeep could negotiate the path, and a high wire fence kept mountain climbers at a distance. We spent the days on the terrace, chatted, sat quietly in the sun, or went for Greta's beloved walks in the olive groves behind the house. Her daily walks were her religion; she withered when she was deprived of them. I once collected her from Onassis's giant boat and she moaned, "It is too small! I cannot go for my walks!"

For years she had lived in New York, because that was the one place where she was left more or less in peace. There she could take her regular morning walk in Central Park, though always disguised in an old hat and raincoat and dark glasses. The story goes that when she asked Stokowski to come with her, the Maestro said in astonishment, "But I have rehearsals every morning with the New York Philharmonic."

"Cancel them," said Greta.

We were expected aboard the *Sister Ann* at eight o'clock. That meant eight—not a minute later. I did my usual Prussian punctuality act and reminded everybody several times that it was time to get out of swimsuits and into slacks. No response. Everybody was on his third martini and feeling no pain.

By the time we finally got into the jeep it was half past eight. During the few minutes it took us to tear down to the harbor, we discussed possible excuses, couldn't find one, laughed a lot, and finally decided on the old story that the jeep wouldn't start.

Five minutes later we arrived, breathless, at the dock. The *Sister Ann* was all lit up. Crowds of people were surging around the barrier at the dock entrance, but Windsor had notified the harbor police and they saw to it that we got through safely. We made for the yacht's little saloon, hoping to mingle with the other guests without being noticed. But there were hardly any other guests. Apart from the hosts, who were sitting stiffly side by side on the sofa, there was only an elderly American couple, a former senator and his wife, who were morosely jiggling the ice in their drinks. Wallis's face was one dark thundercloud.

I bobbed to the Duke and murmured, "The jeep, sir . . . the damned thing wouldn't . . ."

But Wallis wasn't interested. "It's Jimmy," she said coldly, interrupting my stutterings. "He went ashore this afternoon and he's not back yet. He knows perfectly well that the Duke insists on punctuality. It's simply a question of manners, that's all."

At that moment, Jimmy appeared in the doorway, helloing exuberantly in all directions, his arms full of gardenias, which he deposited grandly on the Duchess's lap by way of a peace offering. She swept them to the floor, stood up, and said, "Do you know what time it is?"

Jimmy brought his wristwatch to within an inch of his eyes. "Well, well, what do you know!" he exclaimed. "I'll be damned!"

Head high, Wallis strode past him to the quarterdeck. The Duke, the two Americans, the four of us, and Jimmy followed in single file.

The quarterdeck, where the festive table had been laid, could not be hidden from the people on the dock. We were in full view, though at a distance of some fifty feet. I didn't quite understand the arrangement. On the one hand, the Windsors had called upon the harbor police to protect their privacy; on the other hand, all the yacht's lights were on, and we were spotlighted as if we were on stage, accompanied by an orchestra of subdued buzzing provided by the spectators.

I sat between Windsor and Jimmy, and during the cold soup Windsor and I engaged in a "German lesson" on absorbing subjects like the weather, the swimming, and his three pugs. Gradually, however, we became aware of what was going on at the rest of the table. The senator appeared to be holding forth in what amounted to a monologue, since Wallis was gazing absently out to sea, Schlee and Greta were not interested, and Rex was in a brown study over his soup plate. Not only was the senator drunk, he was stubbornly and aggressively carrying on about his pet aversion, the British, who "over and over again had sacrificed innocent American boys to save their empire." Perhaps he was plastered enough to believe that Windsor shared this hostility toward his former subjects, which was a fatal mistake. The Duke lived abroad, but he felt no bitterness, let alone enmity.

The senator allowed his glass to be refilled. His face was already a dull red. Rex's was red, too, but for a different reason. Every critical remark about England affected him personally, and he stopped eating and looked murderously at the senator, who had just gotten onto the subject of the old destroyers that Roosevelt had sent to aid Churchill even before America entered the war. "That's where it began," he croaked, and I suddenly realized that we were dealing with a die-hard isolationist. "We've always had to pull the chestnuts out of the fire for the British. And what do we get out of it, I ask you? What do we get out of it?"

"The man's drunk, sir," I said quietly in German. "He doesn't know what he's saying."

"That's all right," said Windsor calmly. "These things happen. I just don't listen."

But Rex was listening and about to explode.

I turned to Jimmy, who was engrossed in modeling a battalion of little bread men, and whispered, "Jimmy, I beg you, change the subject this minute or something terrible is going to happen."

Jimmy nodded. "Say, fellows," he called across the table, forcibly interrupting the senator's tirade, "who's coming to San Fruttuoso with me tomorrow? I hear you can get marvelous lobsters there, right out of the sea."

The senator looked at Jimmy as if he were a lobster himself. He'd just got going on Roosevelt, his archenemy, and how he'd been bribed by the British capitalists.

"Oh, well," said Jimmy, smiling at me, "we'll have to try something else." He stood up, pushed back his chair, strolled over to the rail, and casually vaulted over it into the water.

"Hurrah!" yelled the crowd on the dock, which had followed his every move with the same fascination we did. We all sat staring at the spot where Jimmy had vanished, as if he might reappear there, although we had plainly heard the loud splash when he hit the water some fifteen feet below. The crowd, howling with delight and shouting "Bravo," probably saw him surface and swim back to the dock. We couldn't see a thing, because we remained seated.

Windsor was the first to recover his speech. He pointed to the empty seat beside me and said, "But there must be some protocol . . . !"

There sat the ex-King of England, his index finger raised like a suspended question mark. He had been brought up differently from ordinary mortals. In an interview shortly before his death, he said with disarming frankness, "I have never in my life picked anything up. When I take off my clothes, I simply drop them on the floor. I know there is always somebody behind me to pick them up." He was used to consulting an imaginary master of ceremonies, the chief of protocol, about all day-to-day events, but there was probably no regulation covering appropriate behavior when a guest jumped overboard in his dinner jacket.

No one moved. Even the German lesson had no guidance to offer. I glanced at Wallis. Her jaws were clenched and her nose white with shock and anger. "That boy has no manners," she finally managed to say. "I'd like to ask you all not to speak to him when he comes back. We'll act as if nothing's happened."

The shouting on shore suddenly redoubled. ("Three cheers for the brave swimmer!" "The company too hot for you, eh?") Jimmy must have been climbing out of the water. I could imagine what he looked like; the harbor was filthy, full of refuse, dead rats, and condoms. Before he jumped in, he'd been wearing an immaculate midnight blue velvet dinner jacket over a pleated evening shirt, patent leather pumps, and diamond cuff links.

The senator was the only person who hadn't taken Jimmy's departure in. His wineglass was refilled and he was on the warpath again, with Roosevelt still the target. "A Bolshevik in disguise," he trumpeted, "America's ruination, destruction, perdition . . ."

Nobody contradicted him, because nobody was listening. The Duchess signaled to the steward, who distractedly handed the dishes around again, although our plates were still full. Suddenly Wallis said loudly and rudely, right into the senator's lecture, "Of course it's all his mother's fault. It's all Jessie Donahue's fault. On the one hand she pampers him, and on the other she keeps him so short of money that he doesn't care what—"

"And when he was elected for the third time . . ." said the senator.

"Elected?" said Greta in confusion. "Jimmy was elected?"

The senator demolished her with one look, but before he could get going on Roosevelt's fourth term, Jimmy appeared in the saloon doorway. He nodded pleasantly all round, as though he were seeing us for the first time that night, and walked to his chair. His hair was still dripping wet, but he had changed into a dark green velvet dinner jacket and a no less immaculate shirt.

"Well?" he said to me quite loudly. "Did it help? Are we on a different subject now?"

As if on cue, the senator bellowed, "Pearl Harbor would never have happened if Britain hadn't been in such a mess. To this day I'm convinced—and I wasn't the only one in the Senate who thought that way—that Churchill and Beaverbrook and the whole gang bribed the Japanese."

"Oh, for God's sake!" said Jimmy, patting me consolingly on the shoulder. "We'll just have to try again." He stood up and made for the rail once more. This time, however, he didn't bring off his vault quite so elegantly, because Greta had jumped up and was hanging onto his trouser leg. "Don't! Don't!" she pleaded. "Not again! You'll get sick. Stop! Ouch!"

He had given her a vigorous push, knocking her backwards onto the deck. Then he jumped over the rail, laughing, and disappeared into the black night.

Splash! The people on the dock broke into frenzied cheering, "Bravo! Hurrah!" or simply aboriginal screams of delight.

That did it. No hope of rescuing the party. Though the least concerned guest, the Russian George Schlee made a brave try. He stood up, raised his glass a bit too high, and called out, "I propose a toast to the British Empire." Whereupon the senator could do nothing but struggle to his feet and empty his glass, muttering something unintelligible. The rest of us were already standing, glasses raised, repeating passionately, "To the British Empire." It was good to be able to stand up and do something.

Wallis didn't sit down again, so we got no dessert. She went straight back to the saloon, with us trotting behind her. There we stood around, because the coffee wasn't ready and the hosts and Jimmy had disappeared through another door.

"Let's go," said Greta.

"Without saying good-bye?"

"Without."

I felt I should make at least a gesture to cover our retreat and went to look for our hosts. Hearing voices from the library, I knocked and cautiously opened the door. Luckily they hadn't heard me, because all three were absorbed in a passionate "conversation."

I closed the door as noiselessly as possible. Then Schlee, Greta, Rex, and I tiptoed, crouching, down the gangplank and ran to the jeep.

"I need a black coffee," said Greta.

"I need a brandy," said Rex.

And the jeep roared off toward the security of the olive grove.

15

Portofino: Lunch with Helen Keller

❀

WHY DID WE LIVE up there on that rocky path that you could reach only on foot, on a mule, or in a jeep?
When Rex and I struggled up the path for the first time in 1949, it was our first outing on our first day in Portofino, at the beginning of our first vacation in Italy. Everything was overwhelming: the Hotel Splendido high above the blue bay, the palms, the cypresses, the olive trees, the mauve bougainvillea everywhere—Italy, exactly as we had imagined it. The sun beat down on us, and we looked around for a shady place to rest. A few yards higher up was a rocky promontory, and in front of it a little plateau with olive trees. Exhausted, we threw ourselves down under the trees.

When we sat up again and looked about us, our fate was sealed. The view was so extraordinary that neither of us could do anything but stare silently from one side to the other. Far below us on the right lay the blue harbor of Portofino, with its romantic peninsula and the old castle. To our left was the tiny emerald green bay of Paraggi, with its white beach framed by cypresses. Somewhere around here, we decided, we must try to acquire a small plot of land.

"Somewhere around here" turned out to be very close at hand. After stumbling downhill and back to the hotel in a daze, we discovered that the very plateau we had been sitting on was for sale. It belonged to a Contessa Margot Besozzi, who lived even higher up the same path in her Castello Besozzi.

That same evening we went to see the Contessa and bought the plateau. The next year she built our house for us—interior decorating was her hobby—while we were playing on Broadway. The house became a sort of idée fixe in our lives. All year long we marked off the days on the calendars in our New York dressing rooms until June 1, when the Broadway season ended and we could leave for Portofino. ("Don't do that," my dresser Elizabeth said, when she saw me marking the calendar. "You're wishing your life away.")

There was, however, a serpent in our paradise: the path up the cliff. The municipal authorities refused to grant us permission to build a proper road in lieu of the mule track. The only vehicle that could climb the narrow path and negotiate the hairpin turns, the steep incline, and the potholes was an old American Army jeep we had bought in Genoa. It possessed neither springs nor brakes. When you wanted to stop, you went into reverse and backed up against something. But it was indestructible, and you could rely on it in all weathers.

One day Margot Besozzi, who of necessity also owned a jeep, called to say that her cousin had arrived with a companion and that her own jeep had conked out. Would I mind going to fetch the two old ladies in ours? They were at the Hotel Splendido.

Whom should I ask for at the hotel?

"Miss Helen Keller."

"Who?"

"Miss Helen Keller, K-e-l-l . . ."

"Margot, you don't mean *Helen Keller?*"

"Of course," she said. "She's my cousin. My maiden name is Keller. Didn't you know?"

I ran into the garage, jumped into the jeep, and raced down the mountain.

I had been twelve years old when my father gave me the book about Helen Keller written by Anne Sullivan, the remarkable woman whom fate had chosen to be the teacher of the blind and deaf child. Anne Sullivan had turned the rebellious, brutish little creature into a civilized member of society by teaching her to speak. I still remembered vividly her description of the first few months of physical battle with the child, until the glorious moment when she held Helen's left hand under a running water tap and the blind, deaf, and up to now dumb little creature made history by stammering out an intelligible word: "Wa-ter."

Over the years I had read about Helen Keller in the newspapers. I knew that Anne Sullivan was no longer with her and that a new companion now accompanied her everywhere. But the few minutes it took me to drive down the hill were not nearly enough to get used to the idea that I was going to meet in person this mythical figure from my early youth.

I backed the jeep up against a bougainvillea-covered wall and presented myself at the hotel as quietly and normally as possible. A tall, buxom, vigorous-looking woman rose from a chair on the hotel terrace to greet me: Polly Thomson, Helen Keller's companion. Yes, Margot Besozzi had just called to say that I would be coming to drive her and Miss Keller up to Castello Besozzi.

A second figure rose slowly from the chair beside her and held out her hand. Helen Keller, then in her seventies, was a slight, white-haired woman with wide-open blue eyes and a shy smile. "How do you do?" she said slowly and a little gutturally. I took her hand, which she was holding too high because she didn't know how tall I was. She was bound to make this mistake with people she was meeting for the first time, but she never made it twice. Later, when we said good-bye, she put her hand firmly into mine at exactly the right level.

The luggage was loaded into the back of the jeep, and I helped the jolly lady, Miss Thomson, to sit beside it, which was easier said than done. The hotel porter lifted Helen Keller's fragile body and set it down on the front seat next to me. Only then did it dawn on me that this was going to be a risky undertaking. The jeep was open; there was nothing you could hold on to properly. How was I to keep the blind old lady from falling out of the rickety old thing when we took a curve, which had to be done at a fast clip because of the angle and the jeep's general condition? I turned to her and said, "Miss Keller, I must prepare you—we're going up a very steep hill. Can you hold tight to this piece of metal on the windshield?"

But she continued to look expectantly straight ahead. Behind me, Miss Thomson said patiently, "She can't hear you, dear, nor see you. I know it's hard to get used to it at first."

I was so ashamed that I stammered like an idiot, trying to explain the problem ahead of us. All the while, Miss Keller never turned her head or seemed puzzled by the delay. She sat motionless, a slight smile on her face, patiently waiting.

Miss Thomson knelt across the luggage and reached for her hand. Rapidly she moved Helen's fingers up, down, and sideways, telling her in blind-deaf language what I had just said.

"I-don't-mind," said Helen, laughing, "I'll-hold-tight."

I took courage, got hold of her hands, and placed them on the piece of metal in front of her. "Okay," she cried gaily, and I switched on the ignition. The jeep started with a jump and Miss Thomson fell off her seat on top of the luggage. I couldn't stop and help her up because of the steep hill, the jeep in first gear, the dangerous curve ahead, and no brakes. We roared upward, my eyes glued to the narrow path, and Miss Thomson helpless as a beetle on its back.

I'd had plenty of passengers in the jeep, and they'd all complained about the lack of springs. No wonder, with all those boulders and potholes, not to mention the hairpin turns through the olive trees, which only partially obscured the precipitous drop that had unnerved quite a few of our guests. Helen was the first passenger who was oblivious to the danger; she was enchanted by the violent jumps and only laughed when she was thrown against my shoulder. When we rounded the first bend, I heard the luggage rumbling about behind me over the unfortunate Miss Thomson, while Helen actually began to sing. "This-is-fun," she warbled happily, bouncing up and down. I got very nervous at one point, when I saw one of the front wheels in midair as we took a curve; I could see the headlines in the papers if that front wheel didn't come to its senses. "Lovely!" cried Helen by my side. We tore past our house at breakneck speed—out of the corner of my eye I saw our gardener, Giuseppe, crossing himself—and onward and upward.

I had no idea how Miss Thomson was doing, for the jeep's fearful roar had long ago drowned out her anguished protests. But I knew that Helen was still next to me. Her thin white hair had come undone and fluttered about her face, and she was enjoying the crazy ride like a child riding up and down on a wooden horse on a merry-go-round.

At last we rounded the last curve between two giant fig trees, and I could see Margot Besozzi and her husband waiting for us at their entrance gate. Helen was lifted out of the jeep and hugged; the luggage was unloaded, and Miss Thomson upended and dusted off. She turned out to be a gallant old trout and, though bruised and shaken, refused to go and lie down. She knew that without her, Helen would indeed be blind and deaf. (When Anne Sullivan wanted to get married, she postponed the wedding for years in order to find and train the right person to replace her, because without another person to guide and "speak" to her and translate other people's conversation and questions, Helen had no life of her own.)

I was invited to lunch. While the two old ladies were being shown to their rooms to freshen up, Margot Besozzi told me about her cousin and her life. Helen, of course, knew nothing of the average woman's fate—marriage, children, career—but there was at least one compensation: she was famous the world over, and in every civilized country the great and the renowned were eager to meet her and do something for her. Heads of state, scholars, and artists vied to receive her, and she had travelled all over the world to satisfy her burning curiosity. "But don't forget," said Margot, "all she really notices is a change of smell. Whether she's here or in New York or in India, she sits in a black, silent hole."

Arm in arm, casually, as if they just happened to be fond of each other, the two old ladies walked through the garden toward the terrace, where we were waiting for them.

"That must be wisteria," said Helen, "and masses of it, too. I recognize the scent."

I went to pick a large bunch of the blossoms, which surrounded the terrace, and laid it in her lap. "I knew it!" she cried happily, touching them. "What else is there in the garden?"

Like a fool, I began, "Well, there are gardenias and . . . " but I stopped when I saw Miss Thomson quickly look around and then, discreetly and incredibly fast, move Helen's fingers up and down in sign language.

Of course Helen's diction was not quite normal. She spoke haltingly, like someone who has had a stroke, and her consonants were slow and labored. She turned to me, looking directly at me because she had sensed where I was sitting. "You know, we're on the way to Florence to see Michelangelo's David. I'm so thrilled. I've always wanted to see it."

Mystified, I looked at Miss Thomson, who nodded. "It's true," she said. "The Italian government has had a scaffolding erected around the statue so that Helen can climb up and touch it. That's what she calls 'seeing.' We often go to the theater in New York, and I tell her what's going on on stage and describe the actors. Sometimes we go backstage, too, so that she can 'see' the sets and the actors. Then she goes home, feeling that she's really witnessed the performance."

All the time we were talking, Helen sat and waited. Now and then, when our conversation went on too long, I saw her thin fingers take her friend's hand inquiringly, never impatiently.

Luncheon was served on the terrace by a servant wearing white cotton gloves. Helen was led to her chair, and I watched her "see" her place setting. Quick as lightning, her hands moved over the objects on the table—plate, glass, silverware—memorizing where they were. Never once during the meal did she grope about, but reached out casually and firmly like the rest of us.

Conversation during the meal was difficult. Since she didn't know whether anyone else was speaking, Helen would suddenly ask a question in the middle of somebody else's sentence, bringing the conversation to a halt. Miss Thomson, next to her, would stop eating and translate the answer into Helen's hand. Nonetheless I had the feeling that Helen sensed changes in the atmosphere and was sensitive to the vibrations of objects around her. She sometimes went to concerts in New York and would sit there, flooded by a sense of well-being, while the pianist or cellist played.

After lunch we stayed on the shady terrace, surrounded by trailing clusters of wisteria like a thick mauve curtain, the sun below us glittering on the sea. Helen sat in the usual way, head raised slightly as though listening to something, her sightless blue eyes wide open. Her face, although an old lady's face, had something of a schoolgirl's innocence. It was a face that had not experienced, had not been exposed, had not lived. Whatever suffering must have tormented her—and might still torment her, for all I knew—her face showed no trace of it. It was an isolated face, a saintly face.

I asked her, through her friend, what else she wanted to see in Italy, adding that I hoped I wasn't tiring her with all my questions. "Tiring me?" she said, and laughed. "Have you ever heard of a woman getting tired talking?"

Then she slowly mapped out her Italian journey—not her first, of course, all the places she wanted to visit and the people she would meet. Incredibly, she spoke French quite well and could make herself understood in German and Italian. Sculpture was, naturally, her favorite form of art, because she could touch it and experience it firsthand. "There's still so much I'd like to see," she said, "so much to learn. And death is just around the corner. Not that that worries me. On the contrary."

"Do you believe in life after death?" I asked.

"Most certainly," she said emphatically. "It is no more than passing from one room into another."

We sat in silence. The heat and the heavy scent of the flowers were making us sleepy.

Suddenly, Helen spoke again. Slowly and very distinctly she said, "But there's a difference for me, you know. Because in that other —room—I shall be able to see."

16

A Stage Couple

❀

THE 1950s were the last decade of the old Broadway tradition. New York loved its theater as no other city in the world did, passionately and jealously, like a bridegroom. Every premiere was a wedding night.

Those were the days when two individuals, the drama critics of the *New York Times* (Brooks Atkinson) and the *Herald Tribune* (Walter Kerr), could make or break a production, just as the Roman emperors could determine by a movement of the thumb whether a gladiator was to live or die. Both men were incorruptible and unprejudiced. There still existed five other New York dailies, three of them evening papers, but their critics were less influential. Sometimes they ganged up on the big two. The result depended on the type of play; a musical, for instance, could keep going if the five minor critics enjoyed it, even if the *Times* and the *Tribune* tore it to pieces. But no play with any claim to serious content had a chance if the big men turned thumbs down. This meant a quick death, usually by the first weekend. An interesting situation arose when the *Times* and the *Tribune* disagreed, but this happened rarely. When it did, the other five sages suddenly became very important.

In Europe the influence of newspaper critics is not nearly so crucial. A star or a popular playwright can fill a theater however much the critics may carp. But when Broadway still reigned supreme, the critic functioned as a sort of taster to the eight million inhabitants of New York City. If he relished what was served up, the line formed the next morning at the box office. If, on the other hand, he found it indigestible, reservations already made would not be picked up. Thus while there was more rejoicing over a hit in New York than in any other city, the risk was proportionately higher.

For the actor, there were three crucial moments on opening night. The first would come as soon as the final curtain fell. Applause comes in different degrees of intensity: "storms," "clapping," or "scattered bursts." That is the first clue. The second would follow immediately, in the dressing room. The dressing-room door is the index: it can be "besieged" by crowds of ecstatic well-wishers; it can "open repeatedly" to admit an orderly procession of friends and acquaintances; or it can remain virtually closed, admitting only an occasional stray relative or courageous friend, who goes into raptures over the "beautiful costumes." The actor knows what lies ahead but continues to hope. The third, and decisive, moment would come later, at 12:30 A.M. You waited at either a party or a restaurant, because at 12:30 the early edition of the *Times* and *Tribune* appeared, specially delivered to the established rendezvous—the streetlamp outside Sardi's. At 12:29 taxis would draw up and the restaurant door would open. You stood shamelessly under the light and read the verdict, no matter who was watching or reading over your shoulder. The drudgery, the nightmares, and the panic of the last few months were now laid to rest, for better or worse, in two columns of printer's ink.

Rex as Henry the Eighth and I as Cleopatra had riffled through the papers outside Sardi's with equally trembling hands and devoured with equally blissful sighs the reviews of the two formidable critics. We had both been lucky; both shows played to packed houses for a season. When I put away Cleopatra's woolly black wig for the last time, and Rex finally hung up Henry's plumed hat, came the unavoidable question, What now?

For weeks we had been reading scripts. Separately. We had to be careful. Our success could have been a fluke. Our second Broadway season would tell. Doggedly, day after day, we read scripts addressed to Mr. H..or Miss P. and found nothing acceptable.

One day a fat envelope arrived addressed to me. The play was called *Bell, Book and Candle*. The author, John van Druten, had for years been one of the most successful dramatists in the Anglo-American theater. I read the play eagerly—and was deeply disappointed. I didn't understand it. Was the plot supposed to be realistic, or was it some kind of symbolism? My part was a witch, a present-day witch, who lays spells on people around her through her familiar, a Siamese cat. What nonsense. Besides, the male role was so colorless that no decent actor had as yet been willing to consider it.

"Let me have a look," said Rex. "Van Druten doesn't write nonsense."

Two hours later he reappeared, pulling his nose. "You've got to do this," he said. "It can't miss. And I'll play the man. I can make something of him."

The rehearsals of *Bell, Book and Candle* were long and difficult for me. Not that acting with Rex gave me any trouble; we'd appeared together in England, both on the stage and before the camera. But *Bell, Book and Candle* was a comedy, and comedy had never been my long suit. Laughter is a matter of nationality. English humor is especially tricky, because it rests on the famous throwaway technique, very foreign to foreigners. You must throw your lines away without throwing them in the ash can, be cool but not cold, speak casually but not without a certain tension. Above all, you have to "nurse your inner bubble," as Rex put it.

He could do all those things to perfection. Not for nothing had he toured the English provinces as a youth for ten long years, playing the great comedy roles that the stars played in the West End of London. Timing had become second nature to him, whereas I panicked before every laugh for fear it wouldn't come. During the tryout on tour, I felt like running to the footlights before every one of my laughs and telling the audience, "Watch out now! Here it comes!"

Rex could get a laugh with his back turned to the audience as easily as picking an apple from a tree. He was able to squeeze out some that even the author hadn't known about. Even while he was reading the script for the first time, he could mark the laughs on every page.

"How do you know there's a laugh there?" I asked in despair.

"Because it's there."

"But he only says, 'Where's the light switch?' What's funny about that?"

"Because he shouts it first at the top of his voice, and then repeats it full of false charm. That's funny."

Aha!

The first requisite of the comedy actor is the ability to make even anger seem funny. In comedy neither rage nor grief must ever be taken at face value, although they must be played straight.

Aha!

"Aha!" became my leitmotif during rehearsals and during the four weeks of tryouts before we opened in New York.

I felt like getting myself a hearing aid in the hope of improving my "ear." My ears had to become familiar with completely new vibrations. I learned that a fraction of a second can be decisive in producing or killing a laugh. No one can teach you this, but unless you are tone-deaf, you can develop an ear for timing.

I learned too that a surefire laugh, which has rung out night after night at a particular line, may for no apparent reason go AWOL. The worst thing you can do is go after it by speaking louder or serving it up. If you do that, it's gone for good. Instead, you have to force yourself to act as if there had never been a laugh at that place and pass on, even though it breaks your heart. And lo and behold, one evening there it is again, fat and juicy, and you go home walking on air.

The most important thing is to keep it light, light, light as a feather which you could effortlessly blow across the stage. On opening nights that is almost impossible, because you're shaking from head to foot, your throat is dry, and you can hardly hear the cues for nervousness. Rex, too, was always better on the second night.

In this play I had an additional problem—the Siamese cat, Pyewacket, Pye for short. During rehearsals I had tried to get into her good graces by feeding her, taking her home with me, playing with her—all to no avail. She looked at me slyly with her pale blue eyes and clawed at my nylons. But she had talent, everyone agreed on that. When the curtain went up on the first act, I was discovered sitting in the twilight in front of the fire, with the cat on my knee, talking to her. Sometimes Pyewacket would raise her head and meow loudly—she did it on opening night—and the delighted audience was sure she was doing it on cue. They had no idea how difficult it was to hold her quietly on my lap when she wanted to get down. The assistant stage manager, who was responsible for handing Pye to me at the last moment before the curtain went up, wore leather gloves, because she hated him. We had an understudy for Pye, another Siamese (untalented), in case Pye ever became unmanageable. And the understudy had an understudy—and that one was stuffed, a fact that I liked to rub in to Pye. But it had no effect; she was a star and she was difficult.

On our opening night in New York, she behaved with extraordinary perception. The curtain went up with its usual sudden, heart-stopping rustle, and my knees trembled so violently that Pye was jogging up and down. Instead of sinking her claws in my thighs, as I fully expected her to do, she turned her head around and looked at me with an expression of such naked amazement on her malevolent little cat face that I almost burst out laughing and my knees stopped shaking.

Our four-week tryout and my efforts to learn to "hear" had not been in vain, and I didn't have to worry about my laughs. The play's witchcraft bewitched the audience from the very beginning. The applause at the end came in "storms," the dressing-room door was "besieged," and at 12:30 A.M. we read the unanimous verdict of the two dictators: a delightful comedy in which the Harrison-Palmer team treats us to a *pas de deux;* and so on.

The *pas de deux,* in several other plays, lasted another four years. We became a stage couple, something particularly close to the heart of the New York public. Our immediate predecessors and contemporaries were the famous Lunts, Alfred Lunt and Lynn Fontanne, married on and off stage as far back as anyone could remember. The Lunts specialized in "daring" love scenes and physical intimacies that would be considered tame today. For example, during a scene in which Alfred stretched out on a sofa and Lynn took off his shoes, he stroked her face with his feet—in socks, of course, but still a caress that might not have been quite so acceptable night after night from just any leading man to the puritanical American public. Once when the curtain fell on a similar scene, an old lady in the audience was heard to remark with relief to her elderly friend, "How nice to know that they're married!"

A few months after *Bell, Book and Candle* opened, we received an embarrassed call from our New York agent. He hemmed and hawed, and after a lot of beating about the bush, came out with an extraordinary bit of news from his Hollywood office: Stanley Kramer, an independent producer, wanted to know whether we would make a picture for him when the Broadway season ended. Jan de Hartog's *The Four Poster*.

Was the picture to be made in New York? we asked, amazed. Not at all. In Hollywood.

A recent demonstration of Hollywood's hatred—purely personal and therefore undiminished—had shown us that they were not ready to let bygones be bygones. The two trade papers, *Variety* and the *Hollywood Reporter*, regularly carry reports of the New York theater's successes and failures. They had passed over our play in silence. Whereupon Irene Selznick, our producer, bought two full advertising pages right in the center of both papers and used them to reproduce our *New York Times* and *Herald Tribune* reviews in full. So they knew about us in Hollywood, whether they wanted to or not.

We considered. Should we or shouldn't we? The prospect of landing at the Los Angeles airport and finding ourselves once again at the mercy of a mob of reporters wasn't appealing. But could we afford to refuse? We were still paying off our back taxes in weekly installments.

We accepted. It was still winter. The season was in full swing. Summer and Hollywood seemed far away.

Appearing in a Broadway show means six evening performances a week plus two matinees. On those two days you can't hope to do anything except go to the theater and survive. Between shows you sleep in your dressing room. By Saturday evening, the last performance of the week, you're ready to collapse, especially if your part is a long one, like mine in *Bell, Book and Candle*. The play ran for two and a half hours, and I was on stage continuously the entire evening, except for a period of one minute and twenty seconds during which Rex carried on a much-applauded telephone conversation, solo. I spent that minute and twenty seconds sitting on a chair placed in the wings for this purpose, eyes closed, catching my breath. Toward the end of the week, my "inner" performance registered only one impulse: when can I sit down or lean against something?

Nor were the eight weekly shows the end of it. You must pay tribute for a hit in the form of charity benefits, either on Sunday or after midnight on weekdays—benefits for the orphaned children of actors, homes for the aged, or victims of every form of disaster. Every leading actor without exception was expected to devote himself to one specific charity, not just through financial contributions but through active personal effort. No one ever complained, because unfortunately there was a wide range of choice: polio (the vaccine hadn't yet been discovered), arteriosclerosis, mental retardation, the blind, the deaf, and the dumb.

A Broadway actor's weekly schedule leaves him no free time. You sleep late, not because you're lazy but because you go to bed late, unavoidable because you can't eat until after the show. If your voice is to carry to the back row of the top balcony in those huge theaters, your stomach must be as empty as a singer's. "After the show" means midnight at the earliest. It takes that long to receive visitors and remove your makeup. Then comes your one hour of real relaxation. The performance, which you've been dreading all day consciously or unconsciously, is over. Now you can finally eat and, if you can, drink. Drink a lot. You're never home before two in the morning.

Actresses have an even harder time. One non-matinee day has to be reserved for the hairdresser. And, more important than anything else, you want to spend some time every day with your child. It's bad enough that he has been trained to tiptoe past his parents' bedroom door on his way to school in the morning.

Sheer madness, therefore, to undertake a fifteen-minute television show of my own at seven o'clock every Thursday evening. Which forced me to race to the theater like a maniac and left me exactly twenty minutes to make up, dress, and get Pye settled on my lap. I had only one stipulation when I signed my contract with NBC: I would write my own scripts and be free in my choice of topics. As long as I stayed within the bounds of decency, I was not even required to submit my scripts for approval.

Rex disapproved. The entire idea was repugnant to him. A talk show? "What in God's name do you want to bore them with for fully fifteen minutes?" "With all the things that don't bore me!" "God help us!" said Rex.

However, the response of the public and the critics to this show exceeded all expectations. One TV critic wrote that he would like to take a huge sleeping pill, sleep all week, and only wake up for a quarter of an hour at five minutes to seven every Thursday evening.

My themes were exclusively European. I told the Americans about everything under the sun that interested me. About Schliemann, for instance (not so much about the excavations but about the extraordinary man and his extraordinary marriage); about Duse (not about her triumphs but about her strange ethics and her death in Pittsburgh); about Sarah Bernhardt (and her passion for endless, almost clinical death scenes); about Sibelius (and Finnish saunas); about Shaw (and his love for the actress Ellen Terry, whom he met only once); and so on for twenty-six Thursdays. A lot of work, but I enjoyed it.

Once I talked about Plato and his "Symposium." About his idea that there were originally three types of human beings with two of everything we have, i.e., two heads, four arms, and four legs: double man, double woman, and man-woman. Since their physical strength was also double, the gods decided to destroy them, but in the end Zeus generously granted them a last chance by splitting them in half, thus creating single man and single woman, as we are today. At this point I paused and said, straight-faced, "And that, ladies and gentlemen, explains man's eternal loneliness. We are all no more than halves, forever longing for the other—[*pause*]—half."

A bombshell for that day and age. Nicely packaged, but nevertheless a bombshell.

I caught it later from the network. My consolation prize: a letter written by a Capuchin friar from his monastery in Canada, saying that after watching my program he finally understood his problem.

One day our agent telephoned again and hemmed and hawed even more than the first time. Was I alone? Yes, why? Well . . . it was kind of embarrassing, but Kramer had just called. The news that we were going to make a picture in Hollywood had made him feel as if he were "sitting on a volcano." He never thought it would be this bad. The agent was to find out "tactfully" whether I would be willing to make *The Four Poster* with somebody other than Rex. He might be able to get away with me, but with Rex—never. Would I . . . ? I wouldn't.

There was a third call, which Rex answered. It was about a letter the agency in Hollywood had been kind enough to draft for us. They hoped we'd sign and mail it.

A letter to whom?

To Louella Parsons.

Who?

Louella Parsons. Because we'd so mortally offended her when Rex called her an alcoholic illiterate. That had wounded her to the quick, and we'd have to make amends.

"Read it to me," said Rex. He listened for quite a while without a word, but his face grew redder and redder. Then he said something unprintable but absolutely on the nose, and hung up.

After that all was quiet. Even peaceful, paradoxically. All our contractual demands were met, there were courteous telephone conversations to and fro, and the date was set. Winter and spring had gone by all too fast, and June, the end of the season and our contracts, was almost upon us. We had no intention of continuing with *Bell, Book and Candle*, although it still sold out every night.

After our Hollywood caper, Portofino would be waiting! *Bell, Book and Candle* continued without us.

Before we took off for California, all kinds of friends who knew the Hollywood scene sat down with us to brief and instruct and caution us. By the time they were through, we were armed to the teeth.

The plane landed in Los Angeles at daybreak. We peered out the window. The ramp was deserted. We passed through the gate and looked around. Not a soul. We claimed our luggage and came out through the main exit. No sign of life there either. We gave the taxi driver the address of the little house we'd rented on the ocean in Santa Monica and rattled through the empty, early-morning streets. Nobody had recognized us, nobody had even glanced in our direction. Mr. and Mrs. John Doe. Glory be.

17
Carlos

❁

THE HOUSE in Santa Monica was right on the beach. Sand drifted into it, and water, too, on occasion. It was small and comfortable, and if you wanted to stretch your legs, you had only to open the garden gate, which led to the ocean. Early in the morning, before leaving for the studio, and in the evening after shooting was over, I liked to walk barefoot on the wet sand among the dipping, scurrying, and curtseying seabirds. Half a mile to the left and half a mile to the right, breathing deeply all the time, according to my father's advice. He had always breathed deeply when he and my mother went for their daily walk in the woods. He didn't smoke, didn't drink—and died at fifty-seven, almost twenty years ago. What would he have said to us, a man who spoke only German, loved only Germany, saw everything from the German point of view? My mother had lived in England for years now; it had become her home. We three were married to Englishmen. He would have had seven grandchildren, not one of whom spoke a single word of German. He wouldn't have been able to talk to them. And they, in turn, had no feeling that there ever had been a grandfather who had lived in Berlin. When Carey was twelve years old, he spent his holidays there with my mother and me. One evening, on my return from the studio, I asked him what he had been doing during the day. "Well," he said, "we went to visit Granny's husband's grave."

In the early morning and at dusk the beach was deserted. Only the birds, big and small, darted about by the thousands; it was a wonder that one never stepped on them. What would he have said to me if he had seen me there alone, taking my constitutional along the Pacific instead of the Baltic and taking inventory, as he liked to do himself. "You see, *mein Fräulein,*" he would have said, "you should have studied. If not medicine, then something else. Scientific work—that alone is satisfying and enduring, the only thing that can make you truly independent. It's good for you to have to fight. But to struggle afresh every day for something that has no permanence—that kind of fight isn't worthwhile."

Was it worthwhile? The question confronted me more and more. Probably because at long last I had achieved the success I had yearned for. I *had* achieved it, nobody could deny that; but I didn't possess it. You can't possess success.

What was definitely worthwhile was my growing self-confidence, my discriminating ear (at last!), and my independent, critical judgment. Relatively independent, my father would have said with a smile. All in all, *mein Fräulein,* you're a late developer!

Better late than never. Every morning at the studio I had to deliver the goods. There was no time now for experimenting and saying "Aha!" Rex and I were the only actors in this picture. There were no character parts and no supporting roles, not even a dog barking in the background. The schedule allowed twenty-one days for shooting, exactly half the usual number. They expected our teamwork to be perfect, and scheduled accordingly. If the two pariahs had to be rammed down the throat of the Hollywood establishment, let it be done quickly and painlessly, without fuss and without spending too much money.

And that was how it was done. We came relatively cheap, weren't demanding, and gave no trouble. Fellow actors rallied round, of course, entertained us just as they had always done, behaved as though nothing had happened, and never alluded to "it." Actors aren't easily bullied. By the very nature of their profession, they are quite liberal, and they're not apt to join blindly in witch-hunts.

They'll go along if they have to, if it's a question of their livelihood, but they go unwillingly. Those few who persecute out of conviction don't count.

We believed them when they told us that they'd been happy to see Irene Selznick's ads in *Variety* and the *Hollywood Reporter*. And also, of course, the cover of *Life*. *Life* had brought a portrait of the two of us after *Bell, Book and Candle*. (Not without difficulty, because we both had the same "good" profile—the left one—and neither of us wanted to turn the worse cheek on such an occasion. The result was a medallion picture of two left profiles.)

Producers and directors, former acquaintances, began to show interest in us, and invitations were delivered by telegram just as in the old days. The press, though, remained adamant; we simply didn't exist. This situation didn't change until several years later and then radically, when Rex scored the hit of the generation with *My Fair Lady*. And when he added insult to injury by winning an Oscar, the trade papers couldn't ignore him, if they wanted to keep on being trade papers, without making themselves ridiculous. So they capitulated.

Very few monster parties were given in Hollywood anymore. That craze had died down. Television was threatening to cut off the movie industry's blood supply. Taxes were a serious consideration, evening clothes shamefully expensive. The one traditional Hollywood reception we were invited to was to be held at Jack Warner's house. My former studio boss was giving an elaborate party (tax deductible) in honor of Charles de Gaulle's brother Pierre.

When we got into the car for the long drive from Santa Monica to Beverly Hills that Saturday evening, I had no premonition of any kind. No inner voice told me anything. As far as I was concerned, this evening, like so many previously, was going to be a long one. We would say hello to about a hundred familiar and perhaps a dozen unfamiliar people. I would fight my usual battle against sleepiness, defending my single gin and tonic against continuous attempts by hired waiters to freshen it up. I'd probably find a quiet sofa somewhere; Jack Warner's house was big enough.

At about the same time, a young man was leaving Topanga

Canyon, not far from our house in Santa Monica, on his way to the same reception. According to Hollywood custom he had asked beforehand whether he should pick anyone up. "Anyone" meant an unescorted lady. He was a bachelor, one of the few, and was used to performing this service. He didn't mind; the ladies were always pretty. This time, however, the answer was no, please come stag. He didn't mind that either; he liked being on his own and was determined to remain so for the rest of his life. He was independent, came and went as he pleased; nobody asked him questions or demanded explanations.

As he drove toward Beverly Hills he had no premonition either; no sixth sense told him anything. He could look forward to an evening of infinite variety. He certainly wouldn't drive home alone.

Jack Warner's house, in keeping with his status, was like a palace surrounded by a tropical park. At the entrance, illuminated by klieg lights, detectives in dinner jackets politely asked for invitation cards, briefly scrutinized your face, and waved you through. The party was being held downstairs in the playroom. Many Hollywood houses have a room of this sort, used for physical exercises during the day and for parties at night. In Jack Warner's house the playroom was more like a ballroom.

As we went in, I noticed a very tall young man standing by himself at the bar, casually watching the door. When he caught sight of me he smiled with satisfaction, as if to say, "Well, here you are at last." I looked at him more closely, found him worth looking at, but felt sure I'd never met him before and turned away to talk to other guests.

Jack Warner had gone to a lot of trouble and had assembled a special harvest of Hollywood's beautiful women. Food was served at a dozen separate supper tables with place cards. I found myself at Pierre de Gaulle's table, where anyone who could "make with the lingo" (French) tried to keep him entertained. He had the same tin-soldier face as his brother, though less regal.

After supper, when everybody was milling around, Rex appeared with the very tall young man who had been standing at the bar and said, "This is Mr. Carlos Thompson. He has something to tell you." And disappeared.

The young man bent down and said slowly and distinctly, as though he were relishing every syllable, "Juanita."

"What did you say?" I asked.

"Juanita," he repeated with enormous satisfaction. "Do you remember her?"

"Of course I do," I said, amazed. "Why?"

Instead of answering, he steered me purposefully into a corner of the playroom, as far away as possible from the dance orchestra. He took his time, pulled up an armchair for me, and placed one beside it for himself.

"What about Juanita?" I said. "You know her? Where is she? How is she?"

The man was difficult; he didn't answer my question. Instead, he asked me one. "When did you last hear from her?"

When, indeed! I couldn't remember. Before the war, long before, in fact. Before I emigrated, before Paris. Yes, I'd had a letter from her in Darmstadt. The Munich State Theater had fired her (Hitler) and she was going back to Buenos Aires. Her family had already returned there. That was the last I'd heard. After that she was blotted out for me, like so many other people, things, and places.

The young man studied me in silence, and I studied him. Suddenly the penny dropped. Carlos Thompson—I'd read somewhere that Hollywood's latest acquisition was an Argentine film star. The words "Argentine dream boat" had stuck in my mind as particularly unpleasant. So this was the dream boat. I'd imagined something quite different. Maybe he'd just shortened sail. Two light, slanting, shrewd eyes looked at me intently.

"I've known you for a long time," he said.

"Where did we meet?"

"Through Juanita. I know you *well*."

Juanita . . . Buenos Aires . . . Argentine dream boat.

Of course.

"You've acted with Juanita in Buenos Aires? When was that?"

"We've acted together many times. We were friends. Not what you're thinking—real friends. Once she dragged me to a movie. 'You've got to come with me,' she said, 'because a friend of mine is

With Fred Astaire
in *The Pleasure of His Company*,
Hollywood,
1960.

A climactic scene
in *The Counterfeit Traitor*:
I am executed
by a Nazi firing squad.

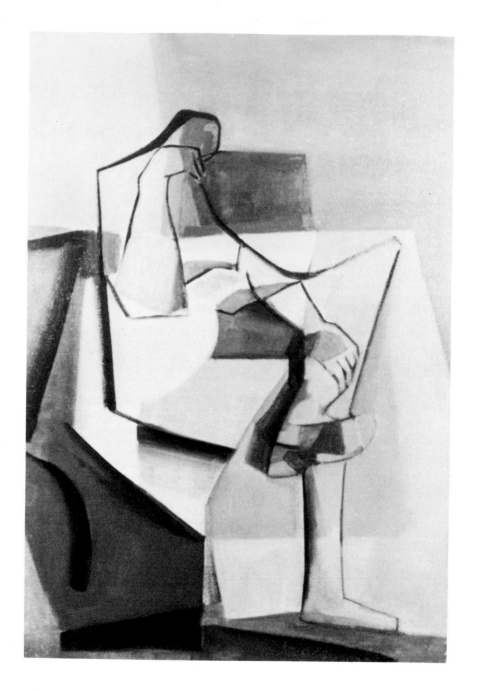

"Sitting Woman."
Exhibition at the
Tooth Gallery in London,
1972.

With Carey on the set,
London, 1967.

First (German) movie
with Carlos:
Between Time and Eternity,
1956.

ew from our terrace
Portofino.

Noël Coward, aged 40,
when I first met him.

With Noël at his house,
"Les Avants," 1972.

house on the top
he hill in Switzerland.

With Carlos
in Switzerland,
1973.

in this picture. She was my friend at the acting school in Berlin.' The movie was called *Body and Soul,* something about boxing, a great picture. But Juanita only had eyes for her friend. 'That's my Lilli,' she kept saying. 'I'd never have recognized her. She used to be a fat, friendly little girl, and just look at her now! Thin as a rake! What made her get so thin? Do you like her?' After the movie we went somewhere to eat, and she began to talk about her years in Berlin, in an unheated apartment at the back of a courtyard, and about her friend Lilli, sixteen years old, who always showed up at acting classes carrying her schoolbooks. Were you really fat?"

"Yes," I said, overwhelmed.

"What became of it?" asked Carlos.

"I don't remember. I suppose I left a pound here and a pound there as souvenirs, first in Paris, then in London—and the rest in Hollywood. Yes, I left the last ounce right here in Hollywood."

Carlos nodded. He had a lot more to tell me. The whole thing was like a fairy tale by Hans Christian Andersen. That evening at the movie had been only the beginning. Little by little Juanita had come out with everything she knew about me, and the more she had told him, the more he had wanted to know. About my family and my life, which had been as strange to her as hers had been to me, about my father's cello, my mother's blue slit eyes and her laugh. He knew the names of my sisters. He knew about our regular three meals a day and about the big yellow lamp over the dining-room table.

The orchestra was making a lot of noise, and the dance floor was getting more and more crowded. The couples edged past us, holding each other close. I watched them without seeing them. Here in Jack Warner's playroom on the Pacific Ocean, someone was talking about my father's cello.

Suddenly Carlos said, "Shall we dance too?" We merged with the milling couples and went through the movements without being able to move. Then we returned to our chairs.

"When I got out of Argentina on a dark and foggy night a year ago and fell into the arms of Hollywood and Metro-Goldwyn-Mayer, I looked everywhere for you, but you weren't living here anymore."

"I live in New York."

"Never mind," he said. "It's happened now. We've finally met."

That was why he had looked at me the way he did as I entered the playroom. Suddenly I could see Juanita in front of me. She was playing Aase in *Peer Gynt,* while we sat on the floor at the dramatic school, holding our breath. When she finished the first monologue —"You're lying, Peer"—we were in tears and couldn't contain our enthusiasm. To bring us back to earth, Frau Grüning asked, "What size shoes do you wear, Juanita?"

Carlos looked at me with a smile. "That's all I know about you."

"It's quite enough. Some of it I'd forgotten long ago."

Then I made him tell me everything he could remember about Juanita. She had scored an immediate triumph on the stage in Buenos Aires and for years had been one of the city's favorite actresses. Then suddenly disaster had struck. Both parents and her sister had died within a year. She wouldn't go along with Perón's dictatorship, distributed anti-Perón leaflets in hallways at night, and suddenly had to leave the country if she wanted to stay out of jail. She fled to Caracas in Venezuela, where she had friends, and earned her living at first by giving German lessons. Again, within a short time she had conquered Caracas and created a theater tradition where there had never been one before. She was now appearing there in all the great roles and had her own dramatic school. She had married, and most important of all, was happy at last. Happy ending.

I nodded numbly. It was too much for one evening at Jack Warner's. Juanita. Buenos Aires. The woman who used to can green tomatoes—dead. Anita, who had talked to Beethoven—dead. Caracas. Juanita married, "happy at last . . ."

We remained in our corner even after we'd finished talking about Juanita. I wanted to know something. Why had he come to Hollywood? Perón? Yes. He too had found it impossible to live under a dictatorship, had refused to play along and had gone to jail for it. Only for a few days, enough to give him a taste. After his release he had still refused to become a party member but was allowed to make films again to support his family. His family? His mother and two sisters; his father was dead. Then suddenly he came out with it: his real passion, his true vocation, was writing. He had published three novels in Argentina. One had received a literary prize; the other two had been banned by both Church and State. Also innumerable short stories and magazine articles. He acted in movies only because he had to; you couldn't support four people by writing. When the chance of a Hollywood contract had come up, he had been up to his neck in hot water politically. Any moment he would be blacklisted, as his father, a famous journalist, had been—Perón's way of exterminating opponents of his regime. The dictator boasted of never having assassinated anyone, and it was true. Under Perón you died a slow, quiet death, even if you were never imprisoned. "I've been here over a year," said Carlos, "but I still can't get used to sitting here, talking, without taking a quick look over my shoulder to see if anybody's listening."

We spent the whole evening in that corner, talking about all kinds of things, intent on leaving an indelible impression on one another. We discovered each other's favorite music, books, and painters. Including Salvador Dali.

"Did you know that there's a portrait of Ann Warner by Dali upstairs in the living room?"

He didn't know. We decided to go and look at it and went up the staircase leading to the big foyer. There stood three imperturbable butlers—two of them certainly hired for the occasion—with arms folded over their chests. I took the young man by the hand and turned to the nearest one.

"Could you please tell us where the Dali is?"

"Second door to the left, madam."

Culture-bound and hand in hand, we opened the second door to the left—and found ourselves in the ladies' toilet.

In the end we discovered the Dali on our own and spent a long time admiring it. Suddenly Carlos unwrapped some more memories of Juanita. Without looking at me, staring only at the portrait, he said that Juanita had told him repeatedly and insistently that if we two ever met we would inevitably fall in love. He had, he said, seen me once before. Six months ago he'd found himself standing next to me in the lobby of the Connaught Hotel in London, but he had resisted the temptation to introduce himself, and Juanita, because I was talking to the hotel manager at the time and appeared to be on edge and annoyed about something and he had felt that it was not the right moment either for him or for me. Even at the risk of never meeting me again. But when he'd seen me entering Jack Warner's playroom a few hours ago, he knew that the time had come.

I laughed with some embarrassment, but he took no notice. Then I looked at him sideways without saying anything, feeling slightly disconcerted. After all, I was married. Actually I knew quite well that I was trying to hold my hands in front of a large hole, but I wasn't yet ready to admit it. The young man seemed to me surprisingly intrepid and sure of himself as he stood there apparently absorbed in the Dali portrait.

When one marries young, one makes compromises without being aware of it. One adjusts without any difficulty to the life-style of the stronger partner. One loves, and nothing else matters. "Day people" live with "night people," the city person finds himself in the country, liking it, and vice versa. A lover of classical music goes to rock concerts night after night, and the jazz fan spends his evenings listening to Bach. This doesn't seem to get on anybody's nerves; on the contrary. "Opposites attract"—but that's true only of young people. If you find a new mate in the second half of your life, the two of you must be of one mind. During my first marriage, it was only love that bridged the gap between our minds.

It took me a long time to get to the point where I was ready to end my marriage. For fifteen years I had single-mindedly and stubbornly invested everything I had in it. For the last few years, I'd been wearing a sturdy pair of blinkers. The only thing that distinguished me from ordinary horses was that I'd put them on myself; I treasured my blinkers and wouldn't allow anyone to take them off. When they were abruptly and roughly removed, I got bogged down in a dark tunnel.

I had known for some time that Rex was "restless." Once I found an unsent telegram in a jacket that was going to the cleaners. The old stock farce situation: a telegram to a beautiful Hungarian lady. (This was a permanent handicap of his; he often forgot to mail his missives. In 1945, for instance, when I was finally about to pack away his RAF uniform, I found in one pocket a letter to his brother-in-law, David Maxwell-Fyfe, congratulating him on his appointment as Home Secretary—two years before.) The thing with the Hungarian lady was of no importance, but it was obvious that he was waiting for something to "come around the corner," as he himself put it. Coming around the corner was Kay Kendall.

Rex had been champing at the bit for some time. He began to hate New York, our little apartment, our Americanized life. "I'm an Englishman. I belong to England." Maybe that was it, I thought; maybe England would cure his restlessness, his constant dissatisfaction. He used to remind me of the German folk song about Hans: "And what he likes he hasn't got and what he's got he doesn't like."

Once we had sold our New York apartment and arrived in England, the timing was diabolical all round. (Or was it fortunate?) We had "broken up" our home, so to speak, had put the furniture in storage, had left Carey in a boarding school, had no home of our own, lived at the Connaught Hotel—when Rex started his first British film after an absence of several years. It was called *The Constant Husband,* and Kay Kendall was one of his leading ladies.

And where was I? I had flown to Munich to make a film, my first German film, my first prolonged absence from Rex. He hated to be alone; he was quite incapable of spending an evening on his own. I was well aware of that but I thought that now, after fifteen years of constant togetherness—perhaps too much of it, since we weren't only living together, we were also working together—it might be a wise move to be apart for a couple of months and find out how much we missed each other.

18
The Return

❀

THE PLANE broke through the clouds and prepared to land.

It was coming from London, and the stewardess spoke English over the intercom. Then she repeated her instructions in German, and I sat up, alarmed. My mother, in the next seat, also stiffened. We looked at each other. Why the fuss? The place we were approaching was Munich. They spoke German in Munich; what else? It was just that we hadn't heard a public announcement in that language in—how many years? This was in 1954. Well, then—more than twenty. We spoke German rarely and badly, mixing it with English expressions which were so much shorter and more to the point. My German vocabulary, my own personal one, had vanished long ago. During the war the language had been all but outlawed anyway, though one day when a bomb fell into our garden, I'm supposed to have spoken German on the phone, according to my mother. I hadn't noticed. The way you automatically return in your dreams to childhood streets and playgrounds.

I was to make a German film in Munich, my first. With a German director and German actors. I had asked my mother if she would come with me. "To Munich?" she had asked in dismay. "Munich! I . . . don't think I could."

She knew Munich only too well. Two of her sisters had been

married in Landshut nearby, and she had spent a couple of years there during the First World War. (With me still in the carriage.)

Emigration had been much tougher on my mother than on me. Having left Germany "forever" when I was quite young, I had quickly learned to plant my roots in other countries and pull them up again when necessary. I was an old pro at the foreigner-status game, and could calmly watch other people's eyes grow moist when their national anthem was played at solemn occasions. Mine remained dry. It was my marriage that was my sheet anchor, my domicile, my kinship. I thought.

My mother was fifty-four when she left Germany, and it wasn't easy for her to start out on a new life. She spoke hardly any English at first but she soon learned enough to get by, though she could never really bridge the gap and get acquainted with English people or make friends with her English sons-in-law. "I'll never get the hang of it," she said resignedly, and couldn't get over the fluent English of her new grandchildren.

And now I had asked her if she wanted to come with me to Munich. Wanted to? Never. She was now seventy-three and regarded every year as a bonus. Why open old wounds? It had taken long enough for them to heal—and never quite, at that. And then she decided to come after all, because she knew that I would need her.

The plane touched down and taxied slowly toward the airport buildings. An entire guard of honor from the studio was lined up at the ramp. Strange faces, stranger even than usual, an extra smile on each one, each greeting extra sincere, or so it seemed to me. A little girl with a bunch of flowers stepped forward. "This is Romy Schneider. She has a part in the film." The girl curtseyed and I laughed. One still curtseyed in Germany. In England, only to the Queen.

There were a number of reporters and photographers. My English and American movies had been shown in Germany and one of them, *The Four Poster,* had been very popular. They had looked in their *Who's Who* and knew how old I was, but that was about all. The questions they asked were harmless enough: marriage, child, last film, last play, future plans. Not a soul said, "And how do you feel now that you are for the first time . . .?" Apparently nobody cared. For which I was grateful.

In the car on our way to the hotel, we talked only about the film, eagerly and optimistically, the way one does in any country before the actual shooting starts. This is called "preproduction enthusiasm." It means that you're received with zest and jollity and flowers and in the snazziest car—and when the last day of shooting is over, you get a taxi and drive quietly back to the airport, alone.

This time there was an extra-hearty vigor in the way we all talked about the script and the music and the cast and the director and the writer and the kitchen sink. Perhaps to cover up the general nervousness. Only my mother sat quietly in the back, put on her glasses, and looked out the window.

I discovered that my German had become very poor indeed. I didn't know a single technical term. How do you say "cameraman," "dresser," "makeup man," "wig," and so on in German? It looked as if I was putting on an act, since I could speak the language itself fluently and without accent.

It was a lovely May afternoon, and I caught a glimpse of the landscape rushing past me. Bright yellow flowering fields, pine forests— and suddenly we passed a sign saying "Dachau." My mother must have seen it too, for she turned her head to look out the back window to make sure. Either our companions hadn't seen it or they were used to it. But it knocked the breath out of me, and my preproduction enthusiasm died down.

The door closed behind our companions after they had convinced themselves that our rooms were comfortable and full of flowers. We were alone. My mother opened the windows and turned to me. "Did you see?"

I nodded and sat by her, and we both looked out silently. Flowering fields, a forest of pine trees. "Come," I said, "let's walk a bit in the woods before we unpack."

We walked through the fields until we reached the trees. Woods have held a strong attraction for me ever since my earliest youth. Even during our holidays by the Baltic, I spent my days in the woods, never on the beach. My Open Air School, too, lay deep inside the woods. Now, standing once again after twenty years of absence under the tall pines, I remained quite still, for the smell of bark and sand and moss attacked me from all sides. There are plenty of woods in other countries, but they smell different. Smell can conjure up memories for me stronger than any other sense. Especially childhood memories. Perhaps because you were that much shorter and therefore closer to the ground and its smells.

We sat down under a tree. Voices from afar. Nazis!

The voices came closer. Children's voices. No Nazis. German children, playing in the woods. As I did, once.

How did I get into that forest? What was I doing sitting beside my mother in a Bavarian forest? "Don't open a can of worms," goes an old saying.

I had opened a can of worms the day the telephone rang in our New York apartment and a voice said, "Frau Palmer?" Not Miss Palmer but *Frau* Palmer, a character who had never existed. Fräulein Palmer, yes. In some dim and distant past before the war, before America, before England, before Paris, there had been a Fräulein Palmer. "A call from Munich for Frau Palmer." And the voice of my old friend Erik Charell, who had produced the still well-remembered operetta *White Horse Inn,* excited and insistent.

"You must come to Munich right away!"

"What for?"

"To make a movie."

"A German movie? Out of the question, Erik."

"If you'll read the script and listen to the music, you'll take the next plane over. Listen to me and don't interrupt. I was dragged to Zurich the other day to see a Swiss operetta called *The Black Pike.* Awful title. I was supposed to make something of it, another *White Horse Inn.* Black pike, white horse—maybe they think I'm crazy about animals. Anyhow, the piece wasn't bad, nice setting, nice music, but no more than that. I said no thank you and left. Then I flew to Juan-les-Pins. I used to have a house there, remember?"

(It was there I had last seen Erik, in 1937. "There's going to be a war," he'd said. "I can feel it in my bones, the way I felt it in 1914." I had looked at him, shaking my head. Poor Erik! The man's obsessed.)

"I remember," I said.

"Now, listen: early next morning I went swimming, and suddenly, way out in the sea, I start singing. I say to myself, what's that you're singing? You're singing something you don't even know! Then I turned over on my back and floated—and suddenly I was singing the lyrics, too. I swam back to shore as fast as I could and made a telephone call, just as I was, dripping wet. If I can sing that song the next day, I thought, it means that the audience will sing it next day in the shower. So I called Zurich and said I was on my way back to take another look at the thing. It's a once-in-a-lifetime part for you—"

"But, Erik, I've never made a German movie in my life. I haven't set foot in the country for twenty years."

"I'm going to sing that song to you."

And he sang. That is, he croaked, without accompaniment or rhythm, hoarsely and exultantly, across the Atlantic, "*O mein Papa, war eine wunderbare clown, o mein Papa, war eine grosse Kinstler.* . . ." It never sounded better.

A few days later a proper recording of "O Mein Papa" arrived from Munich. It really wasn't easy to get the tune out of my head. It wasn't easy to get the idea of Germany out of my head, either.

I turned for advice to the only person I knew who had spent some time in postwar Germany, my brother-in-law David Kilmuir, Lord Chancellor of England. When he was still called Sir David Maxwell-Fyfe, he had been the British prosecutor at the Nuremberg trials, and he and his wife, Rex's sister Sylvia, had spent almost a year in Nuremberg.

Early in the war, his WAC driver had driven him into a bomb crater. Skull fracture. It looked as though his career—at thirty-one he had been the youngest barrister to become a King's Counsel—had come to an end. When the hospital informed his office that there was a possibility of permanent brain damage, his clerk said, "Oh well, then he'll have to be a judge in the criminal courts." His brain, however, was undamaged, although he remained deaf in one ear. Churchill rapidly promoted him from Solicitor General to Home Secretary and finally to Lord Chancellor. Besides being my brother-in-law, he was also my friend. A Scot, heavyset, with black hair and black eyes.

He told me that during the first of the Nuremberg trials, Julius Streicher had protested against his presence on the tribunal. To his certain knowledge, Streicher said, the judges included three undeclared Jews, who would be prejudiced, particularly against him. One of them was even called David. When Streicher was informed that Old Testament names have been in common use in England for centuries, he produced another piece of irrefutable evidence, although this one, he assured everybody, could only be detected by a connoisseur's eye like his own: the prosecutor's distinctly non-Aryan posterior. Streicher claimed to be able to recognize a Jew from the back at first glance.

For over a year David sat on his Scottish posterior in Nuremberg, and his one ear heard what he wanted to know. He was one of the first to see the concentration-camp films. He brought the trial minutes back to London with him and gave them to me to read. That was in 1947, only seven years ago.

"Should I go to Germany?" I asked him.

"It isn't a question of should you go, you *must* go," said David. "Bridges have to be built. We must all help to build them."

Tomorrow I was to start "building." Right now I couldn't see much chance of bridges. The can of worms weighed heavy in my hand.

My life at the studio began early next morning. Screen tests and music rehearsals. My mother had plans of her own. The night we arrived, she had opened the Munich telephone book and found the name she was looking for, a classmate of hers from Dresden who had been her best friend. They had kept in touch until the war. The old lady had wept on the telephone. "Rosl!" she kept saying. "Rosl! I can't believe it." My mother planned to go to Munich the very next day.

The car arrived to take me to the studios. Now, nine years after the war, the Bavaria Studios in Geiselgasteig were as good as any in Europe. Modern buildings, a big lot, gardens, woods. My dressing room had a bath, a dressing table, and a sofa, and was overflowing with flowers and welcoming messages.

A knock at the door. Three girls. My first three German girls. "Come in." They filed in, stopped by the door, and looked at me. What did they know about me? Refugee, formerly German, English actress. Hostile? Friendly? Neutral?

The tallest one stepped forward and smiled. She was Mascha, she said, my dresser. "Hello, Mascha." A sturdy blonde, good-natured though still cautious for the moment.

The other two were still standing by the door. "Come on in." They came in, sticking close together. The small one hastily said she was to make me up and do my hair.

"That's fine. What's your name?"

"Erika." Thin with a pointed little nose, nervous and withdrawn. The third was my stand-in, named Ute. A silent girl whose mouth turned up at the corners as though she meant to smile but couldn't quite make it.

For the next ten years these three girls would be constantly by my side whenever I set foot in a German studio, but I didn't know that then. I never thought that there would be more German films. And not only films, a whole German life. I only knew that I was going to make one picture in Germany. An isolated episode. Then I'd immediately return "home," to New York or London. Rex was making a film in London; I was making one in Munich. What came after was in the lap of the gods.

Ute disappeared to stand in for me so that they could start lighting. Erika silently brought me a few wigs to choose from. Mascha helped me take off my dress, talked about my customers, and carried on as though she'd been with me for years.

On the set things became trickier. When I came in, in full makeup and wig, followed by Mascha and Erika, a hush fell over the set. Erik Charell was standing by the camera, thank God. Our affectionate greetings sounded extra loud in the general silence. Everyone was watching. No point putting it off any longer. I took a step toward the camera as if to say hello, here I am, how do you do, let's get started. Charell took me firmly by the hand, turned me slowly in a half circle and started to introduce me to the stage crew.

So many names, so many people. As each of them shook my hand, I did some fast mental arithmetic. "Hello." He must be about thirty-five, that means he was twenty when the war started. Might have been right in the thick of it. "Hello." That one's younger, twenty-five at the most, couldn't have fought in the war—or could he? They took them at sixteen. Anyway, he must have been in the Hitler Youth. "Hello." This one is much older, pushing fifty. Must have been through the whole thing, possibly dedicated, Nazi party member. Everybody had to be, so they say. Doesn't look like it, though, looks nice. What did a former Nazi party member look like today? He shook my hand and shuffled off. Wooden leg. I nipped my sympathy in the bud. Who knows what he'd done before he lost his leg. He was still looking at me, and when our eyes met, he smiled shyly. No, he couldn't have—"Hello." The next one, gray-haired, tired-looking. He kissed my hand and looked at me urgently as though putting something on record. He was perhaps sixty, therefore about forty in 1933, when it all began. He must have known what he was doing. "Hello." This one was just a youngster, standing in front of the camera holding the clapperboard. He couldn't be more than seventeen, nodded to me, whistling away, casual and indifferent.

A voice from the doorway: "Lillusch! For heaven's sake!" Kurt von Molo ran across the set, pushed through all the people, and hugged me. My old friend Kurtchen. From the old days in London. He and his wife, Beate Moissi-von Molo, had been part of my "iron ration" of friends. We had scrambled eggs together made over the gas ring in my room in London. Kurt and Beate, both non-Jews, were members of the honorable elite that left Germany by choice, not because they had to. Kurt was one of the best cutters in the movie industry, in any language. It was just a question of time before someone put him to work. However, during those questionable days he had had to sleep on a bench in the Bois de Boulogne. Later he managed to get a foothold in England, as I did, and before long he was the only person I knew who owned a car. Until one day, out of the blue, his work permit was withdrawn and he was left high and dry.

Even then he and Beate couldn't bring themselves to return to Germany. He tried to break into the Italian movie industry in Rome, where they weren't so strict about work permits. When war was declared, the Germans grabbed him and put him in the army.

I didn't know any of this, didn't even know that he and Beate were alive. Standing there in the middle of the studio, we laughed and cried until my makeup was a mess. Once again the stage crew stood and watched. Sooner or later we'd have to stop; we were supposed to be working here, not celebrating a refugees' reunion. The silence was becoming noticeable. We hastily broke it up and made a lunch date.

Camera positions. Everyone took his place. The camera lights came on, and I stood in the familiar glare, blind and cut off from the outside world.

Screen tests. Red, reddish blond, and blond wigs. Light makeup, dark makeup. This lipstick, that lipstick. "This is my good side; the other's the bad one."

"What are your best camera angles? Above the nose or below?"

"Above." I knew the answers, knew them in my sleep. Almost twenty years since Hal Rosson had asked me that for the first time and got my vacant moon face as an answer. I kept forgetting where I was, spoke to Mascha in English, and realized it only when I saw her open her eyes wide.

Lunch break. Would I like a car to take me to the cafeteria? How far was it? A few hundred yards. No, thank you, I'd like to walk.

As I walked slowly past the flower beds and lawns, I stopped to look at the large pink daisies. I hadn't seen large pink daisies for twenty years. Or was I imagining it? I looked at them for a long time. They had given it to me in writing that this country, where I had been born, was not my country, its language was not mine but merely lent, its people not my people. And now I was back, having acquired an English passport, an English husband, an English child, an English life. I'd been welcomed with flowers and was speaking

German again. I could digest all that, but what about the people? How was I to come to terms with the people?

Kurt von Molo was waiting in the cafeteria.

The place was crowded with actors, technicians, and musicians. All around I heard nothing but German, German, German; noisy, nonchalant talk and laughter. Well, what else? Had I expected people in this country nine years after the war to slink around with mournful faces, overcome by collective guilt, and quiet, very quiet, so as not to attract attention?

The waiter put the menu on the table. I looked at him, not at the menu. About forty, I thought. Where would he have been during the war? Russian front? And before that? Party member?

"What are you going to have?" asked Kurt. "The *Beinfleisch* [boiled beef] is pretty good." *Beinfleisch*. I hadn't heard that word for twenty years.

The waiter disappeared. "Kurt, do you know that man?"

"The waiter? Yes, why?"

"Do you know anything about him?"

"What do you mean?"

"You know what I mean. Was he a Party member?"

Pause. Kurt laid his hand on mine and pressed it. "Now listen to me, Lillusch. You can't go over this country with a divining rod and see who it points to."

"I can't help it; I can't get it out of my mind. I've got to know. Don't you understand?"

"Of course I understand, but it's useless."

"Why is it useless?"

"Because most people simply don't know anymore what they once thought. Or even what they once did."

"Kurt, you must know these people here in the cafeteria."

"Sure I do."

"Which of them were Nazis?"

"Listen, Lillusch, by and large there were three types of Germans. The ones who were genuinely committed, the 'Nazis.' There were relatively few of those, especially in our business. Many people joined the Party, but they were fellow travellers, opportunists, you know, like most people are anyway, up to a point. And then there were a few who didn't join and didn't 'fellow-travel,' because they just couldn't. That happened too, believe me."

"Kurt, which of the people in my film were Nazis? Do you know of any?"

"Yes, I know a fellow in your crew who was a loyal supporter of Hitler. He believed in the man. He often told me so at the time, although he knew where I stood. And *I* knew that he'd never turn me in."

"Where does he stand now?"

"He doesn't even remember that there was a time when he believed in Hitler the way he believed in God. He lost his son at Stalingrad. That was the first shock. After that his 'faith' went to pot pretty fast. Now he's absolutely certain that he was 'against it' from the start. He can't afford to believe anything else. And he's convinced of his integrity."

"Amnesia."

"Lillusch, let me ask *you* a question now. If you hadn't happened to be Jewish, would *you* have left Germany?"

"I don't know. I've often wondered."

"And?"

"Maybe . . . not. I loved my life in Germany. I'm afraid . . . I'd have stayed."

"You see?"

"But I would never have joined the Party or—or even paid lip service to that insane racial business, or denounced other people."

"Naturally not. But you'd have stayed! And most of the people that you're looking at in this room . . . just stayed."

When I got back to the hotel that evening, my mother was sitting by the open window, staring out.

"Well, how did it go?" we asked simultaneously.

First I had to report about my day, and she listened. Just nodded at the end. Then it was her turn. She had been to see her old friend, who was living alone in a dark little apartment in Munich. Her husband, to whom she had been very much attached, had died a few months before. Their only son had been killed in Russia. She had enough to live on, rarely went out, had a few old friends in similar circumstances. She'd had the coffee ready—real German coffee under a thick cozy, and apple cake. "You know," said my mother, "I haven't tasted that kind of apple cake for twenty years."

"I know," I said, "I've had that sort of thing all day long."

When they had finished their coffee, there was a pause while the two old ladies sat and looked at each other without speaking. My mother had something on her mind which she had to get rid of.

"Erna," she said, "I've got to ask you something, and you must give me an honest answer. You've lived here in Munich, close to Dachau. Didn't you know there was a concentration camp there?"

"Yes," said Erna. "We knew. And we knew that they'd shipped a lot of Jews to Dachau. Late one night I saw a truck full of people, and I thought, maybe it's going to Dachau. People said there was a forced labor camp there and that all the inmates had to work very hard."

"You didn't know what really happened there?"

"Rosl," said the old lady, "you know that I've always believed in an afterlife. You don't, do you? And since Oskar's death, I've been absolutely sure of it. I'll soon be there with him, and I'm counting the days. I swear to you by the most sacred thing I know, I swear by my faith that I'll be reunited with him . . . we didn't know."

My mother looked at me. "What do you say to that? Do you think it's possible? So close to Munich, and they didn't know?"

"It's possible."

My mother remained silent for a long time.

"You know," she said at last, "I believe her."

The telephone rang. A popular Munich picture magazine wanted to know if they could take a cover photo of me visiting somewhere—well, the zoo, for instance. Tomorrow was Sunday, would I . . .?

The zoo. The old lure. I couldn't refuse. Let's have a look at some German animals.

There weren't many about, and the few that stared at me were moth-eaten. We made for the bird house to get a nice color shot with a couple of parrots and cockatoos. I posed amid the earsplitting screeching from hundreds of brightly colored throats. As I was leaving, I noticed a large bird sitting silently and apparently in deep gloom, all alone.

"What's the matter with that one?" I asked the keeper. "Is he ill?"

"The one in the corner? No, miss, he isn't ill. He used to be our prize parrot. He could shout 'Heil Hitler!' louder than any of the others. Got an extra piece of apple every time. But when the Americans came after the war, we didn't know what to do with him, because he wanted his apple and the Americans came running in looking for the guy who had screamed 'Heil Hitler!' Well, we didn't want to kill him—parrot meat is tough, you know—so we hit him with a newspaper every time he opened his beak. Now he just sits there and won't say anything anymore. I guess he doesn't understand what it's all about. He's a dumb bird, miss."

It's amazing how quickly you get used to things.

My second day at the studio wasn't like a second day; it was like any other day. Mascha greeted me as though we'd known each other for years, and even the silent, nervous way Erika pulled my hair about was nothing new, so I accepted it. People were friendly. I was friendly. My fellow actors behaved like actors the world over—down-to-earth, professional, helpful. Slightly inhibited at first but thawing out quickly. Not inquisitive. Nobody asked questions. I didn't ask any more questions either. I made friends with no one and disliked no one. Nobody got close enough.

It took years of working together for months at a time before I asked Mascha why Erika was always so pale and jumpy.

"Oh, dear Lord," said Mascha, "what a rotten deal she had!"

"What happened?"

"Well, she was only sixteen when the Russians arrived in Berlin."

"Yes?"

"They got her. Three of them. And she was lucky at that."

"Lucky?"

"At least they didn't have a disease. That was a break. Ute had it much worse."

"Our Ute?"

"Yes. She had to be cleaned out. Completely."

"Mascha, how old were you when the Russians moved in?"

"Seventeen. But my mother hid me in our bread oven." Thinking back, she laughed. "I spent the first week lying flat on my back. Mother just opened the hatch to give me something to eat." Another burst of laughter. "She only let me out when the worst was over."

I should have asked earlier.

The following weekend, Charell suggested going to Frankfurt. The local theater was still playing *The Black Pike,* the musical on which our picture, retitled *Fireworks,* was based. Would I like to see it?

"Very much," I said. "I'd be very interested. Very interested indeed to see the Frankfurt Schauspielhaus."

We drove to Frankfurt on the autobahn. The entire region, so familiar to me in my Darmstadt days, was unrecognizable. The place names on the highway signs were familiar, but the landscape remained strange.

The Frankfurt Schauspielhaus, like most of the city, had been badly damaged by bombs and was completely reconstructed after the war. Neither the building nor the street stirred any memories. Just as well. We had seats in the managing director's box, close to the stage. The house was full. Two minutes to go.

I looked at the curtain. According to my defunct contract—if I had had the right kind of grandparents—I would have appeared behind and in front of that very curtain. I might have had good roles —might have made my way to Reinhardt's theater in Berlin—no, Reinhardt was gone, of course, but to Berlin anyway. I would have accepted all the blessings of the Third Reich and tried, like many others, to ignore their propaganda campaigns. In the end, like many others, I would have had to play ball, ashamed of myself. Having taken the first step, I would have had to take the second, and as a reward they would, perhaps, have given me a villa on the Wannsee, outside Berlin. And then the war would have come along. And the Russians. Perhaps I would have survived. Perhaps I would now be in the cast of our film and I would look at "her," the outsider. When the picture was finished, I would stay in Germany, of course. "She" would be leaving. Where would she be going? No matter. She was at home everywhere. Could act anywhere she liked. Free.

Those "Aryan" grandparents of mine had done me the biggest favor of my life—by not existing.

The orchestra began the overture. The curtain rose. I began to give undivided attention to the stage only when the actress who was playing the equivalent of my film role made her entrance. She was good. Her voice was much better than mine, and what she did up there would have pleased Elsa. Nice to discover the high level of acting in the German theater. And why shouldn't it be a pleasure to see good theater, wherever it was performed? Should I be put off because it was German theater?

The door to the box opened. A tall, well-dressed man appeared and introduced himself as the managing director. Sitting down next to me, he asked how we liked the show. We were glad to be able to say sincerely that we liked it very much indeed. Yet that didn't seem to satisfy him. He hesitated.

"You're really a stage actress, aren't you? Wouldn't you like to act in Germany? I'd be more than happy to have you spend a season here with us. You could choose your roles!"

I stared at him. Of course, it wasn't the same managing director who had written that letter twenty years ago. This one couldn't have known that I'd once been under contract to the Frankfurt Schauspielhaus. I fumbled for the right words. Couldn't find them.

"No?" he finally said, anticipating my answer. I shook my head.

"Pity. I'd hoped ours would be the first theater to present you on the German stage."

I shook my head again.

"Well, then—good-bye. Enjoy the show."

I saw and heard little of the next two acts. I don't believe in fate, providence, or divine guidance. But there was no doubt about it: I'd come full circle.

A few hours after the clapperboard fell on the final take of *Fireworks,* my mother and I were in the airplane on our way back to London.

"It's a good thing I came along," she said, as the wheels left the runway. We climbed steeply, leaving everything behind and below us within a few seconds. No time for tender farewells.

"But I'm glad we're going back today," she murmured, half to herself.

"Why are you glad?"

"Because I'm too old. Too old for the conflict and the tug-of-war. I want to be left in peace. It was hard enough to write it all off twenty years ago, you know. I can't help you build those bridges. I've had a good look around and I've seen that there's a lot we didn't know about. Erna's lucky; she leaves it all to the Almighty. He knows the real truth, she says."

"Does she believe that He arranges everything too?"

"Yes."

"Arranges or deranges?"

My mother sighed and looked out the window. The airplane banked and made a leisurely circle over Munich.

"Erna doesn't ask questions."

19

The Train in the Dark

❀

URING THE SHOOTING of *The Constant Husband,* Rex fell in love and I knew it, although nobody had told me, because he called me every night (an old habit) in Munich, and I could tell by the sound of his voice.

When I returned from Germany, Rex and I set off together to start our annual holiday in Portofino. I still had no idea who the woman was who obviously occupied his mind. Maybe it would pass. I didn't ask, and he didn't tell. Until a short time later when Kay Kendall suddenly appeared in Portofino, accompanied by her friend Mrs. William Saroyan. All at once, there it was. In the open, clear as daylight. The impact hit me full force.

Carol Saroyan was stunned. "You must believe me," she said in tears, "I had no idea why Kay wanted to go to Portofino. I would never have come."

The immediate problem was our contract with Binkie Beaumont (H.M. Tennent Management) to play *Bell, Book and Candle* in London, starting rehearsals the following month. Binkie was staying with us in Portofino, had witnessed the havoc of Kay's arrival there, and was aghast, not only as our friend but also as producer of the play. Just then, out of the blue, I received an offer from New York to appear in a new play, *Anastasia,* on Broadway. This, I thought, might be my only hope of getting out of the trap, escaping the daily agony of "togetherness," and, perhaps, rebuilding my life.

But Binkie, convinced that Rex would "come to his senses," would not let me out of the contract, and strange to say, Rex, too, was in no way inclined to consider a breakup of our theatrical partnership. Maybe he wasn't sure yet of his feelings either way. Or he was just true to his favorite maxim: "Always try to eat your cake and have it."

After a short "honeymoon," Rex and Kay returned to London, where he and I met to live once again at the Connaught Hotel "together." And start rehearsals.

Sundays Rex spent with Kay somewhere in the country. I used to visit Carey at his school at Sunningdale and give him lunch at Maidenhead nearby. Afterwards we would rent one of the river boats and chug-chug slowly downstream, with Carey at the wheel. Once Rex announced that he would join us at Maidenhead and he did indeed turn up, to Carey's delight. The three of us then made for the boat house and we started our trip, with Carey playing captain and first mate with his father. I sat watching in the back. Suddenly Rex looked at his watch and said that we would have to land, since he had an important appointment. He jumped ashore, and Carey and I chugged on. We watched him walk rapidly over the bridge toward his car, and I saw him suddenly and unaccountably —it was a warm day—pull his coat collar high about his ears as if he were hiding from somebody.

During rehearsals things had been bearable because of the problems and the chaos that prevent one from thinking and feeling and going under. But once the play had opened and was rumbling on like so many office hours, I couldn't cope with my state of mind anymore. I tried to get help from all quarters. First and obviously, from a psychiatrist. "I can't do anything for you," he said, "except give you tranquilizers or pep-up pills."

I tried the church. Opposite the Connaught stands a small church of whatever religion. I used to sit inside by the hour, and left only when the service started. The service disturbed my thinking. Once when I had been sitting there for a while, I felt a touch and saw a gnarled, arthritic hand on my arm. I turned and looked into an old woman's face, thin and wrinkled. "Are you very unhappy, my dear?" she said. I fled.

I went to see my friend Noël Coward. Maybe he could help. He knew, of course; by now, everybody knew. I had moved out of the Connaught and into a small flat around the corner in Mount Street. Friends came to see me, but what was there to talk about?

Noël didn't attempt to make light of the situation or indulge in good advice. "It's about the worst case I know," he said. "I've witnessed fairly bad pickles, but they were always either 'wife sitting in a box watching her husband make love to his mistress onstage' or 'husband in the box watching his wife with her lover.' It's bad enough, and it hurts like hell. My advice has always been, get out of town and stay out—until a decision is made one way or the other. But you and Rex, playing those hot love scenes every night, pretending what was once genuine—honestly, I don't know what to say to you." We sat in silence. Suddenly he said: "Do you think you can hold on for another twelve years?"

"What do you mean by 'hold on'—and why twelve years?"

"Because Rex is forty-eight now, isn't he? Well, I guarantee you that when he's sixty you can relax with him. He'll be tired. Can you hold on that long?"

"No," I said.

How was I going to get through the run of the play? I hated myself for crying and carrying on, giving shoddy performances at night, behaving hysterically in a way I had always despised in other women. I had the feeling that the smell of unhappiness around me ("worse than armpits, dear!" according to Noël) was noticeable to everybody. Whenever I managed to pull myself together and live as normally as possible during the day, I was always undone when I got to the theater. There we were, chained together by a contract we couldn't get out of, embracing each other every night with wooden arms. Once, in my dressing room, Rex said, "Maybe you ought to have a lover. Maybe that would help you." He meant it kindly, not cynically.

Of course my sisters and other friends rallied around. My mother was seventy-five and we told her as little as possible, but there was no need to tell her much. She knew anyhow, and she used to sit in my dressing room watching my dresser taking tucks in my clothes, which had become far too big for me.

One friend, Babs Siodmak, refused to be satisfied with the scanty information I gave her on the telephone. She had known me since childhood, had become a part of my life, sometimes at close range, sometimes from a distance. She knew exactly what was going on. She called me almost every day from Munich, where her husband, the director Robert Siodmak, was making a picture.

"Tell me," she said one day, "haven't you ever, over the years, met anyone you liked?"

"No," I said. "Never. Well, wait a minute—there was a man in Hollywood a year ago. I met him at a party at Jack Warner's."

"What's his name?"

"Carlos Thompson. He's under contract to Metro. But I have no idea where he is."

"I'll find him," said Babs. "Even if he's at the other end of the world."

A few days later she called again.

"I've found him! And guess where he is: right here, at the Hotel Vier Jahreszeiten. He's playing Franz Liszt in a film about Wagner. Here in Munich! What do you say to that?"

I didn't say much because I had no very high hopes, even though the coincidence was astonishing and my recollection of our conversation about Juanita was still very vivid. He had given me her address in Caracas, and I'd written to her immediately. She had answered by return mail, devoting several pages to Carlos and several more to plans for how we could meet again. I'd owed her a letter for months. I'd owed everybody letters for months.

In Carlos's room at the Hotel Vier Jahreszeiten in Munich, the telephone rang. A lady he didn't know, a Frau Siodmak, was inviting him for a drink in the bar. Could he come down right away? Puzzled, he went downstairs. Perhaps it was something to do with a part in a film of her husband's, Robert Siodmak. But it wasn't a part, he realized with disappointment. The lady just wanted to say hello on behalf of Lilli Palmer in London. Strange. Carlos couldn't understand what it was all about. But in the course of the conversation he mentioned that he was planning to go to London when he finished filming.

A few weeks later he walked into my dressing room after the

show. And into my life. We went out to supper afterwards to a small Italian restaurant in Soho. "You've changed," he said. I knew he meant that I didn't look like the woman he remembered from the evening at Jack Warner's but like something the cat brought in. "Your jaws are clenched," he said. "What's happened?"

Next morning, bright and early, I marched to the Connaught Hotel for the first time since I had moved out three months ago, walked up to Rex's room, knocked, and opened the door. Rex was still in bed, his breakfast tray on his knees. I remained standing in the doorway.

"I have something to tell you," I said. "I've taken your advice."

And closed the door. Softly.

Yet at first we barricaded ourselves, each behind his own protective wall, eyeing each other warily and full of doubts and misgivings, exploring and discovering one another. After a series of passionate and dramatic escapades, Carlos had become a confirmed bachelor who enjoyed his peace of mind, independence, and occasional diversions. "Isn't it great that we don't expect anything of each other?" he said, as we walked along the snow-covered banks of the Thames. "Do you know what 'marriage' means? It means come and hold my hand while I watch television." I agreed wholeheartedly. I was still in my dark tunnel, and I didn't believe in a sudden emergency exit. But by the end of the month I had gained five pounds, and the tucks could be let out of my costumes again.

We saw each other every day, and suddenly realized that we were spending every free minute together. A severe case of bronchitis helped. Carlos had to be nursed, so he moved into my flat and happily worked away at his novel, while I continued with my eight performances a week at the Phoenix Theatre. How long could it possibly last? When the snow began to melt, Carlos signed a contract for a film to be shot in Spain. We sloshed along our favorite footpaths, behaving as though his imminent departure were perfectly natural.

Suddenly he stopped and laid his hands on my shoulders. "You know," he said slowly, "you could be my father's daughter."

"And you my father's son," I replied.

After this we remained silent and trudged on, overwhelmed by the momentous discovery.

He flew to Spain, and I showed up at the theater every night as my contract required. We were both harboring, even nursing, our final doubts—until the prolonged separation put an end to the conflict. Letters and telephone conversations could not begin to fill the sudden, gaping emptiness. I talked Binkie into giving me a week's vacation and flew to Spain, while my understudy filled in for me.

As usual, Carlos was living at a distance from his fellow actors and shooting location, in a small hotel on the beach outside Barcelona. The night I arrived, we swam in the dark sea and sat afterwards for a long time on the still-warm sand. Cautiously, tentatively, still jittery, we felt our way into an area we had studiously avoided a few months ago: plans for the future—joint plans.

That night we both wrote a letter to Juanita. "Come to Europe. If there's anyone in the world who ought to be our 'best man,' it's you."

A week later a black-edged envelope addressed in unfamiliar handwriting arrived from Venezuela. In dry tones, Juanita's husband wrote to say that she had died a few weeks ago of cancer. Only a brief illness, thank God. The whole city had followed her coffin to the cemetery. The theater where she had performed up to the very last had been renamed Teatro Juanita Sujo.

One afternoon in Portofino, I told my son. He was eleven years old, and he'd known Carlos for a year. What was the best way to break it to him? What do you say in a case like this? Plenty of women I'd known had had to do it, but I'd never thought that I would, too. One sunny morning we walked up and down in our vineyard, and I explained to him that his father and I would never live together again.

It took quite a while to sink in. Then he said, "I don't understand—you never had a fight!"

I also told him that I was going to marry Carlos.

He frowned. "That's impossible," he said firmly. "I can't have two fathers."

"You won't. You'll always have the same father. But you'll have a new friend."

He accepted that and returned to the game of mini-football he had been playing in his room.

And that's how it worked out. The boy became Carlos's inseparable companion, and I didn't mind that he often preferred being with Carlos to being with me. Men belong together.

I hadn't opened a newspaper for months. I didn't want to see the comments on the breakup of our marriage. I didn't know or care what had become of my German film, *Fireworks.* Until one day a new German manuscript and a letter arrived at my flat in London. There was every hope, said the letter, that this new script, *Devil in Silk,* would be as big a success as *Fireworks.*

So *Fireworks* had been a big success? Well, well. I read the new script and liked it. Maybe this would be a good way to burn my Anglo-American boats, at least for the time being. I pleaded with Binkie Beaumont to release me from my nightly ordeal on the Phoenix Theatre stage, and he relented. Joan Greenwood was willing to take over my part in *Bell, Book and Candle,* and I was at last able to pack my bags.

The new film was to be made in Berlin. Berlin. One more tug—the last one—at my very essence, at all the things I'd locked away forever. Berlin meant our apartment in the Hölderlinstrasse, the Open Air School, my bicycle, the canoe, the drama school, my first boy friend—the entire beloved, know-nothing childhood.

I stood in the Hölderlinstrasse looking up at our balcony, forced myself to climb the two flights of stairs to our front door on the left, bent down, and looked at the dents and scratches made by the walking stick of an irate neighbor whose nerves hadn't been able to stand our piano playing—twenty-five years ago.

One Sunday morning I stood again at the entrance of the Open Air School, and spent an hour walking through the grounds all by myself. The big dining hall with the platform where I had recited my poems was still standing. I even found the tree with my initials.

I went back a second time, hand in hand with Carlos, surprised that he should be so moved. But of course he would be. He too was a DP, displaced and dispossessed.

After that it was all laid to rest for good, and I could drive serenely every morning through familiar streets on my way to the studio to make *Devil in Silk,* with Curd Jürgens.

A few months later I learned that this performance had earned for me the prize of the German Federal Republic at the Berlin Film Festival. I made it a point to accept it personally from the hands of the jury, at the ceremony itself. I had good reason for doing this. I was a burned child.

Two years before I had won the Venice Biennale prize for *The Four Poster,* but had not attended the prize-giving ceremony. The trophy, a replica of the Lion of Venice, was presented to me in London a year later by the Italian ambassador. The celebration at the embassy was a long one. I sneaked away early (to meet Carlos), unnoticed and without saying good-bye, put the box containing the lion under my coat, and slipped out into the street. Before I'd gone five steps, I was firmly gripped from behind by two burly policemen, who wanted to know what I was trying to smuggle out of the embassy. My confused explanation was not convincing. So I was marched back and had to be identified by the astonished ambassador in person before they would let me go.

During the ceremony and the preceding speech, I braced myself. In a minute I would have to mount the platform amid the applause of many hundreds of my German fellow actors. Then I would be given the award for the "best German actress of the year." To me it meant something quite different from the Lion of Venice. Quite different.

My third German film was called *Is Anna Anderson Anastasia?*

This role once again won me the film prize of the Federal Republic. On this occasion one of the guests of honor at the Berlin Film Festival happened to be Gary Cooper. After the presentation of the awards, he pushed through the crowd and tapped me on the shoulder.

"Hey, kid. What gives? Have you become a German movie actress?"

"Yes," I said, dazed. "I think I have."

I had stopped to wonder at the unexpected turn my career had taken. I was quite happy about it; everything fitted in nicely. The New York apartment was gone and the London one too. I suddenly had no home anymore, but I discovered that an old refugee needs only a bit of practice to get back in form. My new home was a hotel room in Berlin, and my private life consisted entirely of letters, because Carlos was filming in Mexico, Carey was at school in England, and Rex sent regular weekly reports.

His letters were deliberately vague about the future, and there was never any reply to my pressing demands on that score. The only thing to do was to go and see him and have it out. He had left for America to start rehearsals for *My Fair Lady*. Kay was his constant companion, and I felt that their relationship was becoming a permanent one. Like mine with Carlos. The time had come to clear the decks.

I financed the flight to New York by appearing on a Perry Como TV show and found out that Rex had just opened in New Haven on his pre-Broadway tour. To New Haven, then. On the way to the hotel, the taxi drove past the theater where he and I had played on our tryouts together. Many times. There, as always, was his name on top in blazing lights and underneath—not mine. "Julie Andrews," it said. Okay with me. That chapter, too, was finally closed.

After the show I went to his dressing room, wedged in among a crowd of people all eager to congratulate him on his unique performance. My visit had a different purpose; I had come to ask him for a divorce.

When everybody was gone, we stayed in the dressing room, and as the hours passed we went through our marriage with a fine comb. I told him I wanted to marry Carlos. He refused to take it seriously.

"You'll only make a fool of yourself marrying a younger man," he said.

"I don't think age has anything to do with it. Look at us. You are just the 'right' number of years older. Did that help?"

Still, he remained convinced that given time we could both come together again and live out our life in "dignity and peace." But I wouldn't budge. When dawn broke, he agreed on a separation. He would not contemplate the final step. Not yet.

We turned off the lights, left the theater, and in the early dawn walked silently back to the hotel.

The following Christmas, during a brief skiing holiday with Carey in the Austrian mountains, I had a special-delivery letter from Rex. Urgent, terrible news: our doctor had given Kay a routine checkup —and discovered that she was suffering from leukemia. He hadn't told her; he had told Rex instead and let Kay leave for Hollywood to do a film there. Would I come to New York? At once?

I arrived a week later. The next morning we drove to the hospital, where Doctor Atchley was expecting us. Atchley had been our doctor for years; now he was Kay's, too.

The waiting room was empty except for one other patient sitting in a corner, waiting for a verdict. Arthur Godfrey. Lung cancer. We chatted for a moment, then fell silent. Nothing was worth saying.

The door opened and Atchley, a tiny, delicate old man, welcomed us. He wasted no time in small talk. "Here's the situation. I don't know how to proceed. You both must tell me what to do. Kay has myeloid leukemia, which means that she has roughly three years to live. All I know, when I questioned her—cautiously, of course —is that she has no relatives she cares about—and that she wants to marry Rex. Now, since both of you are my patients, I find it very hard to ask you, are you willing to get divorced? I must know. Because somebody has to take care of Kay from now on, somebody who knows. If there isn't anybody, I must tell her the truth."

"Doctor Atchley," I said, "you can rest assured that we will be divorced and that Rex will marry Kay and take care of her."

Atchley took our hands, clasped them to his chest, looked from one to the other, and said, "You are both—good Christian people." Which I let pass.

We got into a taxi and drove back to my hotel. For the first few minutes, neither of us spoke. Then I said, "You see. There's nothing for it. You must marry her."

"I can't! You know I can't! You know how I feel about— about it."

About death, he meant. I knew only too well. He had told me

when we first met, when he was thirty-one years old. ("You know that you must die, don't you?" he had said. "I suppose so," I had answered, amazed, "but I never give it a thought." "I do. I think about it every day. And it terrifies me.")

"I can't do it!" he repeated. "I won't be any good at it! She needs a strong person . . ."

"Who? Where should this strong person come from? Besides, it's you she wants."

"I simply cannot do it."

We arrived at the Plaza Hotel and went up to my room.

"How will I live through those years, knowing that she gets closer to death every day, inch by inch—and when it's all over, what will I be left with? I'll be alone. I'll have to start life all over again."

"What's the alternative? Atchley will have to tell her that she has only three years to live. How do you think she will take it? *Can* she take it?"

"She's only twenty-nine."

He sat on the sofa and buried his head in his hands. Finally he looked up. "I could do it—if I knew that in the end, you would be there."

"What do you mean?" I said, aghast.

"I could do it if you promised to come back to me when— when it's all over."

"But I am going to marry Carlos, you know that."

"All right—marry him if you must, but give me your word that we will be together again, in the end."

The more he explored this possibility, the more reasonable it appeared to him. His face had lost its ghastly pallor, and he talked quite rationally. Yes, he would do it, he would marry Kay right away and watch over her so that she would never know—provided that he would be able to have something to hold on to, some "light at the end of the tunnel." He wouldn't be alone; I would be there waiting for him. I would divorce Carlos, and we would marry again.

"By that time you will have got him out of your system and we will be together again, as we ought to be."

We wrestled for hours. In the end, I realized that, in truth, he had reached the limit of his resources. Even with the help of my promise, there would be at least three harrowing years in front of him, well over a thousand days of ever-growing drama, crisis, hopelessness, doom. I felt I had no right to go on my way to a happy new life with Carlos and leave him to cope alone, unaided and in total secrecy, for nobody could be trusted to know. Worst of all, he would be forced to give the best and most painful performance of his life, every day and all day, pretending to embark on a new happiness with a beautiful young wife at his side, himself the "toast of Broadway," apparently at the very summit of his life and without a care in the world. He was right. It was too much. He needed every bit of help he could get.

And so I lied and pledged myself to return to him when all was over. In the meantime we would keep in close touch, write every week, phone whenever possible.

It was getting late; he had to leave for the theater. He got up and put on his camel's-hair coat. He walked to the window and looked out on Central Park for a moment. Without turning, he said, "If you ever change your mind—don't let me know."

As soon as the necessary papers could be assembled, I flew to Mexico and got a divorce. Beyond that fact, there was little the press could report. Although there had been adultery, there was no acrimony and—at my request—no alimony. Rex married Kay, and true to his promise, protected her from discovering the truth. To the world they appeared as a happy couple, enjoying their success, their fame, indulging every whim, living a madcap, jet-setting life, as long as Kay's precarious state of health allowed it. Every week, wherever I happened to be, at least one letter was waiting for me, which told the true story of anguish and often of despair. But the worst were the telephone calls. There would be a transatlantic voice announcing a call from "Mr. Manson," his valet. And then there would be five or even ten minutes of pent-up desperation. Occasionally the voice broke up, and I would not know if he was still on the line.

I answered every letter, wrote time and again variations of the same theme: he must consider his present life as an assignment, like a special mission during the war, one that was vitally necessary and timed to come to an end, however tragic.

Once while I was staying alone at our house in Portofino (Carlos was on a brief visit to his family in Hollywood), Noël Coward came to stay with me. A particularly heartrending letter from Rex had just arrived, which left me, as usual, shattered. And maybe I didn't pull myself together as much as I ordinarily did in Carlos's presence. Noël had a sharp eye, and after dinner as we were sitting in the dark on the terrace looking down at the lights of the harbor, he demanded to know what had so suddenly taken the life out of me. I was no match for him. I collapsed all too easily and told him. The relief of it! I told him the entire story—Kay's illness, Rex's "mission," my "vow." He listened in silence.

Then the storm broke.

"Are you out of your mind?" he shouted. "Who do you think you are, Florence Nightingale? Or do you really intend to go back to Rex?"

"Of course not!" I cried.

"Then what in God's name are you doing? You're lying to Rex; you're lying to Carlos."

"I'm not lying to Carlos. I just haven't told him about it."

"Why not?"

"I *can't* tell him, because he would feel that he is being used. He is a very proud man. I just don't dare tell him. Not yet. Later on, I will tell him everything, of course. By then the whole thing will be over and I'll have a better chance that he will understand why I had to keep it a secret from him. If I told him now, he would just pack and leave. The only thing I can do is to keep my mouth shut."

"That's as good as lying," said Noël. "This house reeks of your deceit!"

"What would *you* have done in this predicament?"

"Predicament, my ass! I would never have allowed myself to be pushed into this ridiculous position. What kind of a cheap melodrama is this?"

"Leukemia is no melodrama. You're fond of Kay, aren't you? Frankly, I'm not—but the facts are that she is going to die in a year or so and that takes the wind out of anybody's sails."

"None of your business."

"Whose, then?"

"Rex's. Let him stew in his own juice. Or are you by any chance enjoying your role in this penny dreadful?"

"Jesus!" I cried. "Enjoying it? I lie awake at night! I thought I might get some help from you."

"Well, the only help you get from me, old girl, is a good hiding. Will you tell me, for instance, what you're going to do when Kay is dead? Have you thought of that?"

"I think of it every single day. It's like sitting on top of a train, and it's going faster and faster through the night and I can't stop it."

Noël didn't answer. We looked out into the black night. There was no moon. Way out, the lights of the fishing fleet shone over the water.

"What a mess," he said softly after a while. "Do you realize that you're sitting on a powder keg? What about those letters? You know how careless Rex is. Suppose Kay finds one? That'll blow the lid right off. There'll be hell to pay for all four of you. How long are you going to spin this out? How long do you think your luck will hold?"

"That's the train I'm sitting on."

Another silence, a long one. He lit one cigarette after another. In the end he said, "There's nothing I can do to help. Except to tell you to send me a cable if the thing explodes. Even if I am at the other end of the world, I'll take the next plane."

He got up to go to bed. I stayed on. The lights of the fishing fleet were slowly moving farther and farther away. Suddenly there were footsteps, and Noël stepped out on the terrace again. I could hardly see him in the darkness.

"You haven't told me," he said. "What *are* you going to do when Kay dies?"

"I shall let a bit of time pass, and then I'll write a letter to Rex. The last one."

"Well," said Noël, "I'd like to have a copy of that letter."

As it turned out, I didn't have to send that cable to Noël. Everything happened as predicted. Kay lived for three years and died in a London clinic. Rex left soon after the funeral. He had gone through such harrowing anguish, particularly during the last weeks, that, as he wrote, he was totally exhausted. I let "a bit of time" pass and then sat down and forced myself to write that letter and made myself walk down to the mail box—and drop it in.

There was, of course, no reply. A year later, during a long walk in the mountains, I told Carlos. "You did well not to tell me then," he said quietly. That was the end of my nightmare on top of that fast train through the night.

20

Blue, the Color of Joy

❀

I N AMERICA, when a girl wants to get married, they say, winter him, summer him and winter him again. We had wintered and we had summered three times for good measure, and then we married in the fall. We were both DPs. Two stateless persons, we stood before the registrar in Küsnacht in neutral Switzerland listening reverently as he joined us in marriage. Afterwards, we received the traditional Swiss "guidebook" to marital life, containing not a word about sex but plenty of good advice about all remaining aspects of togetherness: "Don't ask your husband silly questions when he comes home tired." "Don't ask your wife to bring your slippers. She is tired, too."

We had no idea where we were going to live. Neither of us had a home or roots. Carlos, like me, had lived wherever the wind blew him. We spoke to each other in English, the second language for both of us but the one that came easiest. We wanted to settle somewhere. Where? What country? What city? We thought of drawing lots or tossing a coin. And then we did the next best thing and went to the place where I was going to work, which happened to be Munich. What about Munich for the time being?

"For the time being" stretched into four years.

Right from the start, that night on the warm sand in Spain, Carlos had been learning German, his fifth language. "Never marry a woman whose mother tongue you don't understand," a wise friend had warned him. He bought a set of German language records and respectfully practiced his first German sentence: "Come here, doggie. But doggie won't come. What a shame!" After a while the doggie did come, and he could accept his first German film role without being dubbed, as most foreigners are. As a result, he became a "German film star" right from the start.

We rented an apartment in Munich, two rooms in a new building. Empty. We owned no furniture, not even an ashtray. So we decided to get a car and head south. Italy was still cheap: years ago we'd found beautiful old pieces for the Portofino house for little money. We stopped for the night in Verona and couldn't tear ourselves away. There was an antique shop in a Via Anatasia which reminded me of the film I'd just finished. Did they have any . . . ? Signor Negrini, the fat antique dealer, shook his head. There was nothing worth having in the store, but he did have a warehouse . . .

In the course of that one morning, in a smelly old barn, dimly lit by a single weak light bulb, we found everything we needed. We pulled old tables out from under dusty mattresses, matched up sets of chairs, hunted for missing legs, tore away cobwebs the size of tennis nets, and rolled out cupboards and chests that even the fat little man had forgotten about. Our best find was an ancient oval table put together with wooden pegs. It would be our dining table, though right now it wobbled. We held it steady and looked at each other across the top. That was how it was going to be from now on. That was how we would sit and eat and look at each other.

A month later the shipment from Verona arrived in Munich. Our treasures, unrecognizable after being cleaned, stripped, varnished, reglued and renailed, were unloaded into our rooms and filled them. We had set up a household.

Carlos's first German film was a hit, and for the next ten years he shot an average of two a year, doggedly, conscientiously, though with an increasing lack of enthusiasm. One single picture pleased him, based on a German classic called *The Tavern in the Spessart Mountains*. The reason he liked it was not so much the script but the cast, which consisted, to a large extent, of animals. I discovered that he was even crazier about animals than I. He would have invited the tame bear to our apartment ("Just once! For tea.") if I'd let him. He'd already put down a deposit on the barrel-organ monkey. When he had to relinquish both of them, he brought a Spessart Mountain hedgehog home with him. Noses were his special study and enthusiasm—bear noses, monkey noses, hedgehog noses. He put the hedgehog on its back, waited until the little face with the caviar eyes peeped out, and exclaimed ecstatically, "Nose! Nose!" as he stroked the little pointed muzzle.

"You're choking him."

"He likes it."

The hedgehog didn't like it and bit his finger. He lived in our bathroom, sleeping during the day in Carlos's left driving glove. At night he woke up and climbed around, falling into the tub or the toilet, and in the end we had to set him free in the woods around the Munich Studios. We let him keep the glove.

Our next boarder was Ciancito, the pig. Someone had persuaded Carlos that you can housebreak pigs. Not true. Ciancito was given notice, and Tomasita, the mountain goat, moved in. Carlos had acquired her soon after she was born, and she regarded him as her mother because he fed her her bottle. She followed every step he took, crying piteously if he left the room without her. While he was taking his morning shower, she would stand outside the curtain bleating her misgivings. One morning she couldn't stand it any more, and disregarding her antiwater instincts, pushed boldly through the curtain right into the jet of water. The screams that ensued bore no resemblance to goat language.

At night we wrapped her rear end in a plastic bag and she slept in our bed, in Carlos's arm, her head on his shoulder. During the night she would wake him up a couple of times to be taken into the shower, because she was house-trained. She had no liking for me and gave me baleful looks out of her yellow eyes. Whenever she could catch me, she butted me from behind, knocking me over. One day, inexplicably, she had a heart attack. Her lips turned blue, and she died. Carlos was inconsolable.

We loved Munich and its surrounding mountains and lakes, and our tiny apartment with the tall old trees in front of it, under which the hookers strolled back and forth, calling our dog Biene by name. But our need to live in the country grew greater every day. "My great-grandfather's calling me," said Carlos, taking out the old cuckoo clock that had made the journey from Switzerland to Buenos Aires a hundred years ago in the baggage of his grandmother, the good Swiss citizen Margarete Schaffter.

There is such a thing as a farmer's agent. Farmers who want to buy or sell land go to him, and he gets a commission, just like an actor's agent. The well-padded Herr Dornbierer looked exactly as he was supposed to look, bursting with ruddy Swiss health, dressed in lederhosen, and smoking a pipe. He showed us half a dozen farm properties, but they all had some drawback or other. We'd gone through his whole list except one, "and that's a long way out." A long way out? From where? "It's a good three-quarters of an hour from Zurich." Three-quarters of an hour! That's how long it took every day to drive to the studios in Hollywood.

Herr Dornbierer drove us along the Lake of Zurich and suddenly turned off sharply into the mountains. We passed a couple of small towns, then a village, and then there was nothing but mountains and forests and flowery meadows. Carlos and I looked at each other and nodded. This was it! We knew it even before we reached the ancient farmhouse. Further up the road, stables, horses, pigs, cows (cows' noses!), tenant family, tenant farmhouse, barns, and meadows full of hip-high, nodding, waving wild flowers. We waded through, all alone—Dornbierer had preferred to stay and drink a glass of schnapps with the farmer—until we reached the top of the hill. There we sat down on the grass and looked over the valley to the snow-covered Glarner Alps.

"I'll be able to write again here," said Carlos.

"And I'll be able to paint," said I.

*   *   *

How did it begin? Late. Too late to be decisive, but early enough to become indispensable.

It goes back to the summer of 1945, when the war in Europe had just ended and we imagined everything would be hunky-dory as of next Monday. Rex's old RAF uniform hung in the depths of the closet, and in the entrance hall stood a conspicuously new pair of rubber hip boots. Our first holiday together! It was to be spent in Scotland, on some loch where one could fish for trout. Rex had never done any fishing. He had a vague mental picture of idyllic waters, sudden excitement "when something bites," furious duels in the water, a delectable dinner for the victor—ideal vacation stuff. Scotland was just as the guidebook described it: mountainous, greenish, and misty.

Rex cast his line in a high arc, as he had been taught, but on his first dozen casts the fly never hit the water. It got caught in a tree behind him or a bush in front, or tangled perversely and painfully with his hair, and once, in a truly mysterious way, got hooked in the sole of his green rubber boot. I sat on a rock out of range and watched, weak with laughter. Finally he managed it. A red fly, selected with loving care ("Which one would *you* go for if you were a trout?"), floated on the still surface of the water. Suddenly it disappeared into the depths so unexpectedly and abruptly that Rex almost went down with it. The struggle was brief, the bag small. Still, it was almost ten inches long, pink with black spots.

"We ought to immortalize it!" said Rex. "Shall we have it stuffed?" We were too greedy to do that. Photograph it? Color film wasn't yet available, and it was the colors that enraptured us. "Somebody ought to paint it," said Rex.

In the nearby village I found canvas, oil paints, and brushes. A chair in our hotel room served as easel. The fish lay on the table, stiff and cold. Wild with enthusiasm, I sketched the outlines and mixed red, white, and yellow into a salmon pink. Now for the black spots—and now what? I looked at my work, a small pink oval on a large white background. "Make it bigger," demanded Rex. I made it bigger and then bigger still, mixed a lot more pink, and added a lot more spots. By now it was a salmon, but it still wasn't a painting.

Then it dawned on me: the creature was lonesome! It needed company. Boldly I placed two beer bottles beside it. Better. But still not right. Fish and beer, plus fishhook and wire on the table. Lots of dark brown wood to bring out the salmon pink. I lost my head and attempted a "background," an open door with a glimpse of the loch and the hills—and my first painting was finished! And not a single minute too soon, because the model was quietly beginning to stink. The canvas dried. We had it framed and hung it up at home.

Friends and relatives came and marvelled at it. But that wasn't the point. I suddenly felt the urge to pass once again through the frenzy that had gripped me in Scotland while I was painting the fish. The "painting" I had concocted was beneath contempt, that much I knew. Irrelevant. The ecstasy, the sensuous pleasure of squeezing out large red and yellow worms next to each other on the palette— that I wanted to experience again.

At school we'd been taught to paint in the deadly fashion of the time. Our teacher's name was Herr Prinz. As far as I was concerned, he was one. He gave me an A every year because I produced any amount of garish still lifes from his arrangements of red apples and yellow lemons (made of soap), or, from photographs, flowering almond trees against a blue sky. The main thing was to put your name in the lower right-hand corner in a special way he had invented, a sort of calling card, artistically shaded.

I possessed a certain facility. This facility later became, and remains, my worst enemy. Facility is an obstacle to creativeness. In any art form. You get a nice effect without effort, sometimes by accident, and you're satisfied; but there's nothing substantial underneath.

After the trout, our cook posed for me in a red dress, and Carey in a yellow bib against a blue background. I even tried a nude—Linda Christian on our lawn. A beautiful model, but a pink piece of wood on my canvas. Nevertheless, every canvas was immediately framed to give me courage. Anything looks better in a frame. Tirelessly, I covered a lot more defenseless canvases with bright colors, the way I used to play with decals as a child, full of high hopes but with no idea of how they were going to turn out.

Nonetheless I felt the need to improve. I went to museums and looked at modern paintings with fresh eyes, as a sort of "colleague." I "saw" but I didn't have a clue, didn't even know why I liked any particular picture.

I decided to ask. My best source was Rolf, who was back at his easel, designing the first of the Metropolitan Opera stage sets that established him. I brought him my best effort, a garden with an arbor and a lot of greenery. I knew that Rolf would tell me the truth. He had done it once before, long ago, when we first met in Berlin and I was preparing for my final high school examinations. That time, too, I had picked my very best drawing, and because I wanted his honest opinion, I pretended that it was the work of our drawing teacher at school. "Terrible," he had murmured, "absolutely terrible."

Now he looked carefully at the little canvas and found it neither good nor terrible. "Don't always reach for the green when you're painting a tree," he said, opening up a whole new vista. This became my first and most important rule, for it freed me at one stroke from the fetters of those drawing lessons. So trees could be yellow or even blue! It all depended on what color you put next to them. In my next canvas, the trees were blood red.

In Hollywood I became a Sunday painter. Many stars painted. To kill time, or to calm their nerves. "Are you happily married or do you paint?" the reporters asked. My case was different. I painted out of passion and conceit. I thought myself incredibly talented. Every time I sat down before a new canvas, I was convinced it was going to be a Cézanne. Ronald Colman, a fellow painter, told friends that he once asked me what I did with my bad paintings— did I throw them away or paint over them? "I have no bad ones," I replied.

That was twenty years ago. I painted blissfully and "sincerely" (the way I acted in pre-Elsa days) every time I had a minute to spare. There weren't many. We had left Hollywood for New York and were giving eight performances a week on Broadway. That left only our vacations in Portofino, and there, too, I was rarely on my own, because Rex had no hobby and didn't enjoy reading, so our guest rooms were occupied by a succession of friends who had to be fed and entertained. The easel was put aside, the brushes grew stiff.

They didn't soften up until my marriage broke up. I began to paint again in an attempt to get interested in something. For want of a model I sat down, looked into a mirror, and painted a self-portrait. That was a mistake. What looked back at me from the mirror made the bright colors on my palette shrivel. White and a little green were all I could use.

Not until Carlos came into my life a few months later was the palette brought out once again. The mournful colors were scraped off, and bright blue was squeezed out of the tube. Blue—to me the color of joy and serenity. A professional psychiatrist among our friends said, "Shall I tell you why you use so much blue in your paintings?" "No," I said hastily, "I don't want to know." I didn't want to be reminded of whatever it was every time I reached for the blue tube.

Carlos was the first person to take a long hard look at my work. "Make up your mind," he said. "Either you go on dabbling and remain an amateur all your life or you pull yourself together and *learn* something. That means painting several hours a day, every day. That means going into battle and sweating."

A new artistic life began. The first thing I noticed was that Elsa's "iron rules" for acting held good for painting too. "Don't show me your talent," she used to say. "Talent" was all I had to offer on my canvases. If a composition was successful, it was an accident. Very slowly, like a devout pilgrim taking two steps backward for every three forward, I began to accumulate a stock of "iron rules" which gradually became second nature.

Carlos made some decisive contributions. One day he was frowning at an Italian landscape I was sweating over. "I think the old wall over there would stand out better if you'd get rid of all the undergrowth."

"How can I do that?" I asked indignantly. "It's *there!*"

"So what? What's to stop you from leaving it out? Do you want to paint a picture or do justice to the bushes?"

I got rid of the undergrowth and for the first time became master of my canvas.

In one field, however, neither hard work nor inspiration could help me overcome my lack of academic instruction: drawing from life, an indispensable part of every painter's training. Many great masters draw nude studies every day for a few hours, just as ballerinas practice at the bar, to keep in training. So while I was filming,

I attended the local art school. Whether in Hollywood or in Vienna, I would show up on free days with my sketchbook and charcoal and sit down in the back row. On my very first day in a life class in Hollywood, I made a discovery. I had finished my sketch of a nude, a black girl, in a five-minute pose. Suddenly the teacher appeared behind me.

"Where have you worked before?"

"This is my first time."

"I know you're new here, but where did you study?"

"I've never studied. This is my first life class."

He didn't believe me. "How do you know how it hangs together?"

"I can see it."

"Good eyes!" he murmured and went on his way.

Not that I had produced anything interesting, but my sketch had come out "right." That was something. The charcoal shook in my hand. No doubt about it, in the brief time allotted, I was able to "solve" every pose the girl took up. Weird to discover this unsuspected ability. When the class was over, I was covered in sweat and convinced that I was a genius. From now on everything could be solved; I'd found the key. Masterpieces would roll off my easel like so many pretzels.

At the start of the very next class, I was rudely brought to my senses. This class was working in oils, and I didn't understand a word of the basic principles the teacher was talking about. What were "warm" and "cold" colors? I guessed. Red must be warm. Yellow too. Was blue cold? Of course, they told me, what else? (Oh, well, it had always seemed warm to me!) And what did the teacher mean by composition and "not letting the design slide out of the side"? I didn't understand a word. Anyhow, I was bored with the still-life arrangement of a cold gray vase and two warm oranges that the class was busily painting. It reminded me of Herr Prinz.

No sense in hanging around here, I thought. I'd rather muddle along on my own. Packed up my things and left.

I painted indiscriminately—anything that would sit still; landscapes, nudes, still lifes, portraits. Portraits were touchy. It made me nervous to keep someone sitting there motionless without paying them for it. When I really got going, I often forgot that the model had been sitting for too long and was getting a crick in the neck.

Also, on my canvases, people looked a good ten years older than they were, and angrier. They rarely showed any desire to own the portrait. Unintentionally, I was copying Picasso. When he painted Gertrude Stein, she protested that she "didn't look like that," and he said, "But you will, Gertrude, you will!" And he was right.

Fritzi Massary sat for me, as a special favor, shortly before her eightieth birthday. Fifty years before, Fritzi Massary had been the unchallenged queen of German and Austrian light opera. Her name on the posters meant a sellout for the season. They had even named a cigarette after her—fifty years ago.

Now, in her old age, she was living in Hollywood. She came to sit for me twice and stayed no more than an hour; I knew her face so well that I didn't need her longer. She sat on an uncomfortable chair, as straight as if she had swallowed a ruler, delicate and as effortlessly elegant as she had been half a century before.

"The last time I let anybody paint me was forty years ago," she croaked in her hoarse, double-bass voice. "He was a peculiar young fellow with a long chin and wild hair. He came into my dressing room at the theater and messed it up with his paints. Three or four times. Then I looked at the thing. Nothing but a lot of green splotches. So I threw him out."

"Can you remember his name, Fritzi?"

"Kokoschka."

Undeterred, I went on mixing my colors.

When her portrait was finished, I drove to her house and showed it to her. "It's awful," she said. Relieved, I brought it back home. It hangs in my bedroom.

About ten years ago, when I was staying at Noël Coward's house on Lake Geneva, he invited somebody especially for me: Oskar Kokoschka. He had placed a photograph of my portrait of Fritzi Massary on the mantel, where the painter could hardly fail to see it.

Kokoschka came and saw. He recognized Fritzi at once. Maybe the memory of his hasty exit from her dressing room was still green.

While he examined the photo, I asked whether Fritzi's story was true. "Oh, yes," he said, and laughed. Then he asked what I'd been hoping for: "Show me more." At that time I carried photographs of my paintings around with me the way other people carry snapshots of their children.

Then he said something of crucial importance, which applies not merely to achievement and fulfillment in any artistic field but to life in general: "The question whether—and the fact that—you have talent is irrelevant. Thousands of people have talent. I might just as well congratulate you on having eyes in your head. The one and only thing that counts is: do you have staying power?"

He didn't know that he was dealing with a tarantula. My staying power becomes a vice, because I can never let go of anything. When I sit in front of my easel altering composition and colors and shapes for the hundredth time, I have a mental picture of Jacob in the Bible: The angel has come to pay a visit, but wants to be off again. Jacob, however, clutches the heavenly folds of its garment, crying, "I will not let thee go except thou bless me."

I am Jacob. I never let anything go until I have been blessed. Like a dog worrying a bone, I push and pull my composition this way and that on the canvas until at long last I get it right. This usually takes months, sometimes years. I work on a dozen paintings at a time; I sit down at the easel and listen in to myself, hoping to find somebody at home. Sometimes no bell rings, and the canvas is put back against the wall. But I don't let go of it. Soon it will be brought out and grappled with again. That's what I mean when I speak of a vice. I ought to be able to forget some of my miscarried compositions and save a lot of time and paint. But I can't. Every canvas is a challenge to battle, and you can't come down to supper until you think you've won.

When I'd won about thirty battles, my paintings were shown to the Tooth Gallery in London. Dudley Tooth and his partner put them all next to and on top of each other to get an overall impression. They even used a magnifying glass to examine the quality. Then they gave their verdict; they would give me a show, but not under my own name. The art critics would be prejudiced if they were invited to an exhibition of an actress's paintings. What has she been doodling in her spare time? they would think. If I wanted to be taken seriously, I'd have to exhibit under a pseudonym.

Okay. Suppose I signed my canvases "Lissmann" (my mother's maiden name)? Excellent. Lissmann it would be. Just that; no first name. People would assume that the painter was a man, and that would be a good thing. In any case, my paintings never showed "delicate," feminine qualities. I paint like a man.

"Lissmann's" pictures were framed by the gallery in my absence, and dates were set. Suddenly I received a telegram: "Changed mind stop stand or fall under your own name stop catalogue says Lilli Palmer." "Lismann" dropped out of sight. But my confidence was shaken. The critics had probably seen me in some play in London or in a movie or on television. How were they to know that I was Jacob?

On the flight to London the day before the opening, I sat biting my nails. What had I got myself into? Fortunately Carlos was sitting by my side and reminded me that nearly all painters had been murdered by the critics when they started out. But was I a painter? "Yes," said Carlos. "In your own eyes you're a painter, and that's what counts. Think of van Gogh. He didn't sell a single picture during his lifetime." This cheered me up. At the worst I'd keep on painting, unnoticed and unsold, in van Gogh's footsteps.

The vernissage was at six o'clock in the evening. Well over a hundred people had been invited—critics, patrons of the arts, other painters, and "important" personalities. TV and press had been notified. I felt sick. Sicker than before any exam or first night. An hour before the reception, Carlos and I drove to the gallery. We walked through the empty rooms, hand in hand, looking and marvelling. There they hung, my scruffy children, splendidly framed and lit. I hardly recognized them.

It soon became apparent that I was not to walk in van Gogh's footsteps after all, because I sold seven pictures in the first two hours. All in all, there were twenty-five paintings, of which nineteen found purchasers, plus another three which had been on reserve.

I had a hard time stopping myself from kissing every single red "Sold" label on the frames.

The notices in the next day's papers are the only ones I've ever kept and pasted in a special album. They all said more or less the same thing. But it was exactly what I wanted to hear: she's a painter.

21

Life With My Father's Son

❀

O N TOP of the highest hill on our land, three thousand feet
above the Lake of Zurich, stood an ancient fir tree, around
which we built our house. Mad, of course. No sane Swiss native
would have chosen this lonely spot, utterly exposed to the elements.
But we didn't know about the elements. Blithely we cut a road right
through the meadows, fortified the house with double insulation and
double windows, and wrapped it neatly around the tree. In the
winter, a sturdy Landrover with twelve gears is our only lifeline,
but there are days when even the twelfth gear fails and snow-
storms rage, cutting us off for days on end from the outer world.
No matter. There's a deep-freeze and television to sustain us.

On one such day the telephone rang. Hollywood. As I was looking out the window waiting to be put through, I watched the thick
soup of snowflakes swirling in all directions, obliterating the view
of the lake and the mountains, even our garden and gate—and
suddenly there was a happy, sunny voice at the other end of the
line: "Hi, Lil! Want to come over and do a film for Paramount with
Clark Gable? Is Carlos free to come with you? I have a nice house
for the two of you to stay in, nice pool, nice garden, orange trees—"

All I managed to answer was, "Are they in bloom right now, the
orange trees?"

Carlos wasn't working, thank God. Our only difficulty was how to transport Biene, our boxer dog. In a crate? She'd be desperate. With a muzzle? She'd be deeply hurt. When the storm abated, we took her to Zurich Airport for a private interview with the captain of our flight across the pole to Los Angeles. The man talked to her at some length and finally declared, "You can take her with you in the cabin without a muzzle. She seems to have better manners than some of the passengers I've had to carry!"

I hadn't been in Hollywood since the *Four Poster* days, seven years ago. All my old friends seemed to have moved away; the French set had gone back to Paris, and the British colony was sadly depleted. In any case, we didn't belong to either. All we had was Biene and—never before experienced when I breathed the Hollywood atmosphere—peace of mind. That small swimming pool at the back of our rented house was the first one that I didn't want to drown myself in.

I'd never been to the Paramount studios. Every face was brand-new to me, and I felt like kissing them all, starting with the two independent producers, Bill Perlberg and George Seaton, who were making the film for release by Paramount. They were a rare pair, those two, operating in perfect harmony for twenty years and more, making outstanding films, Seaton writing and directing, Perlberg producing—without ever having signed a contract with each other. They didn't need one, they said.

But Not for Me was the title of my film. I played Gable's divorced wife, who gets him back in the end. I knew Clark, of course, from my former party life. Occasionally he had come to our house, and I remember during the course of one night pouring an entire bottle of whiskey into the glass inside his large fist, and his steadily emptying it without ever stirring from his seat next to the fireplace. At dawn he had walked out of the house, huge, straight, and apparently sober.

I only knew the postwar Gable, the one who had cared so little about his life that he had volunteered to be a tail gunner, the most vulnerable job in a bomber crew. Before the death of his wife, Carole Lombard, in a plane crash, he had been "very lively," people told me, full of fun and fond of practical jokes. The man I met for the first time in 1946 was quiet, withdrawn, apparently indifferent. He still smiled his large-tomcat smile, showing a magnificent array of dazzling teeth. These originated with a dentist named Wallace and were known as "the Wallace Collection." They were easily detachable, and Clark occasionally liked to shock people by taking them out, thus letting his face collapse into unrecognizability.

What impressed me most about him was his sturdy "pro" mentality. Every morning on the stroke of nine he entered the set, knew his lines to perfection, nodded to the director's suggestions, never disputed them, and carried them out. His contract stipulated that he could go home at five o'clock. At five minutes to five he would glance at his watch and call out a calm, firm "Five more minutes, boys!" into the air, not caring if anybody heard him or not. On the dot of five he would get up and leave. Sometimes we were in the midst of a take, and I pleaded with him to let us finish, but he shook his head. "If I stayed on for a couple of minutes just one single time, that would be the thin end of the wedge. I work eight hours a day, like everybody else. No more."

And that was it. We always worked on for another hour without him.

Once when I was standing next to him, being lit for a close shot, he suddenly said apropos of nothing, "You know, I'll only start to touch the first fifty thousand dollars of this epic in two years' time. Funny, ain't it? The boys who take care of me say I mustn't make another cent this year, taxwise." He never came near to touching that first fifty thousand, for he died a year later at the age of sixty, happily married once again and missing the one great event he had been looking forward to with excitement, the birth of his son, born a few months after his death.

But Not for Me was no blockbuster, but it got me back into Hollywood film-producing circles. My second film for the Perlberg-Seaton ménage, a year later, was *The Pleasure of His Company*, opposite Fred Astaire. With trepidation, I read a scene in the script —quite a long one, too—calling for me to dance with Fred. Dance with Fred Astaire! The last time I "danced," I had ended up in a heap at the feet of those chorus girls at the Moulin Rouge in Paris.

I took the script to George Seaton, the author-director, and said,

"Mr. Seaton—sorry, but I can't dance. Could this scene take place somewhere else? On a sofa? Under the Christmas tree? Must it be played dancing on the parquet floor of the living room?"

"Yes, it must," said George. "We need the music, for one thing. For another, we're grateful for every chance to show Fred dancing. Surely you can do a little something! Anybody can dance with Fred Astaire!"

Well, apparently I wasn't anybody. When the dreaded moment came, and Fred, according to the script, had to grab me and "sweep me off my feet," he certainly swept me off in a wonderfully elegant gesture, but I landed squarely with both feet on his, stopping him dead in his tracks. "Good Lord!" said he, amazed. "I warned you!" said I, feeling a certain satisfaction that I had been able to pin down the great Astaire, if only for a moment. The second time he swept me off, he never allowed me to land at all and I just hung suspended in his arms, trying to remember my lines while bereft of the support of terra firma.

During the shooting of this film a remarkable event took place. The unions went on strike. They had threatened to boycott the studios if their demands were not met, and the big companies had remained obdurate. They just couldn't believe it would happen, but it did. For the first time in the history of Hollywood, the lights went out in every studio at six o'clock one Friday night. At Paramount, it happened right after a scene on a sofa in which Fred bestowed a chaste kiss on me from several becoming angles. We rose, said a bemused and subdued good-bye to everybody, and made for our dressing rooms. Nobody knew what it all meant, how long it was going to last or whether we would ever be able to finish the film.

I took off my makeup and climbed into my car. We had been told that the main gates were already closed and to please drive out at the back. Where was "the back"? Slowly I cruised up and down several studio "streets." Strange—only now, when I saw those streets dark and silent for the first time, was I aware of the vastness of the compound. Not all of the giant sets were as yet closed up; some were still wide open. On other days I had whisked past them amidst the bustle and the noise, eager to get home. Now I took them in for the first time. One showed the decor of a medieval castle, another offices in a modern apartment building, a third looked like poverty-stricken huts against a mountain backdrop. There were no lights whatever, but the moon was full and guided me. I drove slowly in the eerie silence. Where was "the back"? Once or twice I thought I saw somebody bending down or carrying something, but when I called out I got no reply. I passed the wardrobe departments, the first aid stations, the vast storage halls, more sets, more units, more office buildings—the expanse and wealth of that studio made itself felt for the first time now that it was out of action.

I found the back entrance, but there was nobody in the guardhouse to check my exit. Anybody might have walked in. Could it possibly mean that Hollywood studio life would die one day? Inconceivable. Yet no doubt about it, some sort of knell had sounded.

As it turned out, it was not the death knell; not yet. The fabulous patient had only fainted for the first time.

A week later some compromise was found, and we resumed work.

The Pleasure of His Company apparently gave pleasure to a lot of people, and I was signed for a third film by the same team, by now my friends. I was to play the part of a German resistance fighter during the Hitler years in a film called *The Counterfeit Traitor*, a good story. What's more, a true one.

It seems that in 1942, when the tide of war had turned in favor of the Allies, they managed to blackmail a Swedish businessman named Ericson into doing some all-important spying for them, a task for which his yearly business travels inside Germany fitted him perfectly. His "contact" in that country was a devout Catholic girl called Marianne von Möllendorf. Inevitably they fell in love. In the end Ericson, played by William Holden, could escape to Sweden, but Marianne was executed in the infamous Moabit prison in Berlin.

We started our location shooting in Hamburg, for it was there that Ericson hid from the Gestapo in one special and well-known block in the red-light district called the Herbertstrasse—just one single block of houses facing each other across a narrow road. At each end of the road there are barriers through which only one person at a time can squeeze, watched with amiable disinterest by a policeman. Hundreds of sailors from all corners of the earth squeeze through in the course of a night, and then saunter slowly from one house to the next, looking upwards all the time. Every house has two stories, and windows reaching from floor to ceiling. The windows are floodlit, displaying the "merchandise" to advantage: girls in all colors of the rainbow, more or less nude, booted or barefoot, brandishing whips and other pleasant accessories and calling down encouragement into the sea of upturned, staring faces.

Perlberg, Seaton, Bill Holden, and I squeezed through the barrier and joined the throng. Perlberg grumbled the entire length of the block. He had had several meetings with the madames of the various establishments, since he intended to hire the Herbertstrasse for one night and shoot his sequence right there. The madames stood firmly united on their terms; no "business" for one night would set Perlberg back $100,000. He declined.

As we were slowly moving with the tide of sailors, staring upward as they did, one fat lady in green corsets leaned out a window, pointed a coy finger at me, and started to sing "Oh, Mein Papa." I tried to shrink into nothingness while a couple of her neighbors looked down, recognized me, and joined in the song. My three companions looked at me with new respect. "They seem to know you," Bill Holden said. "How come? Have you . . . er . . . worked here before?"

Old Ericson, by now in his seventies, a red-faced giant of a man, stayed with us during the shooting to make sure that the details were correct. Once during our location work in Berlin, he took me to a nondescript gray street and pointed to a narrow wrought-iron balcony on the third floor. "That was where we used to meet," he said. "We had two rooms up there—and that's where they caught her in the end." He stood for a long while with tears streaming down his face.

The old prison in Moabit, Berlin, is still in use. Some three thousand major criminals live there, a lot of them for life. Our action shots of Marianne's execution were to be filmed at the very spot where she died, in the center courtyard, entirely surrounded by the main cell blocks. The inmates had been told what we were to do during our three-day schedule, and were allowed to watch from behind their barred windows, provided they kept quiet.

I was handed a piece of clothing that the frugal Germans had preserved from the days when it had been "in use," one of the many colorless old garments that had not been destroyed by blood. But I thought I detected stains, and I thought I found bullet holes. I put it on. I was to be "executed" with two other traitors, all in similar outfits. I walked out into the cobbled courtyard and watched while the cameras were being set up. There was the wall against which I was to stand. It was scarred by hundreds of bullet holes. They were the real thing. The wall was the real thing. Marianne had stood in front of it early one morning, had been snuffed out in a few seconds—and then somebody had hosed down the wall and the courtyard.

I looked up. Hundreds of faces were watching me from behind their iron bars. The assistant director called "Ready" and I walked across to the wall. My knees were shaking, my hands dripping wet. I said to myself almost audibly, now don't be a bloody fool. *She* faced the SS firing squad. *You* face the cameras!

No scene was ever easier to act. It played itself. I did nothing— just let myself go. The only difficulty, the usual one, was doing it several times over. In the end I had stopped shaking and had become an actress again.

The inmates, watching, enjoyed themselves immensely. After we had shot the last gasp and the cameras were packing up, they gave us a loud "Bravo" and, for comic relief, they, too, began to sing "Oh, Mein Papa . . ."

After our return to Switzerland, Carlos took stock. He had made some two dozen German and French films and a long English television series, and had enjoyed them as little as his earlier American and Argentinian ventures. High time to quit, to put an end to what he called "a nylon existence." Throw away so as not to lose, says a German proverb.

He had never really belonged. He'd always kept himself apart from his fellow actors, taking refuge behind his desk whenever he could. He had written two novels in Spanish and dozens of short stories and articles. It was high time to break away completely. "Every day in the studio makes me more stupid," he would say.

On the door of his study in our farmhouse, he tacked a poster he'd painted of a snarling bulldog and the words: "Caution. Dangerous Dog. Enter at Own Risk. No Admission Except for Postmen with Money Orders." He then plunged into the unfathomable depths of a new book, emerging only for meals and a bit of mountain air. He had finished the first hundred and fifty pages when they were snatched away and replaced by something quite different—an adventure, a mission, a mandate.

It began in front of the fire one evening with Laurence Olivier.

My friendship with Olivier dates back thirty years and has nothing to do with acting. People make friends quickly when they're on stage or on camera together. You discover and take to each other with enthusiasm, spend time together on weekends as well as working hours, and are convinced that you've enriched your life with a permanent new friendship. When the play or the film ends, you go your own ways, meeting again only when your contracts happen to coincide. You find that the forced intimacy of collaboration— closer than in any other profession—was only circumstantial and had no real roots. Once in a while, though, it lasts, and these friends then become part of your minimum daily requirement, part of your life. Olivier is that kind of friend.

He called up one day and asked if we had snow and if Carlos would teach him to ski. He had a week free and felt he absolutely must get away.

"But wouldn't you rather lie in a deck chair in the sun and rest?"

"No. If I lie still, the National Theatre will fall on top of me and bury me. I need something to concentrate on, something that will keep me too scared of breaking my leg to think. And then—the fresh air! Skiing is exactly what I need."

He arrived with his wife, Joan Plowright, and Carlos started them off on short skis. On their fifth day they were ready to ride the T-bar lift up the ski bunnies' slope. An instructor rode up with Joan; Carlos had his arm around Olivier. "Hold me tight!" roared the most famous voice in England at full pitch. He made it to the top. As he shakily snowplowed down the gentle slope, he roared again, this time in triumph.

Sitting by the fire that night, relaxed and content, he suddenly began to speak of the problem that was bothering him. Kenneth Tynan, his artistic adviser, had recommended a new play by Rolf Hochhuth called *Soldiers*. Tynan was dead set on producing this play; to him it was a kind of crusade. Olivier, managing director, administrator, and leading actor of the National Theatre, was against it. The play dealt with the death of General Sikorski, leader of the free Polish forces in England during the war. It maintained that in July 1943 Winston Churchill had had the general, one of his personal friends, assassinated by arranging for the airplane that was bringing Sikorski to London from Gibraltar to crash. The "accident" occurred shortly after takeoff. Hochhuth's play investigated Churchill's "tragic guilt" or "justification" in the political murder of his friend. In a preface, Hochhuth stated that documentary "proof" for the murder had been deposited in the safe of a Swiss bank, but would not be available for public scrutiny for fifty years.

Olivier didn't want the play produced at his theater. He thought that the National Theatre was not the right place to accuse the savior and hero of the Second World War of such a crime. He had brought the script with him and wanted to know what Carlos thought of it. Fascinated, Carlos read late into the night and declared himself willing to meet Hochhuth, take him to see Olivier in England, and interpret for them.

When he hugged me good-bye at the airport, he intended to be back "in a few days." The few days grew into two years. But as I drove home alone, I had no inkling of this.

Nor did Carlos. He had no premonition of the mission he was about to undertake when he shook Hochhuth's hand for the first time. At first it was just a matter of being helpful, because Hochhuth didn't know any English. Carlos interviewed people, questioned witnesses, checked newspaper clippings and documents. The few days lengthened into weeks, and I was still alone up there on our mountaintop. We talked on the telephone every night, as we always did when we were separated. One day I detected a new tone in his daily report from London. It seemed to me that he was no longer just being helpful; he was now carrying on his own investigations, independently, for purposes of his own. Finally he flew home. Not to unpack; to repack. Not just one suitcase but several, as though he were setting out on an expedition.

That's just what he was doing, as he told me quite frankly. He'd made discoveries, pried open leads that he simply had to follow up, was more and more convinced that there had never been any plot to murder Sikorski. The plane crashed as a result of a mechanical defect. The "ghastly slaughter" that the British secret service was said to have perpetrated among the occupants of the airplane never took place. But he intended to collect his own evidence on the spot, digging it out like an archeologist. His equipment: a tape recorder.

Above all, he needed time. He would have to travel, travel long distances. How long? No idea. When would he come home? No idea.

So began Operation No Idea. I was left behind, somewhat disembowelled. I had to adjust and reorient myself and live on letters and telephone calls. And collaborate as much as I could. It went on for two years, two long years. The letters and telephone calls came from all corners of the world, and our postman's stamp collection grew rapidly. Stamps from Gibraltar, Prague, Belgrade, Chicago, and finally from San Francisco, where Carlos at last ran to earth the "dead" pilot of the ill-fated plane. Now he was sure of his ground.

The endless dragging months came to an end, and he returned home. The suitcases had increased in number and were crammed with hundreds of cassettes, the testimony of witnesses, the trophies of his two years on the warpath. He spent the next few months in his study behind drawn shades. He had no idea whether it was sunny or snowing. He was listening and typing, listening and typing . . .

He called his book *The Assassination of Winston Churchill*. Shortly before it appeared, he took me along to a secret meeting at the Hotel Connaught. At the last minute he told me that we were going to have lunch with Milovan Djilas and his wife. Djilas? Tito's former friend and vice-president? The man Tito had kept in jail

for twelve years after their political split? The very man. How did
Djilas get to London? Tito had given him a passport and a travel
permit in the wake of the Prague Spring. So Djilas was a free man
now? No, but he was allowed to "travel" and lecture abroad on
Yugoslavia.

"How do you know Djilas?"

Carlos smiled and didn't answer. The stamps from Belgrade . . .

The two men embraced each other like old friends. During lunch
I ventured a few questions, not really knowing what was permissible
and what was taboo. Djilas answered readily. Of course he was happy
to sniff the air of the outside world again. It was all new to him. He
was now living with his wife and son in his own apartment, but
ever since his release from prison he had been practically cut off
from the outside world, like a leper. Only a handful of people knew
where he lived. But one day—he paused and smiled—the doorbell
had rung.

"I open. Stands there—strange man." He pointed to Carlos, who
was talking to Mrs. Djilas. "I say what you want? He says I want
speak with you. I look into man's face. I think, whole man is in
this face. I say come in."

After lunch, both men took a pill from little boxes they carried
with them. It turned out to be exactly the same digestive pill. One
pill came from Belgrade, the other from London. Carlos's pillbox,
an old snuffbox, was a present from me. Djilas had a dented old tin
box that had never left him throughout his twelve years of im-
prisonment. Both boxes were laid on the table and solemnly exchanged as a token of friendship. Djilas's tin box is Carlos's most
precious possession.

Carlos's book was published in England in May 1969. The
London *Sunday Times* carried a long, enthusiastic review: "Apart
from having written an enthralling book which is great fun to read,
Mr. Thompson has performed a valuable service to history. No one
can say quite how the Hochhuth version might have distorted, as
time goes by, posterity's picture of Churchill. Human credulity has
scarcely any limit; the strangest insinuations, the oddest innuendos
can find acceptance somewhere unless they are rebutted by someone

who knows his job and can test the evidence before it disappears. Mr. Thompson has done this. His book leaves nothing for the Day of Judgment."

We felt that it had all been worthwhile.

22
Noël

❦

THERE WAS ONE THING I had completely forgotten when Carlos
and I were planning our life together: the theater. There was
simply no room for it in our future plans. Movies? Yes, of course,
anywhere, any time. In the first place, movies were the best way to
earn money, and anyone starting over from scratch, as we were, had
better work hard. In the second place, it doesn't take long to make
a film. Important for us, because we didn't want to be separated
any more than was strictly necessary. But Broadway! My Broadway
season! "That's all over now," said Carlos. "You'll just have to
accept it." He was right. I couldn't possibly ask him to sit and twiddle
his thumbs in New York for a whole year while I appeared on the
stage every night. A woman's place is wherever her husband's work
takes him, not vice versa. This is not a matter of "making sacrifices"
but of asking yourself, Which means more to me, my career or my
marriage?

Our conversation took place during a lunch break in the Hamburg film studios, where we were making our first picture together.
I still remember the strawberry yogurt I was eating at the very
moment when I realized that the theater chapter of my life was
over.

From 1955 to 1966 I refused every play offered, no matter where
it came from. I didn't even read the plays and returned the fat

envelopes unopened. Which merited no halo. I found it unexpectedly easy to give up the theater. It had completely vanished by the time I had finished that strawberry yogurt. I was living a totally different life, spoke different languages, saw a lot of new people, made films in Munich, Berlin, Paris, Rome, and, if Carlos and I had to be separated, spent the evening on the telephone to him. When I was asked if I didn't miss the legitimate stage, the "live contact" instead of the "artificial atmosphere" of the film studio, I quite honestly said no, I didn't miss it. Neither the rustle of the rising curtain nor the rare moments of genuine rapture on stage, nor the applause. Now if I went to the theater and went backstage to greet a former colleague after the show, I would pause for a moment as I crossed the stage to breathe the familiar smell of the wings—the same the whole world over—but it was like a chance meeting with an old friend to whom you haven't much to say after the happy first greeting.

Then, in the spring of 1966, Noël called up.

Noël Coward died in March 1973, and the English-speaking theater world on both sides of the Atlantic went into mourning. I was in Nice at the time, making an English television series with John Mills, an old friend. His wife, Mary, called me at the hotel and broke the news. That evening the four of us, Carlos and I, Johnny and Mary, went to a restaurant somewhere outside Nice on the Corniche and ate, drank, and laughed until long after midnight. We laughed until we cried, telling stories about Noël. Mine begin in 1940; Johnny's date back to 1929.

In the end we noticed the tired faces of the waiters, mutely asking us to get the hell out and continue our celebration elsewhere. Okay, we're leaving. We paid and drove back to our hotel, looking down at the thousands of lights along the Riviera—and stopped laughing. Suddenly we all recognized that an irreplaceable element of joy had vanished from our lives.

As we said good-bye, Johnny said, "You know something—I'm absolutely sure that this evening has been exactly the kind of memorial service Noël would have liked. This is just the way he would have wanted to be remembered."

So Johnny had known him eleven years longer than I had! I was jealous. Stupidly so, because when Johnny was first appearing on the stage with Noël, I was still a fat senior in high school. Years later, when I started to get a foothold in the English theater world, Noël's star shone from a glamorous distance. I had never even caught sight of him. Not true—I did see him once, sort of, at a first night. I was sitting in the orchestra, and somebody pointed to a box and said, "Look who's over there. Noël Coward." I felt a little shiver of awe, although all I could see was a silhouette with rather protruding ears. The sugar-bowl aspect of his ears was the only defect in Noël's outward appearance. Once when somebody he didn't know was supposed to meet him at a railroad station, Noël sent a telegram saying, "Arriving 4:30 stop easily recognizable stop tall divinely handsome in gray."

When I was finally privileged to see him close to, he wasn't divinely handsome, but he was still tall, with clean-cut English features, Chinese-lidded eyes, nicotine-stained teeth, a jerky, almost convulsive, laugh, and small, feminine hands. Except for his hands, there was nothing about him to suggest that he was homosexual. A hundred percent so.

Later, after we'd become friends, I asked him once, "Haven't you ever slept with a woman, Noël?"

"Never!" he replied, in his staccato, slightly nasal voice, raising his finger menacingly. "Never. I was once assaulted by a woman, though. Gertie, of course." (Gertrude Lawrence, his favorite partner all her life.) "She was twelve, and I was eleven. We were both angels in a Christmas pantomime. With wings, which complicated matters considerably. The whole thing took place in the ladies' lavatory behind the stage. After that I never again strayed from the path of virtue."

Indeed, his pet aversion was homosexuals who had been "saved" by various (and determined) females. When I argued that a "reclaimed" one could make a good husband and, as in the case of a mutual friend, even a father of two children, he would have none of it. "That proves nothing," he declared. "Except that he lashed it to a toothbrush. Twice."

Our first meeting took place in my dressing room in London.

After the show someone knocked at the door. "Come in," I said, and there he was.

Noël was an inveterate dressing-room visitor. He never tried to get out of it. He knew that the stage manager would have made the rounds with the message "Noël's in the house." Even if he didn't like the play or the acting, he came backstage, knocked, walked in with finger raised, and began his diatribe, never pussyfooting, often merciless and sometimes devastating. He was a theater fanatic, took the profession seriously, and would climb four flights of stairs, panting, to reach the dressing room of some unknown actor who had caught his attention in a small part. Then he would knock and deliver his splendid praise, leaving the recipient in a happy trance.

Throughout his speech to me, I was in just such a happy trance and all but fainted when he finished with the words, "I'll write a play for you." But I had to wait twenty-six years for it.

Like most people meeting him for the first time, I was so nervous that I didn't speak a word, just stared at him ecstatically. It wasn't just the extraordinary array of talents that had made him unique. His work was irresistible, but the man himself was a masterpiece. His biting wit cut through any kind of phoniness like a razor blade, spurting out spontaneously with pointed, brilliant precision. Yet he wasn't one of those prima donnas who insist on being the center of attention at every party. There was no better listener than Noël. "Oh! Oh!" he would exclaim, raising his tiny hands in delight when a story or a remark tickled him. The best moment came when he sat down at the piano and played and sang his own songs, old and new. He didn't have to be coaxed. Whenever he entered an unfamiliar room, he automatically looked around for the piano, complaining only if it wasn't properly tuned (like ours). Countless times I watched him bent over the keyboard, his head slightly raised, accompanying himself as he sang in his high, nasal voice, clipping his syllables.

His background was modest, but he was lucky to have had a mother who sensed the child's genius, although she didn't know the first thing about the theater. When the ten-year-old boy bent her ear demanding to appear in the Christmas pantomime (for which a public audition to discover talented children is held every year), she took him to the theater and bravely turned him over to the stage manager. Noël had worked out a little song and dance number of his own and was promptly hired. The stage manager brought him back to his mother and said, "Well, Mrs. Coward, shall we say two pounds ten a week?" Mrs. Coward turned pale. "I'm sorry," she stammered, "but we couldn't possibly afford to pay that much."

Noël scored an instant success and maintained it for fifty years. His first hit play (1924), *The Vortex,* was a sensation. Half a century later his early comedies were revived as if they were classics. He became a legend in his own lifetime. All his life he worked like an ant, meticulously and rapidly. He wrote *Private Lives* in four days, *Blithe Spirit* in six.

He had a vast circle of friends, inevitably star-studded, though he wasn't in the least snobbish, probably because he had already met a basinful of celebrities while he was still a young man. He took it as a matter of course that he should spend weekends at country houses with people like Churchill, entertaining and amusing them. In the middle of the war he received a telegram from Washington, where Churchill had flown to see Roosevelt on a secret mission involving the solution to a particularly knotty Allied problem. The telegram read, "What's the beginning of the second verse of Mad Dogs and Englishmen stop answer essential to settle bet stop Churchill and Roosevelt."

Discipline was his religion, and he allowed himself no weaknesses. From his early childhood he was afraid of animals, and later of flying. So he forced himself to enter bears' and lions' cages at the zoo, accompanied by keepers. Inwardly paralyzed by fear, outwardly nonchalant, a cigarette dangling at the corner of his mouth, he treated the animals with the exquisite politeness he would have used at court. He finally brought his flying neurosis under control by traveling always by air, never by train.

"But why?" his friends asked. "Why force yourself?"

"My two Prussian cows understand why, don't they?" Noël replied, with a smile for me. I was one of his two Prussian cows; the other was Marlene Dietrich. "The only difference between the two of you," he would say, giving me a reproachful look, "is that

Marlene always carries my suitcase when she meets me at the airport."

Every so often I would feel an urgent need to see him, a need for a large dose of his humor, wisdom, and warmth. Then I would drive to his house near Montreux, spend the weekend, and fill up. We would stay up until all hours—I never felt sleepy then—and he would treat me to his conversation, which was perceptive, devastatingly honest, by no means always kind, unsentimental, profoundly wise. And always funny. I laughed with Noël the way you laugh in childhood, until your ribs ache.

For instance, his description of the scene at Buckingham Palace when he was knighted by the Queen. This happened only two years before his death, because Noël did not meet the primary requirement for this honor: he didn't live in England, and had freely admitted in interviews that he lived abroad because he couldn't afford British taxation. Queen Elizabeth, who had known and admired him since her childhood, made an exception. As a seventieth birthday present, he received the famous summons to the palace. Dressed in the obligatory black cutaway, striped trousers and top hat, he waited in an anteroom with several other candidates. A court chamberlain appeared and explained the rules: they were to bend the left knee to the floor, extend the right leg sideways, and bow the head. The Queen would then tap each shoulder lightly with a sword, saying "Rise, Sir So-and-So." Then came the most important part; they were to back toward the door until their posterior touched it. Only then might they turn around and leave the room. "Here is a chair, gentlemen," said the chamberlain. "Hold on to the back and practice."

Full of apprehension, Noël watched as, one after another, the rest of the candidates, none of them in the first bloom of youth, clutched the chair and practiced, breathing heavily. He'd never gone in for sports; knee bends were entirely beyond him. When his turn came, he declined. "I can't do it," he informed the perturbed court official. "But I trust Her Majesty will manage without my gymnastics."

Somehow or other he succeeded in getting down on both knees, while the Queen looked on apprehensively. The sword tapped him, and he rose to his feet, without any help from the monarch. As he edged slowly and carefully backward, the Queen watching him anxiously, he stumbled. "Oh dear!" exclaimed Queen Elizabeth, clapping her hand over her mouth. Then they both burst out laughing, the Queen still clutching the sword and Noël, having regained his balance, hanging on to the door handle for dear life.

When he called and said he was coming to see us bringing three brand-new plays, it was eleven years since I had appeared on the stage. That had been with Rex, in *Bell, Book and Candle* in London. Too long. I had forgotten everything—voice projection, timing, everything—because film technique calls for the exact opposite of stage technique. I told Noël all this before he began to read. He just gave me a long look and opened the script. A refusal? Out of the question. He had decided that I was to play the role and play it I bloody well would. There were three plays, one full-length and two curtain-raisers, which he proposed to alternate.

I can't stand listening to plays being read. I can't concentrate, because I'm distracted and influenced by the reader. But here, as everywhere else, Noël was an exception. Carlos and I listened fascinated for a whole evening. The fact that the London run was to be limited to four months was decisive for me. Noël never played indefinite runs, because he always got bored after four months, and there was no place in his life for boredom.

He wanted to have his face lifted before we began rehearsals, because, as he said, plucking at his droopy eyelids, he looked like "an old Chinese character actress." To avoid hospital press releases, the operation was performed in the doctor's consulting room. Under the anesthetic, his heart suddenly stopped, and the doctor, panic-stricken, had to thump his chest vigorously to start it beating again. When Noël woke up, he complained that his ribs were sore, and they had to tell him the truth. He laughed. "That would really have been something," he exclaimed with delight. "'Noël Coward Dies During Face-Lift!' Could I have asked for a better exit line?"

In addition to the usual confusion and excitement, our rehearsals brought me a new experience: I quarreled with Noël. For the first and last time. It was almost a brawl. I'd been told that he was difficult and demanding where his own plays were concerned, that many a personal friendship had gone by the board. That he could be like a raging tiger. My friend Noël? Impossible! Not at all, they said. Remember Claudette Colbert! While that excellent and beautiful, though perhaps somewhat short-necked, actress was rehearsing with Noël, he had yelled at her, "I'd wring your neck, if you had one!"

He wanted to wring mine, too. First because I wasn't always word-perfect during rehearsals, an unforgivable sin, and second because I insisted on the full four weeks of rehearsals stipulated in my contract. Noël had had enough after three. "I'm getting bored," he declared. "I need an audience." It was all very well for him; he knew the script inside out, having written it himself. There were only three characters in the plays, played by Noël, Irene Worth, and me. When Irene and I protested vigorously against any cuts in the rehearsal schedule, particularly since there was to be no pre-London tour, all hell broke loose. In any altercation Noël had the advantage, because his blistering vocabulary made short work of any opponent. The present quarrel was no exception. "I'm bored!" he shouted in the end, like a spoiled brat, and that was the end of the matter. We had to give in, gnashing our teeth with rage. So we opened a week early, and the result was predictable. I was mediocre (and jittery) and it took another month before I gave a decent performance. I knew that I could have done better, took vast umbrage, and refused to speak a word to Noël off stage.

He put up with it for a week. Then one night after the show he grabbed me by the shoulders and steered me into his dressing room.

"What do you want?" I asked crossly.

"I want my friend."

"You've got enough friends," I said. "One less won't make any difference."

"I want my friend," he insisted, forcing me to look at him because he knew I'd have to laugh. And he'd won again, as usual.

On stage he was the ideal colleague. He took what was his and helped me to mine; that is, he served the cues for my laughs so skillfully that they couldn't miss. And then something took place that had never happened to Noël before; he "dried up." He forgot his lines. His own lines! In the fifty years of his stage career, such a thing had never occurred before. The text had always been sacred. Woe to the actor who forgot his lines. And now here he was forgetting them himself. Every evening.

The first time it happened, I was as flabbergasted as he was. We were facing each other across a table, downstage, right at the footlights, "having supper." (Mashed prunes in lieu of caviar.) Sudden silence. My stomach turned upside down. Was it *my* turn to speak? Had that been *my* cue? No! It was Noël's, no doubt about it. But he remained silent and just sat there with his mouth open, staring at me in bewilderment. I took my courage in both hands and whispered his next line over a forkful of salad. He heard it, thank God, and we carried on as if nothing had happened. "Thank you, darling Prussian cow," he whispered as the curtain came down, and I felt I'd evened the score for the countless actors he'd been harassing over their lines all his life.

The next night it happened again! At a different place. This time I was braver and came to his rescue sooner. From then on it became a daily routine, and in the end we became quite saucy. "What?" he would sometimes ask, when he hadn't caught what I had whispered, and I would calmly repeat his line. The stage manager, Irene, and I wondered, of course. (Hardening of the arteries?) But we didn't mention it, and the audience never noticed anything.

There were variations even in this new routine. Once, during our famous downstage supper, Noël suddenly paused, gave me a meaningful look, and tapped his teeth. I promptly whispered his next line, but he ignored it and continued to tap his teeth. I bared mine, and all but spelled out his next words. He didn't react, just kept on tapping. Hiding my mouth behind my napkin, I bellowed his line. If he didn't get it this time . . . ! He got it and spoke, but instead of his normally grateful glance, I got a frosty one, which perturbed me so much that I nearly dried up myself. Luckily the curtain fell a few minutes later.

"What's the matter?" I asked anxiously. "Aren't you well?"

"*I'm* fine," said Noël, "but you've got spinach stuck between your teeth."

The four months finally drew to an end. All three plays had been spectacular hits, the theater sold out every night, and the line for standing room stretched a whole block along Shaftesbury Avenue. Almost as if people had known they would never see him again.

The last night came. Thunderous waves of applause, innumerable curtain calls. I stood holding his hand and bowing. For the last time. (My last time, too.)

Not long afterward he began to fail physically and spent most of his time in bed, refusing to make any effort to improve his condition (circulatory trouble) and prolong his life, not giving up a single one of his forty cigarettes a day. He had never compromised, and he refused to do so in the face of death.

His condition was no secret, because in the last year he could get about only in a wheelchair. He was wheeled to airplanes and into theaters (as a spectator) and proclaimed that he enjoyed it. Let other people rush about to their heart's content; he wasn't going to! Riding in a wheelchair was much nicer than walking—if only he'd known about it sooner!

In November 1972, one more party was given in his honor. The big ballroom at Claridge's in London was rented, and people flew in from all over the world. Some two hundred of his closest friends showed up. We found him sitting in a corner of a sofa under a huge crystal chandelier which lit him becomingly, though he looked a bit shriveled. The wheelchair was nowhere in sight.

The room filled up with stars, composers, writers from all over the world. I hadn't seen so much glamour assembled in one place since Hollywood in its heyday. They stood in line to reach the sofa and dropped on their knees to embrace him, because he couldn't stand up. It seemed perfectly natural. They were paying homage.

Then the tables were turned, and *we* tried to entertain and amuse *him,* as he had tried all his life to entertain and amuse others. People like Burt Bacharach, Alan Jay Lerner, and Frederick Loewe sat down at the piano and played and sang their latest and best numbers.

Suddenly Noël stood up. Involuntarily several hands went out to support him, but with an abrupt gesture he refused help. Then, like a wound-up clockwork toy, he very slowly tottered over to the piano, each faltering step a separate maneuver. He made it. At the last minute Laurence Olivier jumped up and pushed the piano stool under him, or he would have sat down on thin air. The ballroom was absolutely silent. Noël at the piano! I never thought I'd see it again.

For a while he just stared at the keyboard. We sat motionless. Everyone was asking himself, can he still play? Then, hesitantly, he raised his frail hands, struck a few chords, and a sigh passed through the room. Everybody recognized those chords; everybody knew what was coming.

In 1929 Noël wrote his most popular operetta, *Bitter Sweet*. The story is dated, but the songs are as familiar to every Englishman as "God Save the Queen."

> I believe in doing what I can,
> In crying when I must,
> In laughing when I choose,
> Heigho, if love were all
> I should be lonely.
> I believe the more you love a man,
> The more you give your trust,
> The more you're bound to lose,
> Although when shadows fall
> I think if only—
> Somebody splendid really needed me,
> Someone affectionate and dear,
> Cares would be ended if I knew that he
> Wanted to have me near.
> I believe that since my life began
> The most I've had is just
> A talent to amuse.
> Heigho, if love were all!*

In a high, almost inaudible voice, Noël began to sing it for the last time. Not the whole song—that was beyond him now—the last half-dozen lines. When he came to the words "The most I've had is just . . . ," he paused for a moment, looked slowly around the circle, smiled, and continued, "a talent to amuse. . . ."

I wasn't the only one crying. Not by any means.

Four months later he was dead.

23

The Sum Total

❀

OUR "MEMORIAL SERVICE" for Noël had lasted until two in the morning, and I had to be up at six as usual. I slept a bit more—on the way to the studio, under the dryer, and while I was being made up. Finally I staggered onto the set, taking my hangover with me.

"Tsk, tsk, tsk!" murmured the cameraman reproachfully as he adjusted his lights and asked for an additional one to hide the circles under my eyes.

My stand-in took my place while the rest of the cast was lit, and I dragged my chair into the farthest and darkest corner of the set to catch another nap. My name was printed on the canvas back of my chair, but the French prop man had spelled it "Lily," which never failed to irritate me. "Lily" didn't refer to me. My father had named me after Goethe's young love, Lili Schönemann, and the registrar had added an extra *l* to my birth certificate, which wasn't what my father had in mind. He knew nothing about it, though, being already away at the front.

> What a menagerie my Lili has!
> The weirdest kind of zoo.
> And how she coaxes beasts into their cage
> Is quite a puzzle too. . . .

wrote the young Goethe. What about *my* menagerie? Well, my beasts certainly weren't tame, I thought drowsily in my dark corner. And that was as it should be. Who wants a tame husband? "All your life you've chosen difficult men," Carlos had once said to me. True. Difficult, "weird" creatures. I thought of a Rhineland proverb of my mother's: "A man in any of his forms reveals the wonders God performs."

"And how she coaxes beasts into their cage Is quite a puzzle too. . . ." Now, that was certainly true. A puzzle to me as well. But Carlos, wise as an old Chinese sage, always said that these things are not really puzzling, because nothing happens that is totally alien to your nature. "You yourself are the cause and the instigator," he said. "And in the end you harvest the sum total of all the right or wrong decisions you've made."

"Miss Palmer!" called a cheerful voice, interrupting my reflections. Our press photographer stood in front of my chair and proudly handed me a photograph. "Look what I've got for you. Had it specially sent over from London. Out of the files. What about that?"

I held it at arm's length, trying to see something, but my arm wasn't long enough. "It's too dark here," I said. "Who is it?"

"A picture of you when you were making your first film, *Crime Unlimited*, at the Teddington Studios," said the publicity man triumphantly.

I didn't want to disappoint him. "How do I look?"

"Terrible!" he exclaimed enthusiastically. "Absolutely terrible. If it hadn't been for your name on the back, I would never have recognized you."

"Get me my glasses, will you, please?"

He got them.

"And here's a picture I took of you yesterday," he said, laughing. "For comparison." He left me alone, holding a photograph in each hand. One showed a round-faced girl combing her hair on the set during a break, the other a woman sitting on a terrace gazing out to sea. My sum total.

I studied the old photo. Remembered suddenly that first film at the Teddington Studios, remembered the very scene, the very moment. For a second I was again that fat child who owned only one nightdress (awkward when it needed washing) and bought bath salts out of her first paycheck.

Did I ever imagine then how things were going to turn out? No, thank God. Why thank God? Had it been that bad? No, of course not. Only quite, quite different.

Just as well one doesn't know in advance.

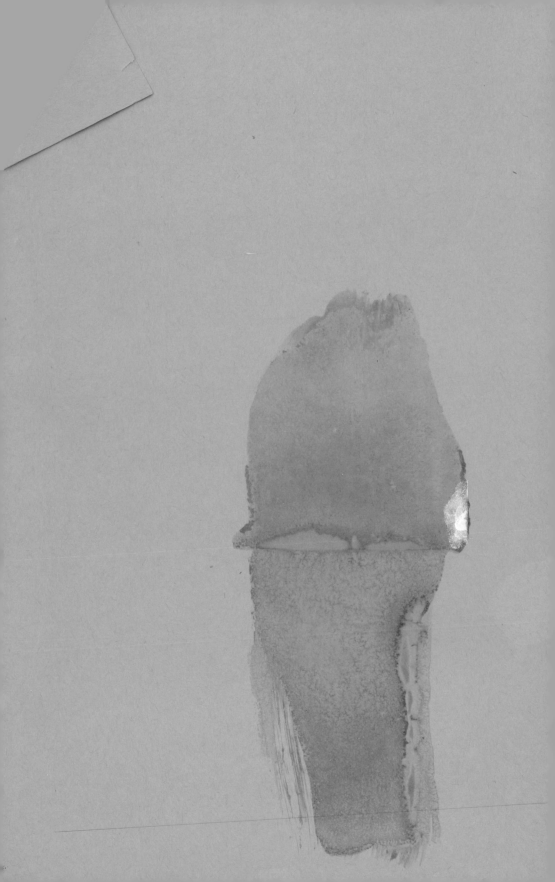